A Journey Through Afghanistan:
A MEMORIAL

North-West Afghanistan

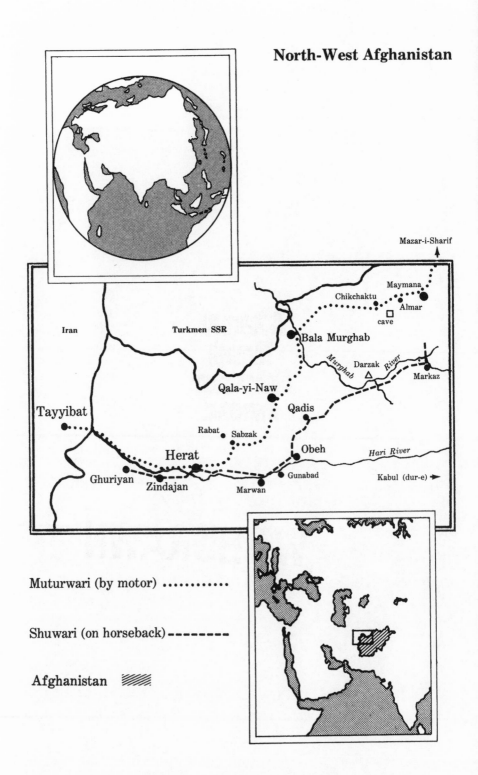

Muturwari (by motor) ············

Shuwari (on horseback) --------

Afghanistan ▨▨▨

A Journey Through Afghanistan

A MEMORIAL

David Chaffetz

The University of Chicago Press
Chicago and London

The University of Chicago Press, Chicago 60637
The University of Chicago Press, Ltd., London

05 04 03 02 01   2 3 4 5

ISBN 0-226-10064-2 (pbk.)

Library of Congress Cataloging-in-Publication Data is available

TO WALI AHMAD KHAN

Such is your portion in this life of a friend:
your portion in your dreams of a phantom.

CONTENTS

FOREWORD

The borders of Afghanistan have been closed to Western travelers for more than twenty years. But at the time of the events and encounters related in this book, Afghanistan was enjoying a peace that had lasted almost a half century. True, the material culture of Afghan society was strikingly sparse, particularly to the traveler arriving from the confident and oil-rich Iran of the late shah. The signs of the country's scrappy economic life, however, were everywhere: in the rows of hotels along the city streets advertising to the Western traveler in roman letters; in the high-sided trucks piled with men and goods racketing over poor roads; in the stalls of small-town bazaars, where one might find stacks of watermelon or, at another season, mounds of watermelon seed, raisins, plump rounds of village bread, its crumb always lightly flecked with straw, and *qorut* (dried milk curd) in mushroom-sized balls, representing the surplus production of the nomads' summer camps. In the north, one was apt to hear Russian spoken on the streets and turn to find a team of fair-haired Soviet geologists or engineers bargaining at a fruit stand. Every teahouse, every low-ceilinged room with a samovar at one end, seemed also to have its battery-operated cassette player. Every valley, every opening between the folds of the mountains, had its system of ditches, visible against the denuded hills, to lead water through its orchards and gardens.

It was also a time, in the mid-1970s, when Afghanistan had a relatively open society. Its cities were cosmopolitan. The functionary from Kabul, a Pashtun, shared the sidewalk with the Uzbek trader from the north, the Hazara porter newly arrived in the city, the Tajik landowner. Schoolgirls walked to school in blouse and navy skirt, their mothers hovering behind in *burqa*. The mosques were well attended, but then so were the movies.

It was a time when a pair of young Americans, armed with a modest knowledge of the language and culture, could wander off the high road in Afghanistan and land in the rich and intricate web of Afghan society. As travelers with stated duties and dispensations, they were called on to explain themselves and their culture, and to hear in turn the boasts, the grievances, the misgivings, and the grudging acknowledgments of their Afghan interlocutors. More than once after a night of discussion, in the guest house of a hamlet in the central provinces or by a fire on a windy ridge, the author of this book was asked—as it was my privilege to witness—if he would not take a wife from the local people and settle among them.

But there were indications even then, had one known how to read them, of the storm gathering over the country. There was Muhammad Daud, Afghanistan's president, who had seized power from Zahir Shah in 1973, following the prolonged drought of 1971–72. Daud would prove to be only the first of a series of strongmen to use the military's backing to gain power. And in the summer of 1975 there had been a coup attempt against Daud by Islamic fundamentalists, who fled to Pakistan when their coup failed. By 1978, Daud was gone; in December 1979, Soviet troops invaded Afghanistan. Opposition forces rallied across the border in Pakistan—Pashtun tribal leaders, Muslim clerics, and sympathizers from the wider Islamic world, including the young Osama bin Laden, fresh from his radicalizing exposure to the religious thinkers at the university in Jidda. With U.S. and Saudi backing, these mujahideen mounted guerrilla operations against the Kabul government.

During the ten years of the Soviet occupation and the further half decade of brutality and chaos that followed, Afghanistan suffered huge population losses, widespread civil disruption, the severe degradation of its infrastructure, and the near-total flight of its educated and professional class. What elements of the life described in this book survive in the Afghanistan of today is an open question. Many of the structures the author visited—the mosques, the pilgrimage sites, and even the private houses—were razed during the years of war; many of the people he befriended were killed or driven into exile. The nomads were settled. The *kariz,* or ancient irrigation tunnels, were in many instances converted into shelters and munitions depots by guerrilla groups. And hundreds of thousands of mines were laid.

When the Taliban movement gathered force in the mid-1990s and was able to impose strict *shari'a* law first on one village, then on one province, it was embraced by the population and its influence quickly spread. Civil order was Afghanistan's highest priority. But the village clerics who formed the Taliban leadership were ill-equipped to gauge the effects of their actions—particularly their encouragement of the opium trade and bin Laden's training camps—on the international community. Where the Taliban saw a citadel of Islam, much of the world recognized a center of contagion for drugs and terrorism.

Yet the day will come, sooner than later perhaps, when the Afghans will face the task of rebuilding their country. The evidence of this book suggests that contrary to the cardboard image of the Afghan as mujahideen or Taliban extremist, the Afghan people draw on a rich fund of Persian and Islamic culture, and their natures are varied, humorous, shrewd, and generous-spirited. Their history has taught them to look coolly on good fortune and calamity alike.

WILLARD WOOD, OCTOBER 22, 2001

This book is a recounting
of a journey
through Western Afghanistan
by two young Americans who
wanted to explore and
experience the lonely,
hermetic world of the
Afghan nomads—a world
now upset by recent
events which have brought
so much suffering and
change to a people who
thought themselves hardened
to any fate.

DCC

1.
PORTALS TO A LAND

Islam Qala

We sat in the teahouse, my friend and I, drinking tea out of palm-sized cups, sweetening the acrid taste of the drink with soft white candies.

Across an empty space from the customs bureau, the crowded teahouse washed in the tide of travelers passing back and forth from the bureau, and the gunning buses loading and disgorging passengers and goods. On the porch overlooking the traffic sat the grand merchants, freshly returned from Iran or ready to embark, I could not say which, lazing against the bolsters of the carpeted porch, but intent on the spectacle of stuffs paraded from customs. Bales of old clothing, rugs, crates, even, *barikollah!* a Mercedes-Benz sedan passed through the view of the porch. No, I saw neither the relief to be returned nor the eagerness to be off in the faces of these merchants, only each one intent on calculating his profit and his loss, while the ritual of tea prevented discussion. The merchants stroked their henna-dyed beards reflectively, showing their hands, finely white, ringed with large and glassy stones, knotted about fake amber rosaries. One of their number lumbered with difficulty to his feet, awash in the folds of his copious *shalwar* and a somber, silk caftan. No one asked why or whither. It was always time to go. A chorus of "Go with grace" followed him out, though no one's eyes darted from the porch view, and they watched, as lazing and intent as before.

Commotion was provided by younger men, chatting noisily in the shadowed rear of the teahouse and hurrying back and forth between the bureau and a seat beside friends. Some were clearly embarking, nervous, full of forced mirth and fear, while others had the braggadoccio, the swagger, proclaiming their return from the wide world in victory. These blades narrated their escapades abroad to the yet untraveled, at which the gullible stood openly agape, while the wiser, cynical youths clicked their tongues in polite disbelief. The stories rambled on, punctuated by laughter; a few easy-going types lifted their turbans to scratch their shaved heads.

At the sound of the laughter my friend and I turn around, listening intently. They, the young men, stare back incuriously, ignoring us and going on with their interminable stories, or rising and going to the door to check on the departure of a bus.

The grand merchants notice neither the rowdy youths nor the two foreigners oddly invading their teahouse.

Indifference, preceded by a volley of stares, marks our taking this innocuous corner of the room. The innkeeper, inhospitable, peers at us with the look of "What do they want here?"

My friend called the boy over, a gangling half-adult in rag-tag clothing and asked for lunch in adequate Persian. The boy looked at us with smug incomprehension, barking a reply in pig Persian and gesticulating wildly. We listened to this demonstration for a spell, then grabbed him by the arms and pulled him over to our table, asking again, nice as cake, for lunch. He heard us; this time, he had listened, and he started back from us as though he had heard a talking dog.

The little interlude had attracted the attention of the youths; again their uncharitable stares, while we waited quietly for our meal. I remembered that the Persian word for foreigner, *gharib*, also means "wretch."

The boy returned to set the table with spoons and forks, but we packed him off for a ewer of water to wash our hands before eating with them. Back again, he set the ewer down and tried to escape, but we made him hold the bowl under our hands while he splashed water down from above. Sticking to the small politenesses slowly had its effect on him. Our lunch was delivered without further awkwardness.

We set to our food, keeping one eye on our plates and the other on our audience, to see how they rated our manners. They were all looking at us now, after our fussing, both the young men and the grand merchants. Their hauteur was chilling, being the stares of an old civilized race directed at barbarians. Barbarians had come often to the land, like locusts, slaughtering God's people and undoing manners and customs of old. The survivors of these devastations never despaired that, eventually, the barbarians would be assimilated, and history had proved their optimism: the Mongols, the Safavids, the Uzbeks, and the Pathans had conquered in turn, only to fall under the spell of culture and be conquered by it. This new pack of barbarians, beardless and hatless, unbelievers and gross materialists, were worse, in one respect, than the bloodthirsty Mongols themselves: they did not look to be ever assimilated. They would destroy the culture before they ever mastered it.

It wasn't easy to practice the grave nonchalance of the Muslims at table. They drank tea with the dignity of royal princes, a memory of the time when tea was a rare and exclusive drink, reserved for members of the court. A plate of rice merited special consideration—a luxury, even in recent years. With a single motion they wafted a morsel of rice off the top of the plate, rolled it into the palm of the hand and popped the ball of rice into the mouth without losing a single grain. It was manners like these which justified the hauteur of the cafe's patrons, their high self-opinion. Manners were only common sense, really, a simple acknowledgement that everything enjoyed was of God's providing, to be consumed slowly, gravely; to be relished. Bread was treated with almost religious respect, as the first gift to *Hazrat* Adam when he hungered after the Fall. The diners passed the loaf of bread before their beards while saying "Bismillah" (in the name of God) and then carefully, as though in sympathy for the loaf, broke the bread into halves. And with the accompanying gesture, a glance in our direction, which meant, "True humanity resides in this."

Islam Qala (Citadel of Islam), despite its high-sounding name, is a small station on the road from Mashhad to Herat, the two principal towns of historic Khurasan. Customs bureau, police barracks, sepulchral hotel, and an array of money changers and beggars suffice to fill its one tentative street lying askew the new Asian Highway, which brings European tourists across to India.

It was summer and the tourists were out in force. Those who had arrived with us by ramshackle bus to Islam Qala hurried onto still more ramshackle buses to arrive in Herat before nightfall. They seemed to know, perhaps by prior experience, not to tarry in Islam Qala. We did not want to rush, if it meant contravening an unwritten code of behavior in our new habitat. My friend, who had been here several years before, saw that we savored what there was of Afghanistan to be savored in Islam Qala.

Afghanistan is an old country, but Islam Qala is less than 90 years old. Old countries have history, which changes people's life in curious ways. In their residual curiosity about these changes, there is something to savor. At the end of the last century one of the innumerable colonial Boundary Commissions established the frontier between Iran and Afghanistan, so that the people living in the area of Western Khurasan became subjects of the Shah in

Tehran, while those living in Eastern Khurasan fell under the rule of the Amir of Kabul. The line, like many colonial borders, caused some confusion in the minds of the local population, villagers whose markets had suddenly become foreign territory and nomads whose pasture grounds had been split in two. With time, however, men who had called themselves indifferently *Musalmanan* (Muslims) began to refer to themselves as Iranians or Afghans. And they still spoke, in their discussions of the demarcation line, as though a broad stroke of calligraphy truly lay, somewhere, scratched across the desert.

Iranians, on the wealthier side, had little reason to cross the line. Afghans, drawn by the high pay of industrial work in Iran, crossed the line in such numbers as to cause both governments concern. They went illegally; they worked without paying taxes, avoiding military service. They lived beyond the law. Those whom we saw in Islam Qala were the very few who go aboveboard, having done their military service—the young men eager to work in the factories of Iran and return wealthier at the end of the season, and the grand merchants willing to pay the "gifts" and blandishments required to obtain the prized exporting passport. Grudgingly they were let out of the country.

And grudgingly let return. We waited in the cheerless customs bureau of Islam Qala. Foreigners, tourists, were passed through the line with cursory inspection—it's what they take out of the country that worries the authorities. Because we did not want to hurry, we lingered back with the long-enduring crowd of re-entering nationals. We sat among those turbanned faces. Hennaed beards were stroked and sidelong glances thrown at us. We had a long time to sit, as the willful officials picked over the untidy bundles of their countrymen.

It was not difficult to start a conversation with strangers, any personal matter being fair game for the queries of the curious. One's neighbor might ask how much one paid for one's coat, what wages one was paid at work, and among the still more curious, whether one was married, how many times, how many children. I used to be offended by these questions, until I slowly learned that by the devotees of this game of question and answer, the right answer was not necessarily the truth. My friend played the game well.

"You were in Iran?" asked a silver-haired merchant, fingering his passport like a talisman.

"Yes, for several years," he replied, obviously reckoning that to admit to a short stay would be face-blackening.

"What did you do there? Trading?"

"No. I worked in oil." Most Afghans found their way to the

Gulf, working in oil. It was easier to tell him this than to explain the whole plan of the journey.

A young man, swaggering, dressed in a fine silk caftan but wearing shiny, square-heeled Iranian-made shoes—the kind London mods used to wear—interrupted us. "I worked in Iran, too. Were you in Abadan?"

"There and other places," my friend said evasively. He had not been to the Gulf, in fact, at all.

"I have been in Abadan, Bandar Abbas, Kuwait, Oman. Abadan is best of all. At night, the silos of oil burn like lanterns hanging at the end of poles. You cannot see the stars at night for their brightness."

"As if I hadn't seen it," snorted the merchant. Not to be outdone by the younger man, he went on: "You can't see the sun at noon for the smoke. A benighted kingdom, this Iran. Tea costs fifteen *rupees*, meat fifty *rupees*—and it stinks. There's nought but tyranny in Iran."

I pointed out how much higher the wages were in Iran. The merchant peered at me impatiently and concluded, "Aye, Afghanistan is the poorest country in the world. If only we had oil, like Iran, we would be rich."

"We do have oil," said the young man, knowingly. "In Mazar-i-Sharif. But the *Rus* (Russians) take it out of the ground and keep it for themselves."

"That is what Islam has come to. And for all their oil, what is Iran but a nation of unbelievers? It is the month of fasting, yet I saw people smoking on the streets of Tehran, and eating, too. They say the Iranis eat pork."

I assured him that the Iranians abhor pork, but the young man asked me pointedly, "Are you a Muslim?"

The blame for Russia's draconian licensing of the Mazar oilfields, the injustice of Iran's scandalous wealth, and all the other insults swallowed by the proud Afghans abroad settled slowly on our heads.

"*La'llah ila'llah . . .*" murmured the merchant, as though the presence of unbelievers required him to reaffirm his faith. Then conversation continued, the unbelievers quietly excluded, mixing deprecations on Iran, envy, pride, and the doleful refrain: "Aye, Afghanistan is the poorest country in the world."

The customs inspection was interrupted for lunch. Because of the delay, we missed bus after bus, full of travelers, setting out from Islam Qala on the last leg of the journey to Herat. I looked after them enviously, impatient to be off, but my friend remained unperturbed. He said, "This is what's so great about the place. You appreciate it for what it is, rather than hurry on in search of something better. Just look at it," he said, gesturing at the quaint features of Islam Qala: misspelt signs, dozing sentries, would-be blindmen staring into the contents of their cups, money-changers in mournful, heavy robes watching tourists troop off to the newly-established branch of the National Bank to sell their *rials.* A few dust-colored flowers—somebody's afterthought—grew beside the bank, while the sign "Kepe off the floures" shaded them in three languages. It was not Darius's trilingual inscription at Behistun, but it was Afghanistan, said my friend.

The fact that we had crossed a line and no natural demarcation suggested the difficulty of defining Afghanistan. The ancient history of the land was a rich but ambiguous legacy. Here Iran, Central Asia, and the Indian Subcontinent abutted one another: much of present-day Afghanistan moved, at various times, in the orbit of Isfahan, Samarkand, or Delhi. At other times warrior clans, emerging from its mountains and deserts, succeeded to rule in place of their former overlords.

The most enduring of these clans came from the Pathan homeland in Southeastern Afghanistan in the eighteenth century. In 1747 a young chieftain named Ahmad Khan—or Ahmad Shah *Durrani* (Pearl-Splendored) as he became—gained election as paramount chief of the Pathan-Afghan tribes and began to conquer neighboring Khurasan, Turkistan, and the Punjab. The nominal founder of modern Afghanistan, Ahmad made *Afghanistan* (Land of the Afghans) the center of a tribal empire stretching from the northern boundaries of Khurasan to the Indus Plain.

Under succeeding princes the tribal monarchy grew weak, enabling the Persians to advance from the west, the British from the south, and the Russians from the north. The head-on clash of the three powers was avoided by a tacit principle, developed in the course of the nineteenth century, that no one power should come to dominate the Pathan Kingdom. This principle effectively stalemated the Persian invasions of 1838 and 1851, numerous Russian feints, and the famous British campaigns of 1838 and 1879.

Afghanistan was given a breathing space. Under the rule of Abdur Rahman Khan (1880-1901), the kingdom gained in internal cohesion what it had lost in territory. The "Iron Amir" took up—but did not complete—the process of transforming a tribal confederacy of Pathans, client Uzbek khans, subjected Persian cities, and rebellious Hazaras and Kafirs into a centralized, bureaucratic monarchy in the Persicate tradition. With his financial reforms, effective administrative machine, standing army and police force, as well as his grand mosques, formal gardens and hillside palaces, Abdur Rahman provided the country with an era of harsh but purposeful rule; he improved the country materially, as one keeps up a patrimonial estate, and his son, Habib Ullah Khan, continued his policies. Aman Ullah Khan, Abdur Rahman's grandson, who seized the throne shortly after Habib Ullah's assassination in 1919, proclaimed Afghanistan a neutral nation, and established the first diplomatic relations with the outside world, including the Soviet Union. In 1926 he took the title *Padishah* (Great King) in affirmation of the royal pretensions and enhanced sense of power of his dynasty. With a view towards modernizing his state and subjects along Anglo-Indian, if not Western, lines, the *padishah* began to introduce innovations such as public education, conscription and westernized dress. These reforms were unpopular with most Afghans; they increased the tax burden, interfered with local affairs, and raised suspicions about the piety of the monarch. This broad opposition, combined with the desertion of the tribal warparties which were the real mainstay of the monarchy, forced Aman Ullah into exile in 1929.

Aman Ullah's fall taught his cousins and successors (starting with the next *Padishah*, Nadir), the limits of royal power. They could continue to rule Afghanistan as a family fief, improve the roads, raise light taxes, buy up choice farmland. But to create a strong nation state and army remained beyond their power. Nadir was assasinated in 1933 during a prize-distribution for school children. His 19-year-old son Zahir succeeded to the title, while various senior members of the family ruled. A familial *coup d'etat* in 1953 brought prince Muhammad Daud Khan to power as prime minister, under the aegis of younger princes and other courtiers who felt that Afghanistan resembled all too well a family farm. In Daud they found the image (though little else) of a progressive statesman. He gave them a "national cause," the liberation of ethnic Pathans in neighboring Pakistan. The Soviet Union, happy to nurture this nationalist nuisance on the border of pro-Western Pakistan, offered to arm Daud's army. There ensued a family feud of decisive consequences not just for the great-great grandchildren of Abdur Rahman Khan, but for much of posterity. The older, cautious princes told Daud not to play with fire. Daud said, in effect, I can handle the Russians. The old guard forced Daud from power for ten years, between 1963 and 1973, but fell into their old habit of running the country like a fief and treating the government like a bailiff, something only old Haile Selassie was still doing by that time. Popular revolution returned Daud to power in 1973, this time as President of the

Republic, with many, but by no means all of the royal house put out of the picture. The Soviet Union was gratified. The United States was cautious.

How successful Daud's latest revolution had been in transforming Afghanistan could be measured by the familiarity my friend felt for this border station. The poor turnout of the soldiers, the prevalence of *bakhshish* in the custom's proceedings, the awfulness of the Tourist Hotel in Islam Qala, none of this had changed since the revolution. If Daud pressed his revolution forcibly, he would wind up like Aman Ullah, presuming too much on the toleration of the Afghans for any government. If he did nothing, he might wind up like his cousin the king, also an exile in Rome. As far as we could see, Daud chose to feign the former course while pursuing the latter. His revolution was largely one of words.

In the customs bureau banners in Pashto (the Pathan tongue) and Afghan Persian or Dari (the *lingua franca*) proclaimed the principals of the revolution in Daudian rhetoric, partly radical and partly the homilies of an old Afghan *khan*. One sign promised equality for all Afghans, ruling Pathans and subject races. We are all Afghans, this one proclaimed. Another sign urged all Patriotic Afghans to love their dear Afghanistan. Every Country must have people who love their country, it explained. All of this seemed rather funny to me at the time, suggesting a visit to a desert *kakania*. My friend, however, quickly disallowed this suggestion, remarking that as a state of mind Afghanistan was immistakably not funny, but harsh and powerful.

The contrast between the images of humor and severity gave me something to think on. A diplomat, one of those people for whom Afghanistan remains an unimportant enigma, once described to me how his section received with great fanfare a special diplomatic pouch from Kabul containing a massive leather-and-gilt tome entitled *The Constitution of Afghanistan*. He had been waiting for this ever since the latest about-face in Afghan affairs. Article I, Section I announced: "The Flag of Afghanistan shall consist of two parts, the flag and the flag staff." That was the beginning and the end of the diplomat's interest in the country. But what happens if you have the misfortune to *live* in such a country? Does the fact that the flag and the flag staff remain distinct matter to you at all? And if all your government does is legislate a two-part flag, how do you feel about this? I have heard people argue that it makes a great deal of difference if the flag is red or not. Why should people who live in the direst poverty care about the color of their flag? The flags, the uniforms, the postage stamps (which would disappear, along with our letters, into the pockets of underpaid postal workers), how often did these change, and how little did they alter anything in the lives of the people they symbolized. There was hardly anything comical in that.

We cleared customs, found a berth in a crowded bus returning migrants, and set off for the city. It was dark, and the few revolutionary banners strung across the street were like ghostly portals of a *sarai*.

Dasht, Bagh, Bazaar

A plain of gravel extends towards the indistinct horizon. The soil, a fine, fawn-colored dust, covers the rocky flatness of the landscape with a monotonous unity of hue. Only when the eye adjusts to the sunlight does the flatness of the landscape appear uncertain. Irregular features delineate themselves, depressions, rises, foothills, and finally mountains, bracketing the horizon. How far away these mountains lie is impossible to tell, with only a single position in view and no stable reckoning point. The horizon wavers before the eyes over a maddeningly elastic expanse of wasteland. This is the *dasht*, the wasteland which stretches trackless for hundreds of miles in every direction, punctuated only by a few, distant hulks of black mountains.

The eyes light on a gully, a shallow path of smooth stones, some of them oddly colored, blue and green. They lie in the belly of the depression, scattered like a row of sown seeds. On the edges of the path, tufts of grass, like gnarled strands of hair, lie close-cropped against the earth, bleached white by the sun. Only the roots of these grasses are alive, cool in the depths of the earth, underneath the pebbles and fine dust. The withered blades are dead, for nothing grows here now.

It is when the spring comes that the snow on the high peaks of the mountains in the Safid Kuh range begins to melt. The run-off, with no soil to absorb it, slides down the rock-face of the mountain with the force of a waterfall. The sound can be heard even here in the *dasht*. A low rumble provides scarce warning of the onrushing flood. The torrent pours onto the plain, carving the earth into stream beds and carrying with it a weight of bright pebbles. Every spring water recuts the face of the *dasht*, arranges gravel into aquatic patterns, the loose sand in the shape of waves.

Almost as soon as the thin soil gulps its first mouthfuls of water, dormant vegetation, wild flowers and spiny grasses bloom. The fleshy roots of these ephemerals soak up the flood as it spills over them and through the next fortnight the plants go through their life cycle. They sprout, seed, and wither. The green meadow of grasses and wild anemones with which the spring carpets the *dasht* is then subjected to the sun's relentless bleaching. Very soon, it reverts to its present fawn-colored scape of dust and pebble. Water, the source of the spring's brief florescence, sinks into the parched soil. The table of ground-water is below 30 meters.

There are few human inhabitants of the *dasht*. Their lives resemble both in their nature and mechanics the tenacious ephemerals of the spring. They have learned to sink wells, primitive rope and goatskin affairs, tapping the deep ground-water. Since this water is shallow, the wells must be spaced far apart, not to drain one another. And since each well is quickly exhausted in a given season, those who live in the *dasht* must migrate from well to well, according to the rigid periodicity they establish among themselves. Sometimes, coming towards a well abandoned for a long dry season, they find it collapsed, lost in the stony waste. It is said they can scent the wet sand and the water many meters down; or they wait for desert fowl to find the well from the air and dive into its depths to drink. Then they re-excavate the well, lining it with bramble bush to shore up the walls. Water and the poor pasturage of grass and thorns provides their herds of camels with the two means of subsistence in the *dasht*. These people live here, they claim, in order to avoid the inequity of government—taxation, conscription, and the abuse of the true religion. Theirs is a hard-won independence of the outside world. The beauties of their way of life, their crafts, their ingenuity, their formal, stately speech, are all spread thin against the monotony of the *dasht*, as thin as the ephemeral's spring blossoms.

After a long journeying across the *dasht*, the eye distinguishes something rare and unnatural, asymmetrical. A line of elevations, only mounds of dirt but tracing a definite line through space, rises to view. Each mound is a crater of dark, turned-up earth, concealing a clayish, yawning pit, indeterminably deep. Rumbling issues from below, and the scent of water, running water, rises sweet and cool into the acrid, dusty air. These craters trace the line of an underground water channel, man-made; the pit had been dug during excavation.

The source of this water must be higher ground, and in fact, the line of craters can be seen running off toward the nearest mountains. There the ground-water is at a high elevation, many meters above the surface of the plains. The underground channel taps this ground-water at the very skirt of the mountains and then, carefully planing its descent onto the plains, brings this water to the surface miles away from the mountains. The flow of water is very nearly constant. Starting in March when the sun melts the winter's snow and releases a spectacular flood of water, the increasing heat of the air thaws the higher and more solid ice of the highest peaks, until finally, in autumn, in the cooling air, the supply of water tapers off. That flow of water, collected in the underground channels and brought out to the flat arable plains, provides irrigation for a half-year growing season. It is exactly enough, no more, no less, to allow for permanent settlement in the *dasht*. No matter how parched the waste, it is not desert: the soil will bear crop where watered. The presence of the mountains and the construction of these underground channels permit another way of life to exist in the *dasht*, in some ways more sturdy, in some ways more tenuous, than that of the camel nomads. The channels are called *kariz*.

Where the *kariz* surfaces, water sparkles into view and flows through a stone-lined canal. A row of willows grows along the banks of the canal, extending the linear symmetry of the water's flow more visibly. Wide-girthed trees with leathery, sun-hardened leaves, the willows spread their roots into the soil around them, protecting the canal from erosion and preventing evaporation with their shade. Under them, the air is cooler by degrees, with a moistness you can cut with a knife. A few wild grasses twine in the mesh of the roots, and in the treetops, here and there, rests a harlequin-feathered hoopoe.

All this life—the trees, the birds, the cool air which seems itself a living thing—has a fragile dependence on that *kariz*, running more than ten miles under the earth. In order to excavate the channel, and to keep it in constant repair, a special profession of men has to be willing to risk their lives working underground. These men are particularly skilled in rough-and-ready compassing and planing. They sink the first pit, the deepest, up in the hills, carrying out the dirt, keeping one hole in line with the next, all the miles of the route. They must keep the water from flowing into the *kariz* before it is completed or they will drown. More often, while they are underground, the tunnel collapses, and they are suffocated. The few who are good at this work are marked from birth by certain peculiarities of disposition and, risky as the life is, naturally go into the business. But they are well paid, being indispensable to a system of cultivation on which the whole civilization depends. They are the bedrock on which everything else is raised.

The green row of willows continues for a mile, then it meets with other rows, the signs of other *karizes* converging from other points on the mountains. At the point of convergence, a riot of trees springs to view: orchards of pomegranates, quinces, and olive trees, lying dark and green behind mud walls. A hedge of poplars keeps the wind and dust off the cultivated fields. As the lower branches of these poplars have been continually pruned for firewood, the trees grow straight up. Silver and grey, they reach to impossible heights, looking like a row of spears. Within the tight hedge of the poplars the soil is very different from that of the *dasht*. The color of the earth is varied—black patches of soil where the tuber crops are grown, whitened patches with the pale-green stalks of melons. The size of each plot is small, like a garden, and that is what they call it, *bagh*.

Running water makes a pleasant noise, bubbling over the rills between the plots. Dozing villas, adjoining the fields, flake off years of mud and plaster. More and more mud barriers divide the view, a thread of silver and yellow clay running between the compact fields and houses. Everything is hidden from view, only suggested by the outline of the walls, by the worn jointures in the clay. The landscape is like a Chinese brush painting, divided and concealing, yet unified. Life is simple here; its needs are easily served. Along a broad path stands a row of shops, mere shacks, vending the bare necessities, soap, matches, sugar, oil, tea. A few wrinkled melons lie on the dusty thresholds of the shops, concealing an exquisite, sharp sweetness. Against a mud wall leans someone's bicycle, used to bring goods from the bigger markets. The *bagh* looks rural and remote, but actually is very close to the city. From here on the road begins to be paved.

The paved road is lined with feathery blue pines. Under their evergreen shade a sweet soporific odor falls on the air. A hiatus in the sense of movement while one concentrates on the change here. The open boulevard is wide and empty. Houses, two-, three-storied, stand in shuttered silence behind the screen of trees. A gutter of green water, choked in dust, lies still, and dust hangs, as though no one would ever disturb it, on the trunks of the trees, and masks the sidewalk. Grey-green rinds of melons and scraps of food lie underfoot. One, two strollers appear from the discreet doors of the houses and steal forward with a sure sense of direction. They walk down the paved road under the green trees, pleasant but heavy, as though hurrying to be clear of their shade. At the far end of the road the sun shines through hotly.

But the strollers accumulate here, flowing with the inevitability of water through the *kariz*. The road narrows, and squeezes between rows of shops, tiny, identical cubicles. The pressure of the flow increases. The shops are swamped by the amount of traffic on the street. This is where all the people have gone, leaving the two- and three-storied houses behind shutters. This is where all the belated strollers were hurrying. A narrow pedestrian-way elbows with people. They stumble and fall off into the stagnant gutter or spill onto the cobbled streets, where hansom cabs and ancient Mercedes-Benzes creep along in greater style. The flow of people is oppressive. Porters bear down on the crowd with wooden crates on their backs; others roll pushcarts doggedly into the crowd. A lone horseman makes his way with a firm hand on his mount's frothing bit and a stout whip to displace laggard passersby. Herdsmen drive their sheep under the feet of everyone.

Everything converges here. The village produce lies heaped up in musty-smelling shops at the foot of the narrow street. Behind them, the butchers receive the shepherds' lowing animals. The air is aswarm with flies and reeks of dried blood. Mixed in with other scents is the odor of sesame and honey from the pastry shops. The bakeries are covered with black soot, the oven doors are constantly opened and shut as cooked loaves come out and balls of soft dough go in. Dry goods are next—in one square the old-clothes sellers have heaped the garments up three feet high, while the buyers wade into the heap, rummaging through for finds. Around the old clothes are grouped stalls of fabric sellers, the gaudiest synthetics blowing in the air beside homespun silk, a milky white. Among the shops are warehouses, high-vaulted, where lumbering trucks, gorgeously painted, disgorge oranges from Kandahar, clarified butter (*ghee*) from Pakistan, sacks of rice from Iran, while cursing porters make gangways through the crowd with their great burdens of dried seeds, tea, and raw wool. Travelers bargain with the driver for spare seats on his return haul.

Market is a weak word to express the spirit of the bazaar.

Everything is the bazaar.
"Where are you going?"
"The Bazaar."
"What's news?"
"The Bazaar."
"What should we do?"
"The Bazaar."

They stroll, they go for no other reason than to mingle in the living theater and imbibe the spirit of the place. They know that every tangent, every movement in the *dasht* and *bagh* around the city must resolve and flow, whirlpool-like, into the bazaar. They do not feel the need to spend their lives elsewhere but in the bazaar.

The danger of losing the thread, the visual integration so strong in the landscape of the countryside, is allayed by the order of the city. The bazaar flows into a central square with four principal radii. Water flows down the four bazaar-ways and gathers in a domed cistern, which feeds, in turn, roof tanks, sidewalk gutters, and fountains. Everywhere water informs the patterns of the city, preserving the sense of flow, the unity of order. Society in the bazaar makes use of water as a mystical union within the pantheism of lives secluded behind mud doors and alleyways. There is everywhere water for washing, water for bathing, water for cooling the dry air, water for brewing tea, which oils the machinery of polite social intercourse.

Water occupies the place of pride in the cathedral mosque, filling the wide green pool in the center of the cobbled courtyard before the towering wall of prayer. At the specified hours of worship one must perform one's ablutions, wash one's feet, one's arms up to the elbows, blow water through the nose, cleanse the mouth, splash water in the ears, and only then recite the prayers. The whole city joins in this ritual washing, touching the single, flowing force of life together.

A city boasts of the purity of its water foremost. To say a rival town is benighted it is enough to say, "The water there is brackish."

And when one recites the prayers in the courtyard of the cathedral mosque, the millenium-old edifice of shimmering blue and green faience, surging with powerful arabesques and subtler arches, it is easy to forget the diversity of strands in the chaos of the city and its environs. The fragile tenure of the city in the *dasht*, the rivulets of snow melting too far away to see, the hundreds of underground *karizes* and the wild men who work them, the crisscross of walls in the villages, the crush of traffic through the bazaar-ways, the curses of porters in the warehouses, here are all condensed, distilled into the pure water which the worshippers splash on their bodies at the side of the pool in the company of their fellows. In the swirl of lapis and turquoise tiling, the vision of the artisan proclaims the same message as the crier emerging from the portal of the prayer wall, THERE IS BUT ONE . . .

We outsiders have no eucharist. The oriental street intrudes on our senses as no Western street can do, with only chaos and no order. The force of bodies shoving by, fat and lean, silky long caftans and foul-smelling rags. Sheep meadowing at our feet, drinking the green water of the gutter before they are slaughtered. The makeshift corrugated roofing of the shops, casting shadows over the street, yet burning to the touch. The crumbling brick cistern with the soaring facade, concealing in its depth brackish cool water. The vendors, taciturn Turkomans with cheap rugs thrown over their shoulders. Pathans, who are not vendors, with somber-colored capes on their shoulders looking like biblical patriarchs. Soldiers, yellow-skinned recruits from the Hazarajat in the Hindu Kush painfully walking in second-hand boots. Others despising the uniform and afraid of it. A pile of sheep's-heads on the sidewalk: Tamerlane's hill of skulls outside Damascus. The urchins in ragtag clothes hopscotching through the alleys. Dark eyes of the gazelle. Beggars, sound and lame, some without faces, some with extra limbs. And the rich sound of Arabic prayer, intoned by a man who has no lips.

We picked our way through the crowd, the bustling, swaggering crowd of *bazaaris*. We tried to be unobtrusive, but they had developed a sense of us. They spotted us from blocks away, turning, looking at us with a mixture of envy and pity. Some would immediately avert their glances, mindful of the tradition that whoever looks on unbelievers becomes as one of them. Others, the young, try to catch our eyes, to gather our secrets, and we would look back at them, not knowing what they read, not knowing whether to expect a smile, a frown, or a sneer. It got to be wearying, the eye play with hundreds of anonymous faces, adding to our mounting sense of isolation and rejection.

Aimless, we went through the monotonously identical alleys of high walls and narrow lanes. We passed a quarter of dyers, where the ground ran with purplish mud, and past them, wool-carders, swarming with flies. Only waifs and urchins were about, raising an irritating wail of *"Meestar, Meestar,"* and calling out after us obscenities which they scarcely understood. Some stones were thrown.

A door in one of the walls swung open and a dapper-looking youth in a starched white pajama stepped doubtfully over the trail of stains and offal. He saw us, and started, as we at him. Understanding our predicament, he shouted to the children one very choice, bone-crunching epithet, silencing them at once.

"Thank you," I said, a little embarrassed.

He nodded, shyly, still unsure of what to make of us, two *meestars*, deep in the alleys of the bazaar. We looked at one another, we at him, he at us, sizing up the pluses and minuses of further conversation, an awkward silence descending. The youth wore a razor-thin moustache on a sallow, impassive face.

"I'm afraid we're lost," I admitted finally.

"How can you be lost?" he asked, forgetting for a minute our strange accents and appearances. "You're only a few paces from the Kandahar Gate."

After hearing his instructions with a look of helplessness, we threw up our hand. "I'll take you there," he said.

His name was Gul Ahmad, a not uncommon one commemorating the "rose" of Ahmad Shah Durrani. I told him my name, *Daud*.

"*Paygambar*, a prophet," he replied. My friend's name he

took for *Wali*, an Arabo-Persian name meaning "governor" or "friend."

After this exchange we felt awkward. We had nothing to say to Gul Ahmad once he had shown us the way back to the paved street. I had the impulse to thank him and go on our way, just as one would do in America. But friends are made of less than this in the East. As soon as we had told him our names, we had made the decisive gesture. When we reached the Kandahar Gate, a four-way intersection where the paved street began, we were caught in the inertia which governed personal relations here. We stood in the intersection, waiting for Gul Ahmad to speak. "Are you going to Shahr-i-Nau? I'll take you there. We can go by bus."

A rickety school bus painted green pulled up. "No, you really don't have to take the trouble."—"What trouble, I insist"— the inevitable polite exchange. Gul Ahmad paid our half *rupee* fares while we protested. Then we rode in silence, a strained experience for a Westerner who expected to chatter constantly with a new acquaintance, but a natural enough condition here.

When we got off the bus, we stood about again, Gul Ahmad not showing the slightest impatience. Finally, he said, "What hotel are you staying at? Ah, I will come visit you later. I have business in town. Go with God." Of course, he didn't have business in town, but got right back on the bus and rode back to the bazaar.

I knew we should have asked him to join us for tea, but that would have involved waiting until the end of the diurnal fast, and we could not support the intervening strange companying. Tired, raw-nerved, our sensitivity for dealing with strangers had evaporated.

We had gone wandering in the bazaars unadvisedly. Herat's physical layout was designed to spare impatient travelers the awkwardness of dealing with locals, and *vice versa*. We had our own town, Shahr-i-Nau (the New Town) sprung up on the edge of the Old City, like so many hybrid European streets in the East. One takes an old city, like Herat, a famous center of medieval Persicate culture, laid out in classical symmetry, with four bazaars joining in an ornate covered *souq*. High walls and towers surround such a city, while four gates open to each of the cardinal directions. In front of each gate is a pilgrim's shrine. Now, batter down the walls and the towers, pull down the covered bazaar (claiming it is unsafe), run a tree-lined avenue at nose thumbing distance from the Old City, erect flat shops and Hollywood-style villas, add a park in which the dry grass is always bronze-colored, a Stalinesque governor's palace and a football field, and you have the New Town, identical to every New Town in Asia, be it Isfahan, Samarkand, Delhi or Kabul.

The New Town in Herat was particularly infamous. Lying on the Asian highway between the European counter-culture and the promised land of Katmandu, the New Town played the vital role of a *cordon sanitaire*, isolating the foreign tourist community from the bazaars. Its hotels were filled all summer long with east-bound travelers. It also served as the town zoo, something to talk about for those Heratis whose venturing out of the bazaar was as reluctant as our venturing in. They came to see the foreigners with their long hair and bare limbs, especially (though not only) the foreign women. The wise took council, and sold hashish for many times its worth back in the bazaar. The incurious and incupidinous were glad not to have to deal with them, not to be reminded that in this world God rewards the unbelievers with so many blessings, no matter what lies in store for them in the next. It is that feeling that we read in the *bazaaris* gazing after us.

The experience was unpleasant. I remember with shame returning to the New Town, comfortably insulated and feeling quite relieved. My capacity for observing, or being like others, often flagged, giving way to complete retreat from further contact. One made ties binding one to people, only to have them grow tired, seeing no use in the friendship. One turned back on one's friends, who seemed too close to that part which held the return ticket. For all these recollections of unpleasantness, it saddened me, much later, to know that the New Town lies empty of travelers, and the Old City is now a Minotaur's labynth of violence.

We had taken a room in a hotel near the bazaar, the most desolate and remote of the "hippie-hotels," but which had the advantage of being empty. We had not been in the mood to room with India-bound tourists, who notoriously loathed the stopover. A boy, asleep on a *takht* in the shade of a weeping willow, had roused himself from the deep, hungry sleep of the fast and had shown us a room, which we took, then padlocked our bags inside and departed. The boy slunk back to continue his nap.

Now, returning from the Old City, we found the same boy sitting with a man on the *takht*. It was getting dark but we could see the two manipulating a *qalyan*, or waterpipe, the use of which was not permitted until sunset. It was getting very near dusk. As we went inside the plaster bungalow, a cannon shot echoed through the street, the fast ended, a hot coal dropped hissing into the belly of the *qalyan* and the man took a few relieving mouthfuls of smoke, the water gurgling at each drag. The boy drank water. Both actions had been forbidden since breakfast time, except for those of us who had been on the road, traveling more than 300 kilometers. Tomorrow, we would have to deal with the fast.

There was no light in the bungalow yet, the city's electricity running only after eight o'clock, so we sat in our room observing a quiet moment. The man and the boy came into the room, without knocking, and squatted down by the door. I thought this was strange, but said nothing, expecting them to speak up. They kept silent. The boy looked at us curiously, with sideways glances, while the man pulled beads through his fingers.

Several minutes passed like this until the hour of eight. The lights went on all over town, and the single bulb hanging down from our ceiling began to give off a yellowish glow. We saw our callers clearly now. The boy who had let us the room was a child of twelve, with a big, square head and a crew cut. He was looking at us intently with a lively gaze. His companion gave us only sideways glances. A middle-aged man, clean-shaven, with a very thin face, pitted with pockmarks; even in the weak light he appeared extraordinarily ugly.

Since they didn't intend to break their silence, I said, "Who are you?"

"He," said the boy, as though eager to talk all along, "is the *sahib otel*." The *sahib*, or owner of the hotel, had nothing to object to this. He continued to regard us sideways.

"*Meestar!*" the boy went on, since we gave him our attention, "what do you want?"

"Want? Nothing." My friend and I exchanged glances and shook our heads.

"*Meestar!* Hashish?"

I caught the drift of this, but before I could express a preference my friend said with suitable gravity, "*La hawla wala qadra bilallah!*" which is to say, "Satan get thee back!"

Astounded, the boy gave us a helpless look and put out his hand, with a small bar of hashish.

"That is forbidden," said my friend, firmly.

The bar of hashish disappeared into the boy's pocket. The man spoke up, though not to us, "They must be Muslims."

"No, we're not. Do you think that every nonbeliever enjoys what is illicit?" asked my friend.

"*Bi-Khuda*, by God, they are Muslims," said the boy, excitedly.

The *sahib otel* mused aloud, "I have seen unbelievers, for the most part they are, as he says, enjoying everything which is not licit to the believers. Perhaps these are a new tribe of foreigners. They speak Persian."

We explained that we were just an old tribe, the *Amrikais*, and that we had learned Persian in school. At the word school the man's narrow eyes lit up. "Ah, I should have realized, they are *mu'adab* (with letters, polite). Then you will forgive this aspersion. I am, you see, a poor man. I have just bought this *otel* and have yet to see a profit out of it. God is munificent, you came here, I have to cater to the illicit habits of the foreigners ..."

"Hashish," I explained, to console him, "is not strictly speaking illicit, *haram*, but unadvised, *makruh*."

The man went on as though he heard none of this, "In order to support this boy, my nephew. He is going to school, to become a scholar, like yourselves."

"He will do well, he is a devil."

"*Mashallah*, he will do well," said the *sahib otel*, warding off the evil eye.

"What's your name?" my friend said to the boy.

"My name is Abdul Wasi (Slave of Who Spreads). His is Abdul Wahid (Slave of Who is Unique). Your names are what—Daud and Wali? *Bi-Khuda*, they are Muslims." At this the man signalled to the boy, and both rose to take their leave. We asked them to stay and have tea with us, but there was the insuperable obstacle that they were not our guests, nor were we guests of theirs in the traditional sense. In fact, they left so that the boy could change *persona*. He returned with an officiating air and brought us dinner. We asked him to join us in eating it, which would have been absurd, and he adroitly refused. When we finished our meal, we called for tea, in which he consented to join us.

"*Meestar*, don't you take hashish?" he asked shyly, *sotto voce*. We told him no. "Everyone here does, Muslims and unbelievers." When he left we felt like two sanctimonious prigs, but it had served a purpose. The only way to convince people that one isn't a great deal worse than they are is to act as though one is very much better.

Days and Nights in a Fasting Season

One day my friend and I decided to fast. We awoke after sun up and had to go hungry, since breakfasting was forbidden now. Because of the fast, many had gone back to bed after a late, light meal; their shops stood shuttered. These were the wealthy grand merchants of the New Town, who could afford to stay closed until evening. Only the passing of a Mercedes-

Benz cab, bearing some astrakhan-hatted bureaucrat to his office at the *wali's* palace, a ten-minute walk away, interrupted the trafficless aspect of the avenue. The early sun, most dangerous to travelers, shone down on the asphalt, and shadows in the thin dry air were intense, electric. The ordinary *bazaari* had to go to work this morning. Because of the fast, none had had his morning draught of tobacco, and tempers had worn thin. Bleareyed passersby, who had been up all night feeding and passing time, staggered to work. The air was already grown hot, yet one was forbidden to swallow one's spittle. Much hacking and spitting could be heard among the thin crowds.

Beggars were the most active figures to take to the streets in the early morning, for the fasting month was called the month of alms. A man came down the street towards the big crossroads, carrying a young boy over his shoulders, like a sack. At the high curb the man set the boy on the pavement and went off from where he came. The boy had no legs, but fish-like, his torso tapered into a long, flat tail, he raised himself athletically on his elbows and began to call out, "In the name of God, *bi-nam-i-Khuda!*" in a clear, cheery voice. He was nimble, turning to this and that passerby, as they came from all directions, so that each one nearly tripped over the boy and had to give him money. Horrified, fascinated, we watched him, ignoring a mendicant who followed at our heels. "In the name of God, in the name of God," said this one, with solemnity mixed with pity. We went on. "RAMAZAN, RAMAZAN," he invoked the Ramazan, the Muslims' sacred fast, and we finally stopped. He could not understand our reluctance to give, since charity was an obligation imposed by the holy month. When we satisfied him, he showed no gratitude—like a stockbroker, he was helping us accumulate shares in the heavenly kingdom. He snorted at our offering, suggesting that such as we should have worried more about laying up a greater store against our present benighted state. Half-grown boys, having nothing better to do, bandaged their sound limbs in dirty rags or smeared themselves with the blood of slaughtered animals and stood about imploring alms. The passersby saw through these tricks, tapping the gaping wounds with a smile and advising the overgrown imps to "seek liberality from God."

Because of the fast, the fruit vendors eyed their clients suspiciously from the shade of their booths, thinking that anyone who bought just one or two apples intended to eat them straight away, in violation of the fast. The vendors refused to sell; "*Ramazan, Ramazan,*" one barked at us, waving us away impatiently. We pleaded, "We are travelers for whom the fast is not ordained."

"And where came you from?"

"Yesterday from Mashhad and the line." We took two apples and exchanged a coin with him, but walking down the street under the livid glares of the passersby, hungry, unrested, their stomachs fresh to the new fast groaning and making noise, we could not bring ourselves to eat. We hid the apples away in our pockets, looking for some place to be unobserved, but even back at Abdul Wahid's, the boy Abdul Wasi came to keep company with us, hungry, and the apples remained in our pockets.

In Iran, the heterodox Shi'ite kingdom, the street was aware of its heresy: the pedestrians all wore black and the women fine gauzy black veils. The taxis were orange, the mosques decked out in fairy lights and loudspeakers, portraits of saints, of the Prophet Muhammad, of his heir Ali, the Imams, hung everywhere in view, depictions of the knights of old, the heroes of the Book of Kings in gaudy color, slaying storybook dragons, the huge photographs of the Imperial family, and the local weight-lifters, decorated public places. In Afghanistan there were no pictures, no visual representations of things. The streets were brown-grey, the gay colors of people's garments wilted and muted in the hot, dry dust; the few cabs were lackluster, the droshky carriages sported years-old paint jobs. Afghanistan was not picturesque in any sense. The lack of color, form, image, shape, was oppressive, and one's visual appetite was denied.

At evening we broke the fast; food tasted excessively good in the dry mouth. "Don't eat right after the fast, but wait," advised Abdul Wasi, who took only a draught of water to prepare his stomach for food. We were knocked out by the effort of a single day and determined not to fast tomorrow.

So we found ourselves with great reluctance lunching on yogurt and porridge in one of the hippie hotels, while *Ramazan* went on beyond the walled courtyard. Surprisingly, beside the assorted Europeans, Germans, Dutch, Japanese, and French, quite a number of young Afghans surreptitiously broke the fast, embarrassed, at first, to be seen with their fellows, and then entering into a kind of conspiracy of food. One of these fellows, a fine-moustachioed *madrasa* (seminary) student, sat in the shade over a table-top chess set, battling with a German fellow over the game. The German had only one arm, which he waved impotently after losing game after game. That the *madrasa* student should be eating intrigued us.

Curious, we invited ourselves to sit by and watch. When the German finally gave up in disgust, my friend asked for a chance to play. Oriental chess differs from ours in two respects. First, the pawn only moves one square initially; secondly, cheating is heartily approved. For whatever reason, my friend lost all the games, but was so charmed by his rival's joking manner and eagerness to rematch that he accepted all the defeats gracefully.

The fellow's name, like mine, was Daud. His brother owned the hotel, a popular and profitable business, unlike Abdul Wahid's, and both brothers bent their religious scruples to entertain their Muslim friends during the fast. "If I don't eat," said Daud, "I get sick, and if I get sick, I'm legally exempt from the fast, so why fast?" As for the other Afghans, "They are all travelers, if any one asks, so they are exempt from the fast, too." We visited Daud's brother's place often during Ramazan's hungry days, and my friend played many losing games with Daud, though losing less badly than the German, whose single arm did not allow him to cheat very often.

And in the evening, with the fast ended, we fell back into rhythm with the rest of the city, sitting in the yard of Abdul Wahid's hotel and giving in to the fast-induced lassitude of our hosts. Abdul Wasi sat on the *takht*, with his legs folded beneath him, his hands turned up in his lap, a school book—long closed—beside him. We sat in the chairs, reading the small library of books which constituted most of our luggage and tried to relax. In typically Western manner, we moved the chairs back and forth, picked up several books and leafed through them before setting them aside. All the while Abdul Wasi sat still, not rigid but motionless, enjoying perfect calm. It was only when daylight failed, which it did shortly before six, that we began to appreciate the night cool, and the inability to read by the poor electric light, and the benefits of doing nothing at all. Soon we found ourselves as reposeful as our young friend.

Sham, the hour of supper and evening prayer: Abdul Wasi took a deep draught of water, ready at hand, to the sound of the echoing boom of the cannon, marking the end of the fast. A dutiful believer, he spread his short cape on the ground and performed his genuflections, without being the least self-conscious of our watching him, and what was more, without being ostentatious before us. Not for him the waggish sophistry of our friend Daud. Finishing the prayers he looked up at us, saying, "*Meestars*, why don't you pray, pray is good."

"So they say, but we don't know your prayers."

"You don't? It's very simple, first you say, *Alahuabkarala- huakbarashaduannala . . .*" he paused for breath, "then . . ."

"Whoa, *jan*, this is very difficult. We have our prayers, too. They are better for us."

Agreeably, the boy slid back onto the *takht* and resumed his former pose. But for the droning of his prayers, the night was quiet. A city without noise, I reflected, was the sweetest prayer of all.

Abdul Wahid was by trade a sweetseller. We had seen his shop, a tiny booth fronting on the bazaar, with only a few strands of treacle hanging from a nail, some oil tins of hard candies and a plate of doughy, oily cookies. It was hard to believe that this merchant traveled annually to Sham and Stamboul to deal in crumbs, but so he said, and described for us Istanbul as though it were before our eyes. Abdul Wahid was a good talker and a popular man, to judge by the crowd of companions who sat before his store, eventimes, when the sweetselling bazaar stayed open to satiate the denied sweet tooth of *Ramazan*. It was apparent that our friend was not a good businessman, for his guests ate well of his diminished inventory. When it grew very dark and customers were few, one of them lit a lantern and led the assembly back to the hotel, where they continued to visit on the grass under the tree, long into the night. We gradually overcame our shyness, began to stay up late and join them in these sessions, the busy nights of *Ramazan*.

From the first, they were amused to have us, for we offered a diversion unique in their experience. The merchants had gradually accepted the fact of the foreign invasion of their city, while being confirmed in the impression that the tourists were beyond the pale of humankind. Here was their chance to learn what there was to know of the strangers' way.

Abdul Wahid spoke most of the time, his companions deferring to his hostship, and his curiosity was suitably high-minded. "My nephew says you read all the time and that you understand all the languages of the world and must consequently be very wise. Tell me, when *Amrikais* went to the moon, how did they get through the spheres?"

"Spheres?"

"You know, every planet and star hangs upon a sphere of *bulurian*, of crystal. Did they have to cut a hole in it? Explain how you did it, and I for one am willing to admit it could be done, though many people here," he looked at the utterly unconvinced faces about him, "say that they never landed on the moon, but only reached the top of a tall mountain."

"To be sure," said my friend, "I don't think there are spheres such as you say. A planet spins in orbit the way a top spins on the floor." But this attempt to destroy Ptolemaic astronomy was greeted with alarmed skepticism.

"But you believe in God," said Abdul Wahid, waving these fine points away, assuming the theodicy itself rested on the same *bulurian* spheres. "Of course, how can one not? If I drop this stone on the ground, what makes it fall?"

"Gravit—"

"God does. I am glad to see that your great learning has not hidden this fact from you, as it is clear to see that everything depends on Him." I looked up at the sky, which shone brightly with stars, which seemed too close, too real, to be distantly orbiting. One could reach out and grab one, but Someone, presumably, stayed one's hand.

"You are right," I said, eager to accommodate our host, and to placate the few suspicious glances born of my friend's physics lesson.

Too late. One of them spoke up, "But why don't they become Muslims? It is so easy. All they have to do is say the words, *La'llah* . . ." He was a hawk-nosed fellow with a cowl-like red beard and blazing eyes.

Another, gentler fellow said, "A *Faranasavi* was here a few months ago. He was very learned, like you, and a Muslim. He became a Muslim in Marakash. Always fasting and praying, that one, but he didn't speak very good Persian. He went to India afterward."

"Hm. Afterward, I reckon he went to India and became a Hindu," I replied.

"Aye, what he says is true," sighed another man, inured to the ways of foreigners.

"It is better not to leave the religion of one's fathers," said the gentler man, meditatively, citing the tradition: " 'If a man is brought up among idol worshippers, he will worship idols'."

"Then what do they believe? Let them say," demanded the redbeard contentiously.

I fished for the cautious words of Mughal Prince Darashikuh, my favorite authority on toleration. "We say, 'In the name of Him who has no name, by whatever name you call Him, there He is'."

"*Wa, wa,* well said," put in the gentle man. Abdul Wahid looked about to his friends as though to say, "Secretly they are Muslims."

Talk turned to other things. I found it strange that, while they regarded as Muslim anyone who voiced the slightest spiritual aspirations and considered the Westerners to be brainless materialists, they had an unquenchable curiosity about things in this world—chiefly money, and women. The higher tone of our earlier conversation was lost, Abdul Wahid himself succumbing to the general interest. How much did you pay for those boots? Will you give them to me? What about that coat? It is cotton? How much is cotton per *man* in *Amrika*? Could I go there and sell confection? What are your wages? How much do you expect to pay brideprice?

And in a still lower tone—it was late now—they asked, "Are women lawful to you in their time? Do you prefer the front, or the back?" We grew red with embarrassment, to their surprise. Grown men were supposed to be able to discuss such things. The combination of piety and carnality in the same evening's conversation struck none of them as incongruous.

Each civilization accuses the other of being *dahri*, attached overmuch to the world. After they scrutinized our women's ways in unattractive detail, they clucked their tongues, "What sensualists these foreigners are." And we were of precisely the same opinion of them.

Whenever talk grew quiet, a ready hand would switch on the radio-cassette player. The most prosperous of Abdul Wahid's friends always carried one with him, boasting that he paid 10,000 *rupees* for it, though one suspected that the battered machine had cost him (and was worth) half as much. One bought them on pilgrimage, in Kuwait, praise God, and had them decorated in the scrapvendors' bazaar, with black naugahide, appliqués, gold glitter, and glass beads. Resplendent, the cassette player served in our modest assembly for the brilliantly apparelled *nautch* girls of Old Delhi, for the bronze *shamdan* or candelabras of days past. It was beautiful to look at, opening the heart with its rending, reedy song; it could not be long before the poets of the bazaar would weave the recorder itself into the tales of the coy rose and the persistent nightingale, of the flaming candle and the lovelorn moth.

During one such concert they asked us, "do you have songs like this in your country? Sad ones?" Sad always meant good.

"No, not like these. Different, but songs," I said.

"Sing."

I sang for a moment, then the hands reached for the cassette player again and set the tape to wailing.

Abdul Wahid, we suspected, made no money at the hotel, which served him as a more accommodating place than his booth in the bazaar. To understand why he had no European clients except us one had only to look into the courtyard of the hotel after six in the evening. The lawn lit up by a single yellow bulb, surrounded by moths, the smoke of the waterpipe, its characteristic gurgle when dragged upon, the half-whispers of the men, wrapped against the evening cool, squatting on the grass. Long faces, faces that have seen everything, faces that accept nothing, stare up from the séance at the intruder. Outside this tiny circle of light, shadows and indifference fall across the yard.

Though we became acquainted with most of Abdul Wahid's circle, by day we rarely saw them, for they were sleeping—or dozing, at least—in the shade of their shops in the bazaar, or loath, in any case, to be seen talking to foreigners in public. More than once, we salaamed a familiar in the street and he would go on his way coldly. The same night he would smile and greet us as though nothing had occurred. If I mentioned it, he would say, "You must have seen my brother," or "Ah, you know it is the fasting month, and my head is ruined, *maghzam kharab-a*."

They took the fast seriously, these merchants, pious Muslims. Sitting up with them at night, seeing their sallow faces under the lamp, I began to form an impression of their dedication to Islam. The moons of the religious calendar suggested the silver coins of the counting house. The lunar period offered a more convenient record for the accountant. Debts were due on the new moon. Muhammad, the merchant, had expressly forbidden the intercalary months which the agriculturalists had introduced into the Semitic year. We awaited the end of the fast, when the new moon would show over Saudi Arabia, when a new line would be drawn down the ledger books with a Bic pen. After adding up the profits of the month, they would set aside their riches, for the poor, for the refurbishing of a mosque or a bath. There was little to buy in the city, after the wife, the house, and the cassette machine, and there were no direct taxes. Bar disaster, the rising of the new moon wiped the slate clean. Sauntering down the street hand in hand with a friend, or pulling the beads through one's fingers in the cool shade of one's shop, one had all the time in the world to think on God.

Always, the theological discussions. Religion—its purpose—must have been to encumber mankind. Righteousness, the cheerless quality of suffering. The Afghans, in their poverty, championed their asceticism. "According to what you believe, must you keep the fast?"

"Not as you keep the fast, by day alone, gorging at night, but day and night for forty days."

"What do they eat in this *chilla* (forty-day period)?" asked our curious companions.

"Little besides porridge, nothing fresh, no meat, dry bread . . ."

"Ha! They call that a fast in your country? It were a feast for us. You see what we eat in the winter, you'd say that our fast lasted from *Aqrab* month to *Naw Bahar*!"

"Well, they consider it a hardship, who keep the fast."

They knew our country was rich, which was enough to prove it godless. For them, poverty and saintliness were rough equivalents, though they admitted the contradictions in this. When we complained of the lustiness of the beggars and of the religious sorts, they excused them: "Poor men are but bellies, that is all." Poverty brought no peace of mind like riches.

They had their cares, these merchants, for all the insouciance and languor of religious spirit which wrapped around them like a cloud of hashish. "We have trees, gardens, fields, livestock, the best melons in the world," they complained, enumerating the traditional indices of wealth, "yet Afghanistan is the poorest country in the world." It seemed like a punishment for their orthodoxy.

Abdul Wahid often lamented his poverty, which prevented him from doing good. "In the old days, why, money was as nothing. A merchant used to scatter coins in the street. Build a bath, a mosque, give great feasts for the poor, why it was nothing. We used to entertain guests for weeks on end without a thought of reward," he said ruefully, hinting at our position. "Only now, everything is different."

Since the sudden impoverishment of Afghanistan corresponded to the time when foreigners first began to travel widely, the suspicion was that we, the *meestars*, had brought Islam to this pass. How? By magic, by spying, by stealing away national treasures . . . An explanation was demanded.

I did not have far to go for my explanation. Wasn't that cassette machine purchased from abroad? And those ruby-dialed wristwatches which the rich sported like jewelry? When they went abroad, on the *hajj* to Mecca, they returned loaded down with gadgets, none of which was common until recently (they were new to me, so they had to be new to them). Was Afghanistan any poorer, or was its demand for foreign things greater? The country owed the Soviet Union ten *lakh lakhs* dollars for arms, to be repaid in raisins, boxwood and sunflower seeds. A few of the greybeards nodded approvingly at this argument.

"Of old," said one of them, "we would go down to plunder Hindustan, bringing back such wealth as is no longer seen in the country today, gold, jewels, slaves, ambergris. But now Islam is as nothing in the world. The *Hindis* sell us flour and *ghee*, and the *Rus* treat us usuriously."

It was easier to see it as one grand *götterdämerung* than accept a taxing explanation. God had turned His favors away from His people. Instinctively I sympathized more with those who felt thus, than with Abdul Wahid, who suddenly announced, "We must cover the country with factories, as in Turkey and Hindustan." More talk went on along these lines.

A threat that hung over these people made their lives more bearable. Foreigners were coming to shake up their world. Whether the foreign powers built new roads, or their tourists spent foreign exchange, or whether their radios and cassettes sounded disturbing voices, the imminence of change relieved the *Heratis* of responsibility for the outcome of their lives. Their major occupation was talk, their living a spectator sport.

They could sit it out either optimistically or pessimistically, according to inclination. Pessimism seemed the truer sentiment: Islam (but how many other cultural traditions!) teaches nostalgia for its origins and a view of history as a falling away from great examples. Islamic pessimism has the deepest resonance in literature and in everyday expressions. Overlaid upon this was the disorder of their own days, the famines, the debasement of the currency, the revolution, and God knows what "those Pathans in Kabul" would do next. All this made the pessimism of the *Heratis* so real to me.

The optimistic ones sounded a false note. Repeating the clichés of the Pakistani *ulama*, Maulana Maududi especially, they pretended that all was for the best in the best of Muslim worlds, that Islam mandated progress and scientific advance. They were happy with the conversion of prize fighter Muhammad Ali, taking this as a fair indication of Islam's wider role in the world. People have begun to call this militant Islam, a mix of converts' enthusiasm, quaint Victorian positivism and still quainter eighteenth-century rationalism, with only a dim trace of pristine fanaticism. But these "militants," in my experience, proved to be rather feckless, pleasant, ready talkers who enjoyed books. They were optimistic about life in face of all facts.

Abdul Wahid was a little like that, which shows what appealing types I could identify as militant Muslims. With unbending single-mindedness he pretended to believe that we were observing the ways of Islam prior to conversion, although we never led him to think so. Thus he salved his conscience over his dealings with the unbelievers, his sole customers. His optimism was manifested by more than his near-vacant *otel*; he had hopes for the future: he hoped that, when we tired of distant places and returned to our homes, we would take his nephew Abdul Wasi back with us as our apprentice, teaching him the ways of the powerful West. In this, too, he was entirely self-deceived, for more than once we told him how hard it would be for an Afghan to come to *Amrika* and settle there, or even study at school. But he would only say, "Ah, anything desirable is difficult, but the desire makes the difficulties easy."

It was useless to explain to Abdul Wahid some of our real

interest in visiting the country, though we mentioned it to him. I had my first view of the nomad's black hair tents in Herat itself. By the ruins of the *musalla*, where the city tapers off into a field of rubbish, ruined houses and the occasional pauper's shack, three black tents, flapping on their ropes, with patches in their canvas, stood in the windbreak of a ruined wall. I was standing on the bridge over the stream Injil, to get a view over the tents, seeing the broken odds and ends which the tent dwellers had collected from the surrounding scrap heap: metal cans of *ghee* worked into primitive vessels, worn tire trends reworked into shoes and buckets. A woman in a filthy grey *chadri* sat in the opening of a tent and stared out over the rubbish. Her *chadri* had no mask; her expression was one of immobility. A child of these tents caught sight of me and stole up to the bridge. The little girl was dressed in bright rags. She offered me a piece of faience, a fragment off the fallen minarets of Gawhar Shad. I said, "You didn't take this off the minarets, did you?" She understood nothing, but stared at the bit of fragment in her hand and wondered why I didn't give her money for it.

I asked Abdul Wahid who these people in the black tents might be. Gypsies, he told me, and I believed him, until my friend observed that he had been out to a gypsy camp, a gathering of horse thieves, prostitutes, freak-show performers and wild musicians. He did not think these black tent dwellers were gypsies. "After the famine in 1972, a lot of nomads were supposed to have moved to the city because they were destitute."

Abdul Wahid said, tellingly, "Oh, gypsies, nomads, it's the same thing." If the only nomads he had seen were these pauperized refugees, he might as well think them gypsies, but he would never understand that we hoped to join them.

The two of us went back to the bridge to see the tent dwellers, but after an appeal for alms they had nothing to say. There was just the loud sullenness of their poverty.

We didn't expect to see our friend from the Kandahar Gate again, but we overlooked the slower pace of life during the fasting season. One day, after dusk, Abdul Wasi came in to announce a visitor. Gul Ahmad appeared at the door. We asked him to come in, and seated him at the top of the room, the place of honor, sending the boy to fetch us tea and supper. Abdul Wasi seemed piqued that we should have any friends outside his uncle's circle. He was clearly jealous that we should receive this stranger so courteously.

Gul Ahmad, for his part, was a little surprised at the easiness of our welcome, having been unable to raise the courage to look us up for some time. Now he quickly addressed himself as though to old friends, *"Walijan, Daudjan,* I have come by here several times, but they told me you were always out." *Jan,* which meant "soul," was appended to one's name in a friendly way. Gul Ahmad spoke with a note of concern, as though we were long-lost friends, and began to *tutoyer* us.

"We have been busy," I said to reassure him, though I knew he was fibbing. "How did your business go?"

"Business? Well, thank you. Business is very hard, isn't it?" he said vaguely.

We agreed. A repetition of our earlier awkwardness was avoided by Abdul Wasi's prompt delivery of dinner, reheated from yesterday in an oiled cooking pot. We asked Abdul Wasi to join us, but he sulkily refused, staying by the door, though, to watch us eat. He had not provided our guest with a separate bowl, so Gul Ahmad was somewhat put out at the thought of eating. It was one thing to sit with them, but to eat off the same plate as they did was perhaps forbidden. Abdul Wasi looked maliciously on, until we called for a ewer, signalling the end of the dinner. Gul Ahmad had scarcely eaten anything.

"I wasn't hungry." He knew that we had noticed his restraint in eating, a slight to the host. "Hotel food makes me ill." Then he rose, placed one hand on his heart in a sign of fealty, and begged his leave. Now he was running from us, having crossed some invisible line in his dealings with us, wanting to dart back across for the time being. We smiled, mystified, and expressed the hope that we would see him before as great a time elapsed as previously. "Yes, yes, *inshallah,* I will see you soon." And he left.

Said Abdul Wasi, clearing the tea, "That's the sort of friends Afghans make (He meant Pathans, for Gul Ahmad was not a *Herati* by speech or manner; there was race rivalry between him and Abdul Wasi.) They come, they eat, and they leave without so much as a howdy-do."

'But he didn't eat anything,' I wanted to protest to the child's remark. However, I merely clicked my tongue.

Daud was different. With him we could almost forget the hundreds of barriers, linguistic, confessional, and cultural which deafened communication back and forth. Not that Daud wasn't extremely *Herati* by nature. His daily intercourse with foreigners at his brother's hotel had not tamed him, the way so many young men of the town had been tamed to European ways. They wore jackets and trousers, white shirts and heeled shoes, but were difficult to deal with in their own fashion, holding as they did a mirror of our own ideals up to us which we could never possibly realize for them. Daud asked us to be ourselves; he was himself. Whatever was *Herati* or Afghan about him he appropriated to himself alone, taking neither credit nor blame for their expression in him. If he was devious, lazy, hypochondriac or a daydreamer, we forgot these were national shibboleths. If he was unpredictable, that too we never attributed to the fact he was Afghan. We showed up at our usual rendezvous, the brother's hotel, and he wasn't there.

"He said he'd look for you in the Parc Bihzad," said the one-armed German, when we asked for him. The park was only on the other side of town. In the heat, we hurried over.

The Parc Bihzad was a cheerless plot of evergreens and tanbark, on the site of the old *musalla* or place of prayer. The sleepy pines threw everything into shade, unrelieved except for a burn-out, here and there, or the ruins of the *musalla* complex, lonely, free-standing minarets, broken off midway and cracked by faults running up the sides, fallen masonry, the pale domes of mausoleums. Scattered around lay chips of faience, the shattered skin of ruined buildings, which glinted in the rare shafts of lights penetrating the dense tree cover. A *madrasa*, a modern brick edifice, stood at the foot of one of the great monumental minarets. No one seemed to be around, another instance of Daud's unpredictability.

"*Daudjan, Walijan, istauni?*" Daud's pleasant voice called from a clearing in the trees. We saw him sitting in this sunny spot with another youth, school books and pens spread before them. The young man introduced himself as Sayyid Shafaq, an affable, slightly feeble-minded-looking sort with aristocratic grace of manner. His baby face was ever creased by a frown, to make him look older, I guessed, and because friend Daud with a sharp sense of humor always teased him. For his part, Daud constantly twisted his fine moustache, which suggested that his relaxed manner was something of an effort. Daud and the *sayyid* were preparing for an examination.

"*Daudjan*," the *sayyid* complained lazily, "I just can't do it. You sit beside me in the exam."

"*Bi-Khuda*, Sayyid Shafaq, you'll just have to cram." The unhappy scholar began to prime his pen, an expensive German one, and looked attentively, extending his starched pajama sleeve, to Daud's dictation. The two reviewed the details of Islamic inheritance laws.

"Now the collorary is that all brothers and sisters are excluded by the son, son's son, how low soever, father or true grandfather. Half brothers and sisters, on the father's side, are excluded by these, and also by full brothers, from inheritance."

". . . half brothers and sisters," the *sayyid* dutifully copied this into miniscules on his shirt sleeve. His handwriting was wonderfully elegant, with the sweeping downward curves of a master in *Shikasta* style. The *sayyid's* better subject was calligraphy.

The legal lesson ended abruptly when my friend asked, "Can you climb that minaret?"

"Yes, yes," said Sayyid Shafaq, much more interested in climbing minarets than learning about inheritance laws. From his voluminous silk pajamas he produced an elaborately tooled key and led us across the way to the *madrasa*. Inside the school room, the inevitable map of Afghanistan, the pictures of the Ka'ba of Mecca, examples of master calligraphers, worm-eaten copies of books with lengthy Arabic titles, like "The Divination of the Secrets of the Most Sublime Rose Garden of Felicity and the Way of Ascent Thereto by the deceased great Shaykh Ali Khwujagan son of Abi Fazl son of Hasan al-Mushayakh al-Heravi."

"Old books," commented Sayyid Shafaq, seeing me look through the titles. "They make a young man grow grey." We stood before the narrow stone staircase which spiralled to the top of the minaret. Only one of us at a time could make the ascent, so we waited our turn, calling out to each dawdler, "Hurry up so we can all go up!" My friend and Sayyid Shafaq went, then I. It seemed like only a few moments that I was up there.

The evergreens spread at my feet like a green pool of still water, limned by the grey and yellow cityscape of Old Herat. In the green pooling, just below, I saw the mausoleum of Gawhar Shad, a floating dome of polychrome tiles; a smaller mausoleum, not piercing above the green, but showing like a white stone underwater, was the unornamented tomb dome of Amir Ali Sher. Beyond the park, I could see the portals, the twin *ivans* of the shrines of Abdul Kasim and Abdullah Ja'far, white-washed and ghostly, encircled with grey clouds of pigeons, while rising above them, the crumbling walls of the ruined citadel, baked brick, and a few huge tiles of blue and black faience which spelled fragments of a Kufic inscription. Behind that, the sunburst of light on the cathedral mosque, in all its delicate faience skin, blue, turquoise, lapis and green, like another pool of water, in the grey and yellow infinity of tiny domes, flat roofs, ruined houses, still-standing pigeon towers.

"Hurry down so we can go up!" Daud called through the stairwell. I climbed down reluctantly. The spiral staircase was much harder to negotiate going down. Sayyid Shafaq waited for me with brows furrowed on his baby face, as though the view above were something important.

"The ruins of the *musalla* are very sad," I told him. I thereby struck an odd note. The *sayyid* wouldn't see the *musalla* as a ruin at all. Six of the original fourteen minarets still stood, just two of the innumerable mausoleums; nothing of the schools, nor eighty-four foot high portals, nor galleries for students and dervishes, nor cathedral mosque remained, these were all pulled down under an earlier threat of Russian invasion, when Abdur Rahman Khan feared the *musalla* would be used as sightings for the Russian artillery, an attack which never came. Sayyid Shafaq did not think of the *musalla* as a ruin. He went to a school there, on the site of the *madrasa* founded by Gawhar Shad in 1432, and in imagination, he identified the two. There was nothing sad about it to him.

When Daud descended, the *sayyid* insisted he tell us an anecdote about the *madrasa* of Gawhar Shad. Daud consented, though Sayyid Shafaq continued to prompt needlessly. "I say, Gawhar Shad, who was queen in those days,"

"Queen of Shah Rukh, Timur's son . . ."

"Queen of Shah Rukh built this *musalla* and this *madrasa*. She used to come here to inspect the place, at night, of course, for discretion, after she built it. One night when she came to inspect it, she heard a lone *hafiz*, chanting at the gate of the school. You know what is *hafiz*? A reciter of the Holy Qur'an (Koran). He was blind . . ."

"They are mostly blind," put in the *sayyid*.

"Well, this one happened to be blind. But he wasn't reciting the Qur'an as he chanted, no, what was he reciting? He was praying to God for a visitation from a *huri*. You know what is a *huri*? A pretty girl . . ."

"From Paradise."

So Gawar Shad heard the *hafiz* praying to God for a visitation from a *huri*, and she was very amused. She went home and told her slave girl to go to the *madrasa* the next night and visit the blind *hafiz*, telling him that his prayers had been answered. So the next night the slave girl went to the *madrasa* and found the *hafiz*, as before, praying just as the Queen described him. She told him his prayers had been answered. At first he was very pleased. But when the girl kept coming back night after night, he was no longer so pleased. Finally, in desperation he cried out, "Isn't there another *hafiz* in the *madrasa*?' "

Sayyid Shafaq burst into laughter for the first time, "And we still say, 'Isn't there another *hafiz* in the *madrasa*?' It's an expression."

The anecdote and the expression kept the *musalla* from seeming the shattered ruin it was in fact. *Heratis* often seemed to live in the afterglow of a brief century, the rule, 1391 to 1506, of the heirs of "Lame Timur" (Tamerlane). The fashion had popularly been for a long time to throw everything back on the Golden Age, to attribute every building to Shah Rukh or to his Queen; to attribute all calligraphy to the admitted master, Sultan Baysunghur, and every painting to the prince of painters, Bihzad. A man hawking postcards in the street would say, "Masterpieces, real Bihzads," meaning only that the past and the present had not slipped apart in Herat. The names of the Timurids, rather promiscuously, speckled the official city with signs and advertisements, for hotels, for schools, a plastic emanation of folk memory.

Of their downfall, preceded by fratricide, unrivaled debauchery and chronic cirrhosis, followed by the brutal occupation of the Uzbeks, and the long sleepy rule of Iran, the city remembered little. The chief reservoir in the bazaar was the work of the Iranian governors of the city in the seventeenth century, but it had fallen into disrepair. Urban renewal had effaced the splendid governor's palace of the same period. How could the center of the world have been a provincial capital for some far-off kings? It was better not to remember. Besides, during the Persian occupation the city had converted to the national heresy of the Persians, Shi'ism, and many old *Heratis* still clung to it, making the city the scorn of Orthodox Afghans, and making reference to the days of Persian rule unwelcome. Were the *Heratis* really covert Shi'-ites? And were they really sympathetic to Iran? The *Heratis* preferred to pretend that they were absolutely unique, like their poet who said, "They ask me if I am a Shi'ite or Orthodox. I say I am neither the dog of the first nor the stick of the last."

"Let me tell you about the *Heratis*," said Daud, after I tired him with historical questions. "In the days of Nadir Shah, the Persian shah, the Persians wanted to find out what the *Heratis* were thinking. So they sent a spy into the city to see what the *Heratis* were saying. Nadir wanted to know. So the spy came and someone said to him, 'Istauni,' which means 'How are you?,' but the spy, he didn't know. So he wrote it down. And they knew he didn't understand. So they said to him, '*Zanbil-i-sirisht dar bun-i-tu bikana wa tu dar sabil-i-kurshit zipak zipak mikuni*,' which means, 'A bee will sting you in your bum and you'll jump up and down on the crabgrass.' But the spy didn't understand, so he wrote it down too. And he wrote many things like that, in the *Herati* expressions, and returned to Nadir, the Shah. And he said, 'O King, I do not know what the *Heratis* are saying, but here is what I wrote down'. And when Nadir read these things, he was amazed, and he went to Herat himself, and the *Heratis* received him. And when they told him what it was they had said to the spy, Nadir was even more amazed, and he left, and he never came back to disturb Herat again."

The point was, and they admitted it, it was hard to get to know the *Heratis*. "Why, there have been wise men who come among us for ten years, twenty, and they don't understand us. Why don't you get married and settle here, that'll answer your questions," they would say. We were getting to the point where the prospect of staying on made us distinctly nervous. We thought we had better leave Herat before we were too used to this insular, languid life here. Our friends urged us to wait until the fast ended, so as to participate in the Minor Feast (*Id-i-Saghir*). The fast was running out, and lately, people had been tuning their radios to Arabistan, to get word of the sighting of the new moon, for the heralding of the lunar month of *Shawwal*. Activity in the city seemed to slow down even compared to before.

On one of the last nights before the new moon Gul Ahmad came to visit us, hurrying, unwilling even to stop for tea. The popular singer, Hamahang, was performing in one of the grand teahouses, would we like to come see it? Indeed we would, and we followed him out into the night. The reason for this haste was too apparent the minute we reached the teahouse. The street was jammed with would-be concertgoers. Using our greater height to advantage, Gul Ahmad shouldered us into the press, and the force of those behind gradually pushed us through the doors, up the steep stairs, and into the tearoom where the singer would perform.

In the brightly-lit room we found ourselves to be the momentary center of attention, with our awkward height, our odd clothing and glasses. A sea of turbaned heads turned towards us as we stumbled across the room, causing me misgivings for being here. Our intrusions on these people's lives had too graphic a demonstration here, as we looked for a place to sit in the crush, and their curious stares made me despair of ever feeling at ease with them. But as we sat down, elbowing and squeezing into the folds of gaily-colored pajamas and caftans I looked into faces which were not at all isolating or hostile. Among the young men, excited for the singer, for the coming festival, there were those for whom our presence was welcome addition. It reflected well on the fame of the singer, Hamahang. We were packed sinew to sinew, so that every ripple of excitement that passed through the crowd set off a tremor in my knees, my back. We perched atop a table; others sat on *takhts*, on the floor, in the window and on lamp-niches. They waved to one another, smiling, acknowledging greetings. But Gul Ahmad sat quietly with us, not looking for friendly faces. It occurred to me that as a Pathan, a foreigner, he didn't know anyone in the city and had no one to come to the concert with.

We sat in the press for a long time. *Aficionados* had brought their autograph books and waved these in the air, excitedly. Owners of cassette machines were busy arranging them on the platform where the singer would sit, taping their microphones to the floor. A number of men in the audience had brought along a flower, or a note, which they intended to present to the singer. I thought that was a nice touch, unlike so many obligatory bouquets presented to indifferent divas.

Hamahang and his entourage made their appearance amid cheers and cries of *"Wa, wa"* (bravo). The star was a little round man, dressed simply in white, wide-trousered pajamas, and sporting a thin moustache. He wore no hat, an omission his status as an artist afforded him. This was the look of a *shawqi*, an enthusiast, an Afghan who allows himself to lose his self control. His band included a gaunt-looking drummer, a tambourist, and an accordianist, dwarfed by his cloth-swathed instrument. Hamahang adjusted himself on the platform in front of the microphones while his musicians began to warm up. All this time, the audience was calling out requests for favorite songs; a procession of slightly nervous rose-bearers shuttled back and forth across the room showering the star with flowers; autograph books and pens seemed to rain down on the singer. He received all this accolade with good-humored graciousness and little signs of self-deprecation, as he diligently signed all the myriad books. Sometimes, smiling, he flipped through the book to see who else rated with him as a celebrity. Apparently, no one was very anxious that he begin. There was no back-up group to postpone the moment of expectation. He was here; the rapport and enthusiasm had already begun. There seemed to be no reason for him to actually perform.

The excitement of the audience, from pure exhaustion, subsided to a low hum, and Hamahang began to sing. His first songs were catchy tunes, new, full of accompaniment. The difference between Radio Kabul and traditional music was precisely that the music of the capital favored the introduction of Western techniques, keyboard instruments, polyphonic orchestras, accompanied singing. These were pop songs which the young men especially enjoyed. They sang of "modern life" in Kabul, which few of them knew much about other than what they heard in these songs.

The audience warmed up, and Hamahang reverted to more traditional songs, in which the orchestra played only preparatory interludes, each instrument a single voice, followed by the singer *a cappella*.

Persian music is sad; falling scales predominate, and the tenor of the singer is always the voice of the grief-stricken lover. At first, to Westerners, it sounds forced, repetitive, not so foreign as, say, Chinese music, but recalling the music of our own Tudor songsters or the music of Joachim du Pres. The rhythms are complex and variable, while the melodies are simple, but full of coloratura. Improvisation, as well as dialogue between the singer and instruments, as in jazz, plays an important role.

We heard snatches of words, often repeated, the common and affecting words of Persian poetry:

> *Gashtam dar shahr dush*
> *gashtam gashtam madhush*
> *dil az ishq jush-a-jush*

> (Last night I wandered through
> the town, I wandered, mad,
> my heart boiling with love)

The rhymes, the most hackneyed in poetry, had only a rhythmic effect; divorced from meaning, only the sound of the words, the long "U" sound of the madman's lament filtered through the trance induced by the song. It was a *kharabatiyya*, a song about degradation, the misery into which an unrequited lover falls. The singer's voice rasped like that of a drunkard, tinged with the regret of having passed youth, wasted life. I felt sure that Hamahang sang of himself, his face contorted with emotion. For the *Heratis*, whose steady, bourgeois lives had protected them from any depth of experience such as this, the song was like a revelation to them. The singer was a seer, opening a window onto a part of themselves which they had not known. When he finished the verse and repeated the well-known refrain, "*Chism-i-siah yaram, hamisha bidaram*/Dark eyes of the beloved, I am always awake," the room echoed with approving "*wa wa wa*" and "*ihsanat*," and "*muqadir*".

I said the room was packed corner to corner. A latecomer arrived, and the crowd parted, miraculously, to make way. As rapt as the audience was in the music, their attention slowly gathered on this latecomer. A slight, fair-skinned European in a dark pea jacket and blue jeans, the latecomer seemed at first a particularly handsome boy, with a set chin and a petulant mouth. We looked closer and saw a rather boyish-looking young woman, moving shyly through the crowd, as though a lost child, yet with a steady gait and firm gaze. The audience, retaining a guarded dignity, examined her, not gawking, but with thoughtful, probing looks. Only a few young men, less conscious than the rest of decorum, let slip excited remarks and a few shy leers.

Gul Ahmad whispered to me. *"Hamshahri?* A countryman?" And I gestured, "How should I know." As though we all knew one another!

Hamahang, aware of the effect of this woman on his audience, continued to sing, while she took a seat in the back, taking no notice of her notoriety. She simply listened to him, as though nothing could be more natural. In short, she acted so as to attract the maximum amount of attention.

More than anything else I was struck by her coolness. She was certainly alone, the sole woman—as far as she could tell, the sole European. She must have been able to guess with what delighted horror the *Herati* bourgeoisie looked on her. Some were conspicuously disgusted, others glumly prurient. Against them all she maintained an insulating hauteur, ignoring all the gazes focused on her from every face in the room. Here was a traveler, I thought, who was willing to break down barriers, without nice scruples about cultural traditions. Applaud her guts, deplore her insensitivity, I didn't know what to think. I wondered if her intrusion here was any worse than ours.

Hamahang tried to regather the distracted attention of his audience, singing bawdies, satire, standard love songs, but the spell was gone. I have seen this happen in Iran, how the appeal of the classic poetry, with its ineffable feminine mystique, lost its hold on a public no longer exclusively male. The songs seemed tepid and diffuse beside a flesh-and-blood woman. Like a good showman, the singer knew when to quit, which he did to rather belated applause. As soon as the woman got up to go, every head in the room craned to follow her.

"That was a great concert," my friend said to Gul Ahmad. "Thank you for bringing us."

"Hm. I insist," said Gul Ahmad, who had scarcely heard. We went out with the crush of concertgoers. "What did you think of that girl?"

"I thought she was very brave."

"Brave?" The word didn't connect with the idea of femininity. "For a European, is she quite pretty? I would like to marry one of these Europeans."

"Really? How are you at cooking and cleaning?"

He didn't find this funny. "Of course, Afghan women are very beautiful, too . . ." We had not seen one since arriving in Afghanistan. Throughout these *Ramazan* evenings, always male company, the talk always of money, God, and women. Critics of the veil talked as though only the women of Muslim society were victimized. But the men, too, were veiled, in their teahouses, in their

concerts, their tobacco and their hashish. The world of masculine
society was a straitjacket no less than the seclusion of the harem.
Sexes were confined to preserve the world of rigid custom and law
from dissolution "in the uncontrollable mystery on the bestial
floor."

After musing quietly Gul Ahmad came out with a new
thought, "*Daudjan, Walijan*, why don't you stay in Afghanistan
and marry Afghan girls? In Kabul, there are the pretty ones.
You know Persian, so it wouldn't be a problem for you. Of
course, you would have to become Muslim; are you *khatna*? Well,
then, it's easy to become a Muslim, you just have to say the
words."

The idea always disquieted me. "Do you think we should stay
here for the rest of our lives?" Gul Ahmad shrugged his shoulders, disguising with a light-hearted smile a serious purpose.
Here, wherever a stranger found welcome, his host always said,
"Come and be the candle of my dark house. Stay a week, stay a
year." If the stranger accepted the hospitality he had said, in
effect, "Your life is good enough for me." The longer he stayed,
the greater his approval. Since we had started through this journey we had often been asked, "Why don't you stay here?" But we
were always eager to go on, eager to find something new, and our
old friends would conclude we had rejected them. They would
know that theirs were not the only lives in the wide world. I
made a convenient lie to Gul Ahmad, "There's a fiancée."

"Oh, really? Your father sent you on this trip?" That was the
usual *quid pro quo* for a young man's agreeing to a match. "How
much did you pay for your bride? Five *lakhs*? For the girl at the
concert five *lakhs* would be low." I smiled. "Ten *lakhs*? *Daudjan*,
lucky devil!" I should have been so eager to rush home for a ten-
lakh bride, he thought. Wasn't every minute in Afghanistan torture, then?

Restlessness in bourgeois Herat consisted in silent but determined pacing down the empty streets, dimly lit by the yellowish
street lamps. Troops of strollers, their caftans blowing behind
them in the night breeze, passed us by. They were restless too,
but at this hour of night, in the whole city, there was nothing to
do but pace. The cinema had shut down, the cafes, under the
watchful eyes of the guardians of public morals, were emptied.
The city of 80,000 was simply put to bed, no matter how restless
or sleepless any single soul felt himself. We walked, and I thought
of the girl at the concert. We wanted to hire a droshky and clatter
through the streets of the city at top speed. We were going to
spend the night awake in the Parc Bizhad, getting drenched in
dew. Gul Ahmad, ever so quiet, surprised me with his despera-

tion, which was no less than ours. We were all three travelers here.

We had an impromptu *mushaira,* or poetry contest, which Gul Ahmad easily won with this verse:

> We sought the Beloved in the candle's flame
> They found our ashes in the lanes of oblivion.

Then he set off home into the lanes of the bazaar, where only the first few shops were lit by the street lamps and, a few paces on, it was entirely dark.

Celebrating the Feast

The fast ended as soon as one Muslim reported the sighting of the new moon, having gone a little way into the desert to catch sight of it; this was off in Arabistan. Here in Herat, we heard it reported on the radio, a sign that the Minor Feast, *Id-i-Saghir* or *Id-i-Fitr,* had begun.

Early morning in the still grey streets herds of animals flooded into the city, their shepherds cudgeling them forward with staves. Cattlemen stood at the street corners selling *rupee* jugs of *qaymaq;* we drained one between the two of us, squatting among the cattlemen and their earthen jugs. *Qaymaq* was a heavy cream with the texture of soufflé. Still hungry, we sought out the bakery, which we had seen busy only by night. By day it had looked like a charnel house. But this morning it was jammed with customers, women, householders, crowding at the stall window and fighting over their place in line. Shrill calls for their turn. Robed from head to foot in her pleated veils and secure in her anonymity, one cried, "Whoa, son of Satan, haven't I been here longer than anyone else?" She was the most recent arrival, I thought, though all the velvety pleats looked the same. There was no telling; a woman used her anonymity when veiled to visit her lovers. "Give me my turn, I say, God stint your reward!" The women jostled one another, knocking even the men aside, and I momentarily lost all my regret at the single-sex society of Herat. Over the loud complaints of these harpies, we finally got our steaming loaf and hurried off to eat it, tearing it into warm morsels as we went down the street.

The teahouses were overflowing, smoke rising from the brewing of tea and the eggs frying in pungent oil. Troops of comrades pounding the street hand in hand, or holding the empty sleeves of

one another's caftans, thrown over the shoulder like a cape, all on
their way to the bazaar.

Shopkeepers raised the corrugated gratings of their shops now
before these had grown hot in the morning sun. Samovars brewed
tea, the apprentices scurrying about with hot coals in tongs
which they used to heat the morning brew. From the tradesmen's
bazaar the air rang with the rhythm of anvils and hammers,
lathes on earthware, hands, countless hands, tying the warp of
the silk looms. Merchants, ready to recoup the losses of the slow
month passed, arrayed themselves energetically about their new
wares. The stalls were thronged with buyers, poking and examining the merchandise, going through the ritual of bargaining.
They wrapped their money in plastic bags to keep it clean, but
the bills were old and threadbare; the ten-*rupee* note changed
hands so often it looked like a dervish's cloak. We only had to
look at the bazaar scene for a few minutes before we felt used to
it.

The beggar boy shaped like a fish had been deposited on the
high curb, as usual, but the *bazaaris* hurried past him today; he
could not keep up with the traffic, but leaned back wiping his
brow in exhaustion.

To celebrate the ending of the fast the city put on a fair.
Hard by Abdul Wahid's hotel they erected the fairground, a rus-
tic ferris wheel, gun games, egg-jousting, *kutakan*, the coin toss,
vendors selling sweets. They were poor enough entertainments,
but for the ragged children of the neighborhood quite elaborate.
They scampered through our streets, running in high spirits past
the wrapping-cloth tomb of an old saint, a narrow lane whitened
with pigeon dung, where a beggar woman, in black rags, sat
entreating them. Children with a prize cookie, a knuckle-bone, or
a brightly-dyed egg, dashed by her with the cruelty of youth,
guarding the object against the thin-handed beggar woman.

Daud and Sayyid Shafaq were in the crowd, stuffing themselves on cakes and kebabs, guiltily enjoying these pleasures
properly reserved for the children. "Do you want to go up on the
ferris wheel?" asked Daud of the *sayyid*, teasing him. The wheel
was pint-sized, of weathered wood, turned hand over hand by the
operators, hoping every moment against collapse. The highest
gondola rose no farther than ten feet in the air.

The petulant baby face shook his head, "I don't think it's
strong enough to hold me."

We presented our salaams; the *sayyid* took hold of us with
exaggerated concern, "What's this bad news, this disaster? I hear
you are going from us, with grace. You'll see, go to Kabul, Kan-

dahar, Jalalabad, and when you've had your fill you can come back to Herat and settle down."

We walked with them under the lane of trees for a while, the road that led to the *musalla*, their *madrasa*, the road out of the city. They said school was almost over for them, in a few months they would get their certificates. Afghan schools closed in the winter months, when it cost too much to heat the bare brick class-rooms. I couldn't explain how our school year ended in the summer, or how for the last fifteen years I had always associated buds and green with the thought of school getting out. They, for the same fifteen years, had seen the leathery plane trees wither, but not fall, the piles of apples and quinces, red and gold in the fruit stalls, and the thought of school ending. Their planting season, too, was in late fall. I couldn't explain our harvest rites of autumn, when we saw farmers plodding behind their oxen in the grey September fields.

The seasons of life were different from ours. It was odd to see how easily they accepted the unrolling of the months and the years here. After school Daud and Sayyid Shafaq had to look forward to the military, two years of squalor and starvation, which they put philosophically out of mind. Next, the settling into a business, as a wool broker or carpet salesman, in some fancy shop in the New Town. We had seen what sort of existence that was, sitting in the dark of one's shop all day long, fingering one's beads and one's money. "It makes a man grow old," said the *say-yid*, as though that were his greatest worry, as though his smile-less, baby face could ever show signs of age. Then the families arranged marriages. "That's what makes a man grow old," said Daud, cynically. The marriages were endogamous, if possible, in order to preserve family control over estates and wealth. Both sexes rushed into marriages; the groom had the outlet for his energies which shop-sitting didn't provide; the bride escaped the tenuous position of stranger in her father's house. The burdens of married life soon outweighed the blessings, for a newlywed couple was expected to produce, out of nothing, an heir, an ade-quate *sarai* for the entertainment of friends and relatives, while protecting the modest seclusion of the harem. Suitable houses were few and expensive, so the young marrieds, the petty bour-geois, endured the inconvenience of the communal *sarais*, houses without baths, with common wells, full of gossiping women, squalling brats. After that, one merely hoped to get rich.

The struggle to rise above this, to dress one's children in gay clothes for the lesser and greater feasts, to maintain the hospi-tality which one's father kept, certainly no less—these were the strains under which one grew old. The transition was absolute: there were no middle-aged people in Herat, only the young and the old. The poet had said, "Age comes on and the season of youth is out. The hand has no strength to bear the brimming cup."

The consolations of their lives were few: sons who would be no worse than the father, a sure wife, dog fighting, horse races, visiting friends on feast days. Perhaps in the end one would buy an old secluded *sarai* with a garden and a high garden wall. There, behind the walls, if nowhere else, one could escape. The cypress tree growing beside the leaf-clear reflecting pool portended the young and beautiful wife one might marry in old age, the strong son growing up tall, the Beloved, the eternal feminine of the mystics, consoling the predictable monotheism of bourgeois life; it would be the *Tuba*, the Tree of Paradise, which, when all had run its course, one might hope to see spreading beneath His Throne.

These were small consolations, but effective. When we agreed to meet again before my friend and I should leave town, Daud promised us an outing, a picnic outside the city, settling on the next Friday. Then time, which had passed so slowly and so emptily, raced by. My friend and I went to the baths, had ourselves barbered and shaved, went shopping for splendid melons and grapes. We even had our washing done exorbitantly. Thursday evening we went to the cinema to see a Bombay movie. Abdul Wasi declared we had never looked so elegant. The beggars demanded a higher sum of us. But mingling with the crowd of young and gay cinema-goers, we verged on regretting our decision to leave Herat.

On Friday morning Daud drove up to the hotel in a droshky. When he didn't let the droshky go, we started to hurry to get ready. "Don't rush, I've got him for the day. We can go anywhere you want: Gazurgah, the Cave of the Bhang-Eaters, the tombs. We can see all of them, if you like." We stuffed a knapsack with some ground-cloths, grapes, and bread, and got into the droshky. The driver, a big, wide-eyed man, could find no words for himself when we said hello. His name was Abdur Razik (Slave of the Sustainer) and he was a relative of Daud. Abdur Razik moved over to let Daud up on the driver's box and handed him the reins. Daud gave the horse a tap with the long, springy whip, and we lurched forward. Plying the whip on the horse's flanks and calling out "Hoo, hoo," Daud labored to make the horse extend his gait. Finally the lurching smoothed out. We flew behind the effortless, long strides of the trotter as though sledding on ice. Abdur Razik turned to us and announced, like an oracle, "He–is–a–good–driver."

We made good speed down the paved road past the *wali*'s palace, but there jolted onto the rutted country lane heading north. The droshky began to rattle like a clapper in a bell until Daud hauled back hard on the reins. The road led up a steep incline. At Daud's command we scrambled to the ground, so the empty droshky could negotiate the climb. Even then, the horse teetered in ascent. Daud leapt off and gave him a sharp crack under the tail. At last he cleared the top with the droshky. We had to run up and remount. From here we could see the road stretching towards Gazurgah, a famous shrine in the gardens of the city. As we rambled over the way, the shrine loomed larger, the characteristic Timurid structure with a huge, sail-like *ivan*, and tall, finger-like minarets. At the hilltop under the garden wall of the shrine we climbed down, and Daud handed the reins over to a doorkeeper. "That one is a relative, too," he explained.

Inside the wall we passed a crowd of hungry-looking mendicants, to whom, at Daud's direction, we gave a fair sum of money. "You have to be careful about these people. This shrine is a *bast*. That means that criminals can escape here and they can't be arrested.

"If they're criminals, why did we give them alms?"

"It's their due."

The shrine was a complex of buildings, dervish cloisters, royal residences, enclosed mosques, mausoleums, roughly organized around a series of courtyards. At the doorway of the outer courtyard stood a tall portal—an *ivan* with a Safavid sunburst—in front of which, piled up, were a mountain of shoes, a gathering of dervishes wrapped in their cloaks, pigeons. We went through this portal into a second courtyard, quiet, with no one about, grass overgrowing the ancient cobbles. Through the portal to the inner courtyard, we saw the disorganized maze of white marble tombstones, an *ivan* echoing the one outside, more dervishes, more pigeons, and the tomb of Ansari, mystic and exegetist, enclosed in a finely-barred wooden cage with a Chaghatai roof. From his grave a magnificent plane tree grew, or used to grow before petitioners pitted it with nails from which they hung their prayers. The dead tree, heavy with rusty iron, hung over the long, velvet-covered bier of the divine while the cage protected him from too zealous hands. The rest of the narrow courtyard was full of graves; wall to wall, the rulers of Herat: royal Persians, descendants of Genghis Khan, the Amir Dust Muhammad. Each of the tombstones, brought some fifty miles away from the mountains to the east, had been carved with the most exquisite style, the only use of stone carving in the whole city, and one of the finest opportunities for brief poetry:

> The Goal of Pilgrimage
> Is Prayer
> This is my lot today
> Tomorrow it may be yours.

The rhymes tended to repeat, but on the little graves which were only an arm's length long, I found them moving.

But I would have missed the mood of the place if I had settled into a gloomy reverie on the tombs. The courtyard hosted more living than dead, their mood was anything but solemn. They thronged the place, admiring the fragmentary stucco and faience of the *ivans*, sitting in the sunny spots among the tombstones, on the grave of some old *beg*, chatting with friends. Daud knew many here and, leaving us behind discreetly for a moment, went to say his salaams. Much pressing of hands: when Afghans shook hands they didn't let go until they finished visiting. We were all barefoot, having left our shoes at the entrance to the first portal, and it was amusing to see so many people, old and young, stepping gingerly over the pebbly, unswept terrace of the courtyard.

Sayyid Shafaq was there. He drew us aside and said, "Did you see the dervishes? Aren't they sublime looking? This is a very holy place, you know." Only the *sayyid* put on a grave face, for people bowed respectfully to his green turban, and he had to look the part.

Daud detached himself from his friends, stepped over to the plane tree, and almost as an afterthought, tied a small cloth to one of the nails in the trunk. He hurried away, hoping we would not notice, but we mentioned it to him anyway.

"Do you know what's a *du'a?* A special prayer. I am going to to Kabul when school gets out to try to get a passport."

We asked him how he could get a passport without serving in the army, the necessary precondition. He smiled, the facetious *Herati* smile, and twisted his moustache. "*Inshallah,* you will succeed," I said, hopefully.

"Where will you go with your passport, to Iran?"

"Further, God willing, I'll go to *Urupa*, to *Alman* and *Inglistan*, to *Paris*, all the big cities."

We stood outside the wall of the shrine and looked down towards the city. Many had come here for the view, after visiting the shrine. We could see the cathedral mosque, far away, its pearly blue minarets guiding the eyes like beacons. The mosques and citadel of the city rose out of the maze of greys and yellows, the swirls of streets and domed houses around them like patterns of an intricate arabesque. Towers and trees ringed the city and formal gardens spread up this hill, where, not quite at random, somber tombs lay amid flags. I imagined that just possibly the medieval symmetry of the city might correspond, point for point, with the delicate carvings of the tombstones in the shrine. I could visualize the elaborate manners of the *Heratis* at tea as a kind of arabesque, the flowery language of the poor sweetseller Abdul Wahid as another arabesque, the stately genuflections of the Muslim at prayer, too, were the abstract expression of a world view, a view from such a hill. At this distance Herat appeared the capital of a world culture, a stage vast enough for the play of a hundred heroes. It seemed big enough to have the critical mass necessary to make life dramatic, to give it the history and irony which life in small towns and villages lacked. At times, Herat had been such a city. But for Daud, looking down at the same scene, there was perhaps only the rubbish box of a few hundred years of Central Asian backwater, the enclosed gardens where families lived out their lives like flies in a bottle. He was in manner and speech the ultimate *Herati*. But he wanted his exit visa.

My friend asked him if he knew how to get around Europe. Daud replied with an anecdote about a well-known *Herati* jokingly known as Mirza Badinjan (Aubergine, Esq.) who had gone to Germany with a fortune in Turkoman carpets. Since he didn't know the language he couldn't change money, couldn't buy anything to eat and was reduced to starvation, sitting on his pile of carpets. Finally another *Herati*, an interpreter, came on the scene." Mirza, what are you doing here?"

"I'm starving," came the reply. So the dragoman took Mirza into his apartment and fed him. The two of them decided to go into the rug business. The *Herati* who knew German went around with Mirza Badenjan to a big rug wholesaler. After a lengthy negotiation in German the rug dealer and the dragoman smiled, shook, and reached for the schnapps. "What happened?" asked Mirza, excitedly. "How much did we get?"

"He gets 50 percent, I get 50 percent, and you get 5 years for possession of stolen property." The two had Mirza arrested, but in lieu of incarceration he was expelled.

"Eventually," Daud added, "he got things straightened out. *Heratis* are very clever, they have a way of bouncing back."

My friend offered to write his family in Paris and tell them of Daud's arrival. "While you're in Paris you can stay at my house, I'm sure."

Daud said warily, "You are very kind," since promises were only an empty way of imposing obligation, but as my friend went on to talk about his father's house and Paris, Daud realized he was serious and grew abashed at his own mistrustfulness, embarrassed at the thought that he had never made us his guests.

On the way out of the shrine I worried that we would not find our shoes, expensive leather ones, in the heap of plastic and rubber footware at the door of the shrine. We began to look, joined by the dervishes and a few of the mendicants who were enjoying the *bast*, and with the help of all the searchers we turned up the four shoes. "You really should donate these shoes to the shrine," said the officiating dervish, but we declined this fine opportunity to accumulate blessing.

From Gazurgah we drove over to a garden called Takht-i-Safar, once a formal Persian garden of the Timurid princes, but now no more than a relatively well-watered lawn. We ate here, my friend deftly carving the melon into cubes with his pocket knife. These melons, sprung from a hot, dry soil, were acrid, sweet, tart, and juicy all at once. They burned the mouth like very cold ice. "The great *shahs* of old," said Abdur Razik, each word emerging with great effort, "were great drunkards. They used to carry on here, oh, seeing day into night and night into day." Herat used to be famous for wine, though in the whole country now liquor was illegal. Tea, from the eighteenth century on, began to replace alcohol as the prime intoxicant, and when it became convenient, wine was roundly condemned. "But how can one become drunk on tea?" I asked.

"A poor man has nothing in his belly, that's how."

Across the way from Takht-i-Safar was a complex of buildings where, in the fifteenth century, the poet-statesman Amir Ali Sher had built a philosophers' city, stocking it with fellow poets, men of letters, and artists. Now, according to Daud, the site belonged to the civic mental institution.

After lunch we rode to the west of the city, Abdur Razik now at the reins, as Daud had tired of driving. On another rough country lane, we neared a number of impressive graveyards, where we dismounted to wander about. A row of white marble slabs clung to the shade of a charming pistachio tree, which grew out of the barrow of the largest grave plot. This was the tomb of Jami, Herat's foremost poet and mystic, the last canonized poet of the classics. His poetry made cold reading, his verse being effortless and witty, but the Persians and *Heratis* read a deeper meaning into him than I had. Jami was not interested in art as truth or reality, because he deemed mankind unqualified to speak of that. Therefore, whatever one said, true or false, might be true or false without one's knowing. Jami's philosophic skepticism justified the characteristic *kitman*, or dissimulation of the Afghans. He was often quoted in support of lying and double-dealing. But the poet himself was a pious, saintly fellow, who modestly asked to be buried under the open sky, without any elaborate edifice marking his grave. In partial fulfillment of his wishes, his devotees had built an *ivan* some feet behind the grave, to mark it from afar. The gnarled pistachio tree grew of its own.

Beside Jami's tomb lay that of his nephew and pupil, Hatifi. Said Daud, "Do you know how Hatifi died? In the days when the rivalry between the Shi'ites and the Sunnites was very great, Hatifi told the Shi'ites he was one of them; he told the Sunnites he was one of them, too. In the end they found out and killed him. Who? I don't know. Either, or both."

"I thought you said *Heratis* had a way of bouncing back."

Daud smiled, and recited in the wonderful singsong of Persian:

> A lover cannot give up wine,
> Not that wine, exciting love,
> Pour a glass upon this dust,
> Soul and body from the grave arise.

We drove back into the city around dusk and dismissed Abdur Razik at the hotel. Daud suggested that, even though the driver was a relative, we might tip him out of the kindness of our hearts. "When you come back, I'll be in *Urupa*, God willing." We told him we would look for him there, as though it were a small place.

Abdul Wahid was upset at our leavetaking: he was losing both paying customers and, as he had begun to think of us, friends. "You have been the light of our dark existence," he told us. The boy Abdul Wasi took our leaving as a fall from favor, although I began to think their protestations greatly exaggerated, recalling the scene from Tolstoy's *Cossacks*, where—immediately after such farewells—the hero starts off on his journey and the Orientals lapse into sullen indifference. "Come back, at least, for the Greater Feast," said Abdul Wahid.

"*Inshallah*, for the Greater Feast," two months hence.

Gul Ahmad was nowhere to be seen after the Minor Feast began, an absence which annoyed me, because we had agreed to meet.

The strangest thing was that, on the day of our departure, people whom we didn't even know, or had met but once, stopped us on the street to say farewell. "So, *Meestar*, you're leaving us?" "May the trip be fortunate!" "Go with grace."

2.
WAITING FOR TRANSFER

Afghan Truck

The vehicle, the *mutar*, moves slowly, no faster than a walk, as though treading its way conscious of the rocks and the ruts of the road. The driver's boy, one hand on the cab, hangs out over the wheel, calling out, straining to be heard over the engine in low gear, "To the left, slow! Move over!" The driver, the *mutarwan*, manages to avoid the worst parts of the track with tortuous maneuvering.

But the twenty-three passengers occupying fourteen seats feel every jolting of the *mutar*. The *mutarwan*, they grumble, is mad. He has in mind their slow death by fracturing. Every rut passed seems like a canyon we have spilled into. I am kneeling with six other men on a pile of bundles, while the sixteen others, including my friend, are balanced on their narrow seats with their feet twisted underneath them. A jolt causes the big man sitting above me to lose his perch and he slides on top of me. Our discomfort in the cramped, swaying van of the *mutar* takes on a distant aspect. We can talk about it, joke about it, but it never goes away. The next jolt brings the nose of the *mutar* down, the big fellow crashes on top of me again, someone else sits on my ankles, or stabs me with a knee, and we have three more days to ride in this *mutar*. The trip has been roughly nightmarish.

We left Qala-i-Nau, the capital of Afghan Badghis yesterday morning. The road north has been made passable to wheeled vehicles only recently and the introduction of *mutar* service is a source of satisfaction to the provincials. Cheaper and faster than pack animals in former use, the *mutar* has caused a revolution in the distribution of bazaar goods—tea, sugar, and rice, as the local markets fill with these one-time unheard-of luxuries. The *mutars* are Russian military vehicles, rugged, but still sorely used by this road. The track is so bad each *mutar* requires a full and costly overhaul at the end of the run, and the operators are hard pressed to make a profit. They load the trucks with as many riders as police regulations allow, and then, when they are safely outside the town, they take on even more riders, packing them in like livestock, until some of the travelers wistfully observe that the caravans of donkeys were not such bad things after all.

Approaching a steep incline the driver comes to a halt. Everyone must get out and climb on his own power, while the lightened *mutar* takes the slope. The stretch is welcome. We stand around on the firm earth massaging our atrophied limbs, checking to see if anything is broken. Meanwhile, the *mutar* lurches up the hill with a whirring of gears. Some of the passengers quickly rejoin the vehicles at the hilltop. In their plastic shoes and long cotton *chapans* hanging down to their ankles, they pick their way up the slope with the agility of mountain goats. They are the provincial bourgeois, trading across the hills of Badghis. They dress poorly, in used clothes from the city's bazaar, but they are not poor men. The ticket for this trip costs a healthy 300 *rupees*, so they must expect to make a fair profit off their journeying. When they get to the top of the hill they squat patiently by the *mutar*. The mixture of speed and patience is characteristic.

A few lag behind, unused to the climb. An aged *mulla* (Muslim cleric) surveys the slope and decides he cannot ascend unassisted. Although as a pious Muslim he will not speak to me, the unbeliver, he neatly summons me by waving his arms and orchestrates my efforts to help him up the hill. His colleague, a younger man with a handsome black beard, supports the other shoulder, so the old cleric makes the climb with us walking beside him like the wings he expects to wear in Paradise.

Atop the slope we assemble beside the *mutar*, all twenty three of us. The *mutarwan*, having gunned the *mutar* too sharply uphill, has taken a stone in his crankcase. He and his boy are sweating under the chassis to dislodge it. The rest of us, ignorant of things mechanical, take not the slightest interest in this proceeding, not even noting the delay, nor complaining. Some sit on their cloaks to nap, others gather for prayer, while a few retreat discreetly behind rock-outcropping. One would hardly suspect we are stranded in the Safid Kuh, miles from the nearest town, just a few hours before sunset. "It rests with God" says the young *mulla*, blandly, as he rises from prayer.

We look at the landscape spreading around us. It resembles the surface of the moon. The soil, a silverish gravel, covers the land like flint-hued skin, blanketing boulders, and withered grass and brambles. The land looks flat, like the distant moon. Only when the eye adjusts to the starkness of the mountain light does one distinguish the sharp folds and rises in the moonscape. The eye can only see as far as the next rise, as though the horizon had been lopped away with a knife. The blue sky looms just behind the hill.

Yet behind the rise lies another, and still another, flat, low *kutals*, and the track bucks and dives across the landscape like a wild horse, until, exhausted, it settles into the sandy steppe of Turkistan, beyond the stream of the Murghab River.

Moonscape that this mountainside seems, it is full of habitations. Driving across the endless, scrubby sierra, we have spotted in the distance a cluster of silver poplar trees, grown to impossible heights as the result of constant pruning. Silver and green against the grey of the hills, they serve notice that a village, still invisible, lies just below. The natural advantages of the site are few but obvious: the face of the *kamar* shades the ploughland from the west wind; a shallow stream skirts the site, providing water and bearing away waste. Otherwise, the village is a random point in the monotonous landscape.

The village and thousands like it occupy a narrow strip of land which picks its way between the high mountains of the Paropamisus and the low-lying desert. On the high mountains water is more plentiful, but the land is steeply graded and resistant to the plough. In the lowlands, the soil is arable but waterless. Midway, then, the delicate balance of land and water permits the cultivation of narrow plots and compact orchards. In this strip of land, habitation is surprisingly dense. In a morning's journey afoot one can always make out two or three tell-tale clusters of poplar trees from afar. In the smallest village the headman is bound to protect the traveler and serve the single cup of tea.

And that is why the travelers on top of the *kutal* are not the least anxious at the *mutar's* breakdown. At last resort, we'll simply walk. And the wolves? "It rests with God."

The young *mulla* with the handsome dark beard takes note of our prolonged reverie on the moonscape and comments, "What are you looking for out there? Desert, mountain, waste." He speaks with a certain amount of satisfaction. "Are you looking for the tall buildings? The grand avenues? You won't find them here. I have been all over the world, to Iran, *Sham*, *Makka* (Mecca). Of all the countries of the world, Afghanistan is the most backward." Then he smiles.

The driver revs the engine, the wheels spin. The boy perches on the fender with his *danda panj*, a wheel block that looks like an enormous top, ready to jam under the wheel if the *mutar* should stall in the starting. The travelers pile back in the van, trying to reseat themselves more advantageously than before. When everyone thinks he has found himself a secure seat, surprised at the new comfort, we count a man missing. The aged *mulla*, returned from a trip of necessity, demands a seat. Each man slips down one rung in dignity, and the usual discomfort begins again. The *mulla* steps into the van with remarkable litheness, treading gingerly over those kneeling on the bags. We call to the driver, "*Burau bi-khayr*, go with grace," and the old men stroke their beards with a pious gesture. Already, the aged *mulla* is sunk too deep in thought to notice.

The ride goes on, far after sunset. In the dark the jolting in the truck becomes far more serious, since the boy can no longer see the track. Complaints are louder.

"Oh, God," says a weak voice under me, "can't you move off? I'm dying, I tell you, by the Holy Quran, I'm a sick man." Mechanically sympathetic, I shift my weight a few inches, sending a ripple of curses through the length of the *mutar*.

"What the hell are you doing? Get off me," bellowed the man beside me.

"There's a fellow underneath me who says he's sick."

"He's sick, is he? I'll give him something to be sick about," says the man carelessly, somehow landing a blow in the tangle of limbs beneath me. Somebody mews like a cat and falls silent.

We enter Bala Murghab about midnight. In the pitch black, guided only by a spirit lamp, we grope our way into the roadside inn and throw ourselves exhausted to the floor. The innkeeper heaps up the house blankets, covering us like the dead. There is no room for twenty men to stretch out, and we must twist and crouch in the dark for a few miserable hours before dawn.

It is still pitch black out when the innkeeper sends around little palm-sized cups of tea and stale bread for our breakfast. We sit up and eat hungrily. In one corner of the inn are my friend and I, the two *mullas*, the big fellow whose knees threatened my life for the last hundred miles, looking warm and comfortable in his splendid *barak*, which is of wool, while the rest of us are unprepared in cotton clothes from southerly Herat. We drink our tea and talk with chattering teeth, passing time until daybreak.

The big fellow talks of travels, of India and Pakistan, collectively Hindustan, for the Afghans contemptuously confuse their Muslim brothers of Pakistan with the unbelieving Hindus; they are all *Hindis*. "The *Hindis* are great eaters of *dhal* (groats). *Dhal* for breakfast, *dhal* for noon meal, *dhal* for supper. One day I was eating meat, praise God, and while I was getting out the marrow with my teeth this *Hindi* said to me, 'If you eat bones, what do you feed your dogs?' I said, 'We feed our dogs *dhal*'."

Even the old *mulla* smiles at this.

"Yes," says the innkeeper, "they are that way, some are otherwise." A roundish Central Asian Turk with a beardless, child-like face, he imagines himself a great philosopher, having seen travelers come and go on the road through Bala Murghab. He turns to my friend and me with a note of condescension, "*Meestars*, you are so young, yet you have travelled all over the world. What do you mean you haven't? Iran, *Urupa*, *Amrika*? There, you see my point. Tell me, of all the countries in the world, which is the best?"

"There's good and bad in every place," says my friend, to the appreciative murmurs of the rest. To be counted a philosopher in Afghanistan one has only to tell the truth when it would otherwise be in one's interest to lie and flatter.

The innkeeper, though, has set my friend up. "If there's good and bad in every place, *Meestar*, why did you leave your home and come to Afghanistan?"

"Just to travel."

The young *mulla* smiles in his handsome beard. The innkeeper sighs, "Yes, just to travel. If I were like you, young, money in my pockets, I would go all over the world. *Bi-Khuda*, I would never grow old."

Wherever we travelled in Afghanistan, people understood when we said, "Just to travel," though they thought the confession a little bald. Few could afford to travel for mere pleasure, but as merchants or pilgrims they managed to satisfy their curiosity about the world. Even the poorest lads entering the army had the prospect of billeting in some new, potentially interesting post. The rich dignified a tour of the Middle East with a trip to Mecca, the Holy City. Yet all went to travel and see other places, if only within their own province. I once talked with an old greybeard about his environs. He seemed remarkably well-informed, naming towns, headmen, passes, and tracks. I was surprised, and said, "You've been to every town in your province—how come?"

"You've been to every kingdom in the world," he replied, "and you ask me how come I've gone to the places of my own province? Just to see them, to learn the ways of towns and men." The reason was as old as the Odyssey, the rewards of traveling being largely the same now as then.

But the Afghans did not really understand what manner of traveler my friend and I meant to be. When an Afghan visited a place, he did so with a perfunctory view, to have seen it, to pass on to the next town. Tales of travel read like simple itineraries, "After Kushk is Kushk Rabat, which is an old city, with ruins, and after that, you come to Kham-i-Khaj, a rich village, green, of pure water . . ." It was the voice of the medieval geographers telling of roads and towns. The important thing for the Afghan was to have been there, to have stored up memories and stories of distant places. So he collected bric-a-brac, a piece of faience, holy water, anything to serve as a keepsake. Or he would leave his sign upon the place he visited—the outline of his hand, his name. The habit was an ancient one: the monuments of kings were built inaccessibly and the biers of saints were closed off in cages in order to discourage the *graffitisti* and pillaging momento-seekers.

The tourist with a camera made more sense to the Afghans traveling than we did, since photographs made the perfect record, linear, exact, accessible to sharing. "Take a picture of this," they would say. "In your own country it will be a source of wonder." We shook our heads. "What, you have no camera?" Without a camera we were not travelers, we were simply *there*. "You came to Afghanistan simply to be here?" Being? They would not understand. In Persian "being" and "nonbeing" were not antonyms, but finely shaded into one another's meanings. In this hard, hostile land, life was fragile, life was but a journey. Why would anyone want to *be* in Afghanistan?

Light

GOD IS THE LIGHT OF THE
HEAVENS AND THE EARTH.
HIS LIGHT IS LIKE THAT NICHE
WHEREIN IS A LAMP
A LAMP OF CRYSTAL
CRYSTAL GLITTERING LIKE A SHINING STAR
LIT WITH THE OIL OF AN OLIVE TREE
BLESSED, NEITHER OF THE WEST
NOR OF THE EAST
OF A BRIGHTNESS
THAT SCARCE NEEDS IGNITING
LIGHT UPON LIGHT
UPON LIGHT
GOD GUIDES TO HIS LIGHT WHOM HE PLEASES.

This is how dawn comes to Bala Murghab: a grey light—what they call the "wolf's tail"—breaks at about five o'clock. The tall, pruned trees stick up into the sky their long fingers. Nothing else is visible outside. Fog, perpetual fog from the higher mountains, settles down as the temperature climbs and there are still only shades of grey and black. In Bala Murghab there is little to catch the light. The timbers of the inn are grey with soot and ashes. The hard-working innkeeper and his boy dress in plain cotton, grey and coffee-brown, serving tea out of blackened cups, while we sit on reed mats in the grey stuccoed room. The boy wears an over-sized *kullah* on his head, gift of several holidays back, on which a few glass beads of ornament survive. Gradually, the greys soften, the blacks grow less intense. Men begin to relax their muscles, as though the burden of night has been taken off their shoulders. It is that the day is warming up, and there is no longer the need to shiver. A half-grey light floods into the street through a seam in the fog, the glass beads on the boy's hat gleam hotly. We pile out of the inn, standing about the *mutar* stamping against the cold, still. The town is a single lane of mud and plaster booths, worn by wind and rain to look like heaps of ant hills. We climb into the *mutar* and drive away.

On the road from Bala Murghab we pass orchards of fruit trees on which the dew, frozen, has cased the branches in sheaves of crystal. The filigree of ice and yellow leaves screens out the grey sky.

My friend and I—looking, but saying nothing—share the thought, *This is why we are in Afghanistan.*

We descend the mountains onto the plains of Turkistan: passing the Murghab River on a high *kamar* overlooking its deep ravine, we see the valley wall laced with icicles hundreds of feet long, with ghostly white veins of frost patterning the grey rock face. Below, by the river, stand the black hair tents of the nomads, between the stone foundations of abandoned houses. Again, we share the single thought, *This is why we are in Afghanistan.*

Samovar Talk

A teahouse is a very special place. This one, in Maimana, Turkistan, is dominated by a shiny, nickel-plated samovar, bearing the Russian seal "Tulskaya Fabrika, Zolotaya Medal, 1887." The innkeeper boasts that the samovar cost him a *lakh* of *rupees.* "It's a Nikolaev, you know, the best kind." His boy stokes it with spindly brushwood to keep the liters of water boiling for the travelers who crowd the door. The pint-sized boy could take a swim in the great, bellying cylinder of the samovar. A nineteenth-century innovation from Russia, it has given a special character to the townlets of the North, and by metonymy, has lent its name to the teahouse—to the point where only the most deracinated Afghans would refer to the teahouse as a *chai khana* (literally teahouse). *Samovar* is universally understood, and in the North means more than either a pot for boiling tea or the room about it. *Samovar* means the whole world.

We had descended from the *mutar* in the dark. Half the travelers groped their way home if they lived here or went to houses where they were habitually received as guests. Those of us strangers to the town fell in together. "There's a good *samovar* here," said one of our company. The single, wide avenue of the town blew with wind. To open the door of the *samovar* and feel the warm, sweet atmosphere of hot tea, bread, and musty carpets was a tremendous relief.

Smoke from the samovar blackens the roof of the building with soot. Rafters, necessarily few in this treeless country, are massive. From the beams hang photographs, in cheap wooden frames, of the innkeeper, of the Ka'ba, tinted green, of the deposed Monarch Zahir Shah—the revolution had not dimmed the decorative value of his picture—and his successor, Daud Khan: jealous cousins, gazing aloft at each other, while their apolitical countrymen squat on the carpets spread on the floor, or sit on raised *takhts*, supporting themselves on cushions or on bundles of belongings, wrapped in tartan cloth. Dinner, served all around, is *shurwa*. A local pronunciation of Arabic *sharba*, our "sherbet," the dish has nothing in common with sweet cooling drinks; a greasy meat broth, it is served with dry bread, which the diners tear piecemeal and steep in the broth, then eat with their fingers: the fat tastes good in the cold weather.

No one speaks during supper, but afterward the *samovar* fairly ripples with conversation. Etiquette insists on modesty in public, even the donkey drivers practice a restrained demeanor in their conversation. But beneath the outward calm and quiet, conversation is brisk. In the *samovar* one hears the news of the whole world. We, the travelers, even if we arrive empty-handed, have a valuable commodity to exchange with the locals, that is, news of other towns. People from the hills fifty miles up come down to the *samovar* for news of Qala-i-Nau, Qaisar, Mazar.

One of the men who arrived with us, a shaveheaded young soldier on leave, passes a photographic document from hand to hand. "It's called an identity card. The government is giving them to everyone. See, that's my picture."

"Very pretty, just like a girl," jokes one wizened trader, examining the passport. But all wonder. Imagine the government giving people photos of themselves to carry about. And is it free? God is Great!

Traders exchange the news of the markets in the towns of the North, Shibarghan, Sar-i-Pul, Tashkurghan. Given the inadequacy of the roads, a man can make a living just by making the effort to traffic goods from one small town to the next, a marginal sort of life for which a knowledge of most minute details of local prices is a necessity. One finds wool *baraks* in Hazarajat, 1,000 *rupees* apiece. In Mazar one can sell them for threefold profit, buy cooking oil, hurricane lamps, sacks of tea, and return to the mountains. And the roads: "Terrible, a man could get killed." Heroism of the petty traders, sons of Sindbad.

The merchants' conversation is edifying in a business sense. The news they bear, like the clothes they wear, are all imported luxuries. White beards tangled in the folds of their silk caftans, wristwatched, wearing amber rosaries, they say: "These *mutars* are a torture. Do you know what the *mutars* in Iran are like? They call them 'Otobus'; they are long, oh, as long as this very *samovar*, and everyone has his own chair. You get a slip of paper, you see, and you ride, just like so, and it's hardly like traveling at all, wossh, whossssh!" Copious gesture of the hands, and the clincher: "They even pass around a beverage, called *kukakula* . . . Do you know what that is?"

"Yes," says another voice, uncertainly, "they have that in the Capital." Not everyone understands, but few let on. The townsmen and villagers listen silently to this talk, faintly amused by it. "*Kabuli*," what concerns Kabul, means little to them, it is so far away.

After a while, there is little more to say. In years past, one used to go to the *samovar* to hear singing, storytellers, dancing boys painted to look like women. These professional entertainers had low fees, perhaps twenty rupees a night, collected from the customers in a hat, with the *samovarchi* throwing in a free meal. But nowadays the local government regards itself as the guardian of public morality and discourages entertainment. Dancing boys are under heavy attack by the prudish, and most people will not even admit they still exist. Singing and storytelling, hold the ultraorthodox, are forbidden by the Prophet's law. The common people spend too much time idling, runs the theory in higher circles. So after we have discussed *kuka* and Kabul, *baraks* and caftans, we sit and do nothing at all.

Some travelers lie down to sleep on bedding of their own or in the great *luhats* provided by the *samovarchi*, while others reluctantly set out again on their journeying. The *mutar* is going on to Shibarghan this very night. Newcomers are constantly arriving, stamping their feet against the cold. The noise of trucks and donkey drivers saddling their mounts goes on behind the walls of the *samovar*. The door slams open and shut. The boy serving tea slaps his cups onto a tin tray with a regular tinkling sound. But I am so tired that even the commotion lulls me to sleep, under my heavy *luhat*, in the smoke-drugging room.

I woke up a few minutes later. Someone was talking to me, shaking my leg. The *samovarchi* said, "*Meestar*, you can't spend the night here. This is no place for you."

I was still half-dreaming.

"You must go to the *otel*, this place is not comfortable." I mumbled that was nonsense. "You are too delicate, here is no bed, no heater. *Meestar*," he leaned closer, "Police."

In one of those ill-fitting Warsaw Pact uniforms, he lounged against the door, drinking tea watching us. There seemed no point in arguing, so I woke my friend and explained the situation to him. He had fallen into a much deeper sleep. The policeman stamped impatiently while we hurried to get up.

I felt ridiculous, humiliated, to be escorted from the *samovar* by a policeman. Many in the room now waked and stared at our predicament, suspecting all sorts of culpability on our part, whispering, "God prevent it, I was sitting right by them ..." and "Thank God our police are vigilant." Outside I asked the official what this was all about, injecting much rancor and importance into my tone of voice. Disarmed, he mumbled something about the town being dangerous for foreigners, but without much conviction. I could not make myself angry.

Down the windy street through the dark he led his prisoners to the hotel. Unlike the *samovar*, it was isolated, shrouded in darkness behind a menacing wall. A long, barrack-like structure, it was bare and cheerless, no rugs on the floor, broken-down sofa in the foyer beside a formica desk, water stains in the plaster, bare lightbulbs hanging from the ceiling. The heating consisted of Franklin stoves, for which it was necessary to buy wood, very dearly, from the management, while the tariff itself was phenomenally expensive. The stay at the *samovar* had been free. The hotel clerk was absent when we arrived, so we sat on the broken-down sofa and waited. I was sulking; my friend fell asleep again. The policeman said innocently, "When I heard there were two foreigners in the *samovar*, I was curious. I thought I'd go talk to them. Of course, I couldn't talk to you there. But cheer up,, we'll have a good time in this place, though I admit, it looks pretty bad.."

When I got used to his uniform I could see he had a pleasant, wrinkled, open face. He had very red hair.

The clerk wandered in, dazed, wrapped in several blankets, with a desperate look. "I can't check in these two because my hands are too cold to write. Let's do it tomorrow." He shivered a few times. A thin, young man with long, George IV sideburns and an Adam's apple prominent as a rooster's gorge, he looked much less hearty than the policeman. "I sent the lackey out to get more firewood and he hasn't come back, so we've had no heat."

"It was warm in the *samovar*," I said pointedly.

"Don't worry, we'll just get under the *sandali*," said our captor, smiling sadly, and again I had to forget my anger.

In the smallest room in the hotel a brazier with coal was kept burning. We set a table over the brazier, a blanket over the table, then huddled under the blanket. In Iran they called this arrangement a *kursi*, which also meant "throne," while here they called it *sandali*, which meant "chair" in Iran. Only in a civilization without furniture could there be so much confusion in nomenclature. Anyway, after a few moments under the *sandali* our cold limbs grew warm again. The room was lit with a sputtering hurricane lamp. Green twigs had found their way into the coal on the brazier so the smoke which filled the room was sweet and sickly-smelling. We sat up to our knees under the blanket, our feet arranged around the brazier like spokes of a wheel.

"Now don't move your feet. If you knock over the brazier it'll burn the blanket, and it's the last good one we've got," said the clerk, fingering the singed edges of the cloth.

A lackey brought tea.

Kidnapped from the *samovar*, tired to death, half-freezing without and steaming inside the blanket, we began to revive under the tea and the sad, cheerful talkativeness of the policeman. His name was Khalil Ullah (Friend of God). The clerk called himself Surush.

The city was asleep. No one had the fuel to burn either for light or heat to pass the cold night awake. The lodgers at the *samovar* and the townsmen had gone to sleep. The streets, but for a tea-drinking sentry, were untraveled. No light showed from neighboring houses. Tomorrow one rose at dawn for prayer, why spend the night in talking? Given a half an hour, a man could say all that he had to say in full. But we idle folk, the clerk, the red-haired policeman, the two *meestars*, somehow managed to pass the night in talk, fortifying ourselves with tea and sweets. The two Afghans were friends as well. Wakeful people they thought themselves, because they could talk for hours, about the newspapers, politics, foreign affairs, without an onlooker like the lackey understanding a word of it. For instance, when they discussed the constitution of Daud, they said, *mashruta*, which meant "constitution," but to the lackey simply "conditions." Daud's conditions? What would Daud set as conditions. We could not have explained that the constitution would be limits on Daud's laws!

Khalil Ullah and Surush, both *Kabulis*, had been long stationed in the North. They discussed home, the Capital, with its Spinzar and Intercontinental Hotels and Mir Wais Avenue. Lately they had run out of things to talk about.

Surush was trying to learn English. He showed me his book, which was, surprisingly enough, a bit of sizzling pornography. In the margins he had scribbled the Persian for the underlined words in the text, just as I would do when reading the Persian classics. He asked me for the meanings of some of the words he didn't know, which proved very embarrassing. I bowdlerized many of my translations.

Khalil Ullah had no interest in English, but waited until Surush had tired of his book. When he started speaking, his tone was half-ironic, half-cheerful, as though mocking us. "So, *Meestars*, tell me how you came to Maimana, and what can we do for you here?"

My friend answered, "It's listed on the map as a historical site."

"A historical site?" he laughed. "Is that what it says on the map? Nothing ever happened here that I know of. No, let me tell you what happened. Once upon a time the town was full of Jews, so much so that they called it *Yahudiya*. Then Zahir Shah, or really his uncle Hashim Khan, got rid of them all, so now it's called Maimana (the Auspicious Place)."

"He got rid of the Jews, and filled it up with Pathans, which is even worse," quipped Surush.

Khalil Ullah sat quietly for a moment, and then ruminated, in the same ironic tone, "So, that's the sort of people you are. You see a historical site listed on the map and you go to see it . . . a fine life."

Surush started talking about the town in an official, earnest sort of way. A census of the province would soon be taken. Surush explained how they would come to determine the total population of Afghanistan.

Khalil Ullah interrupted, "How many people do you think there are in Afghanistan?"

My friend said, "According to what we read in a book, seventeen million."

"That's the official figure. It couldn't be more than seven million. Did you travel through Ghur? Did you see how few people live in the countryside? So why do they say seventeen million, so the world will think Afghanistan is big and important? No, so the world will think Afghanistan is twice as poor as it really is.

Do you see? The Russians build roads, the Americans build a dam, there are Germans and French in Kabul, I don't know what they're up to. The country gets aid from every foreign government in the world, because they think there's twice as many of us."

I smiled at this cynical logic. Whether it was strictly true or not made no difference, such a pure example of Oriental subterfuge. It reminded me of Chichikov, the antihero of Gogol's *Dead Souls*, who bought titles to deceased serfs in order to appear, on paper, the owner of many souls. Only Afghanistan was doing it to look poor, not rich.

Surush took up his tea cup, sipped it, and frowned. "This tea's gone cold." He called the lackey up from his corner. "Hey, tea's cold! Boil some more water!" The lackey stopped in the door, letting in the draught, for which we cursed him. He was reluctant to go out in the night at this late hour to the cookhouse where the samovar was cold. "Come on, get hot water. Hurry up. And shut the door, it's freezing in here."

We began to talk about the efficacy of aid, Soviet and American. "The Russians built a very good road, from Kabul to their border. The American road, from Islam Qala to Kandahar is no good, full of pot-holes," said Surush, like many young Afghans, a pro-Russian.

"The Russian road can hold trucks up to eighty tons," observed Khalil Ullah. "Well, where in Afghanistan do you have trucks weighing eighty tons? But Soviet tanks . . . it's too convenient."

The lackey returned with two piping pots of tea, black and green, laying them on top of the *sandali*. Then he stood by, staring down at us, snugly under the blanket.

"I think he wants to come under the blanket," said my friend.

"Oh, come on then," said Surush in short temper. The lackey knelt to the floor and edged under the blanket; his foot, touching mine, was stone cold.

In the course of the evening Khalil Ullah grew more serious in his conversation, shedding the ironic manner. It was too bad, I was getting so tired I could no longer follow him, but my friend, sleeping in snatches through the evening, caught the drift of his story. He talked of his family, poor gentry in Kabul, and how, orphaned at an early age, he was unable to get a position in the Capital appropriate to his birth. In order to maintain his social rank he had to settle for a job in the provinces, still supporting his family in Kabul. His was a relatively high rank in the service, but his family's shabby genteel style of living strained his resources. Khalil stopped talking, I noticed sleepily, and reverted to that ironic tone, "You're not listening." And then to himself, "Well, this one isn't listening." He went on. I was too tired to object, "Yes, I'm listening." He told how he had been in Maimana several years now and was due for transfer. He hoped to return to Kabul and home, but that was unlikely. The many towns in the North, Kunduz, Shibarghan, lonely burgs in the steppe, appeared far more likely. There was an expression, "If you want to die, go to Kunduz." He said he felt that his mind was going to sleep in these small towns. "You're not listening. He's not listening." Smiling sadly, he rose to say goodnight.

I woke up the next morning early. It was cold, and the blanket had been burned through by the brazier several hours before.

The Div's Castle

We breakfasted and went out to take in the town, which we had only seen by night. It was surprisingly green. Treading up the road from Bala Murghab came the fertile valley which enfolded the town with shadowy pines, groves of pomegranates, and quinces. The fruits of the valley were famous, especially the grapes, whose vines overhung the walled villas of the town, twisted up wide-girthed oaks, supported on lattices, between the houses. Above the flat-roofed view of the streets peeked Chinese mulberry trees and cypresses. There was no shade in the streets. Behind the town, to the East, sloped sandstone mountains which cut short the greenery with a dull haze. The town's official architecture derived its inspiration from the cliffs, apparently. The main avenue blew dust which flaked off the barrack-buildings, the hotel, the bank, the *wali's* palace, the lycée. The avenue looked more like a path cut through rock, through clay, than a thoroughfare. The official places were of stucco and brick, squat, flat, looking to have killed the pathetic greenery planted about them with the reflected glare of their stark facades.

A strange note was introduced by the movie theater, which perched high on a *tepe* (barrow) in dead center of the town, monolithic in appearence, its flimsy Palladian ornaments, slender columns, capitals, and dormer windows scarcely able to tame the rockish, inhuman nature of the thing. A fantastic landscape complemented the place: a dusty playing field and a purely Chinese garden with bronze foliage and stunted mulberry trees. A *div's* castle looming over the official town, the movie theatre was impregnable and enchanted.

Beyond the dusty field the bazaar began. Newly laid out in the last century with straight streets and well-built shops, the bazaar in Maimana had an orderliness which differed from any we had seen. In the shops lay goods, neatly stacked, chintz, teapots bowls of green raisins and bowls of black raisins. The shopkeepers,neat little figures in immaculate silk *chapans*, stood in front of their shops, animated and business-like, so different from the somnambulant *bazaaris* of Herat. Their *chapans* were silk, hard-edged, with straight, bright patterns of stripes, red and gold, black and green, which, too, lent a certain note of regimentation to the bazaar. These were Uzbek merchants, a race of Turks who retained their Central Asian features, without a drop of Mediterranean blood in them like their *Istanbuli* cousins. The old men had a feminine delicacy, fine skin and smooth features, and the children a shyness which was touching. A strange experience for us, going through the lanes of the bazaar where the Uzbek children played, to see them, eyes downcast and silent, at the approach of the intruders. They looked like beautiful Chinese dolls. The little girls had perfect straight black hair, dark almond eyes. The boys, thin-boned, all had shaved heads, looking as though they were carved out of boxwood. The children's bare feet and hands, though, were like those of old monkeys, chapped and calloused by cold winters. But for that, the children might have been the pint-sized courtiers whom Shaykhzade painted in old Bukhara. The restraint and reticence in the paintings I had earlier thought to be a reflection of the artist's own nature, but now perceived to be the nature of his subjects: these Central Asian Turks.

Maimana had been a prominent Turkish town, the capital of an independent Uzbek khanate a century ago. Before that, Nadir Shah of Iran had camped here on his way to the infamous sack of Delhi in 1739. He put on festivities in Maimana which lasted days. Before that, as Khalil noted, the town had been large enough to have a large Jewish (and Hindu) merchant community. The medieval Arab geographers report that Maimana had a great fortress and cathedral mosque, perhaps the present *div's* castle of a movie theatre, still glowering over the town. Before that, Maimana, like any town in Afghanistan could boast a Hunnish, Bactrian Greek and Guptan heritage. But whoever edited the small-scale tourist map of the country must have been acting out of whimsy when he marked Maimana as having historical monuments. Or perhaps he was from Maimana and wanted people to visit the town. There were no historical monuments here. Thus, from the point of view of the Afghans, we had no business being there. And because the Asian Highway had been built connecting Herat with the east via the southern desert, foreigners rarely traveled *through* Maimana, let alone to it.

My friend had suggested that we go to Maimana because it

might be a good base from which to visit the surrounding countryside of Ghur and Badghis. Maimana was well-situated at the foothills of the mountain country full of tribes and villages (unlike Herat Oasis, confined by the desert). From Maimana we hoped we could come and go easily. This proved to be wrong. The smaller town meant we were more closely watched. The lack of a specific excuse for our being there made us suspect. Multiethnic Maimana was not as easygoing as Herat. We knew no one outside the hotel, and had no entrees into the life here. The Persian speech which we had cultivated in Herat was almost unintelligible here. The local Pathans, Tajiks, Aymaks and Turks all settled on a peculiar idiom which took us a long time to make out. They were not surprised that we should speak Persian at all (as in Herat), but that we should speak it as poorly as we did. As we struggled with this once an onlooker observed to his friends, "They're not stupid. They just don't speak our language well." (Afghans had an annoying habit of talking about one within earshot. One was supposed not to take notice of this.) That was just a part of our frustration. We were waiting for the local branch of the Pashtani Bank to open after the inevitable string of holidays. When it finally opened it proved not to have authorization to buy or sell foreign currencies. So on top of everything else we were strapped for cash.

There is a certain ritual involved in visiting towns which have no special claim on tourists. We fall into this, dumbly, hopelessly, seeing the school house, the local newspaper, the literary and historical society. Here are small revelations. Unlike other high school students elsewhere, Afghans do not crowd around the visitors and mob them with questions (not even about Muhammad Ali Cassius Clay). They stay shy of them while the teachers treat the foreign visitors like parleying warriors. At the newspaper office we met polite, unfriendly, astrakhan-hatted civil servants (the newspaper is government owned) who offered to satisfy our curiosity with statistics on the number of kilowatts, the number of sheep and the number of hospital beds added to the province since by the latest Five-Year Plan. The newspaper prints as news stories not the result of the Plan (which are unaudited), but old projections. In the local historical society one can see pamphlets about Afghan history, the Lodi Sultans of Delhi or the short-lived Afghan dynasty in Iran. Inquiries about the history of Maimana led nowhere. This was not a politic subject.

The reserve which we experienced demanded some kind of explanation. We were willing to attribute it, along with our other bad luck, to some spell cast by the *div's* castle, as though its glowering genie had decided to arrest our trip. To be sure, we had faced reserve, even hostility in Herat, but there it had been disguised by the voluble and cosmopolitan air of the great oasis. Maimana was bare, and its tension was bare.

Old feuds were slow in fading. Even though the last Khan of Maimana had voluntarily ceded his patrimony to Abdur Rahman Khan, Uzbek resentment against the Pathans was fairly bristling. Fights broke out in school rooms among clan enemies. In spite of the softening lines between tribes and peoples outwardly, in a personal realm the sense of isolation from the strangers' tribe continued. Men would recite their ancestors' names to the seventh generation, a Bedouin tradition carried over through Islam. A Ghilzai and a Durrani, feuding Pathan groups from the south, would remain aloof from one another, though both exiles in Turkistan.

Occasionally the tension would erupt into violence. Criminal cases were almost always settled by the voluntary surrender of the participants, especially in crimes of honor. The families involved, without shame or argument, would turn the culprit over to Khalil Ullah, for dispatch to prison in Kabul. If the wrongdoer did not get into prison quickly, he would probably fall victim to the vendetta himself. In this respect Khalil Ullah's job endeared him to both victims and criminals.

People appreciated the government in so far as it protected them from themselves. They knew the potential for violence in the province, how brigandage had only recently been abolished. When asked if the government oppressed the people, a silk merchant told us, "if there's government there's tyranny." This was a saying, *aga hukumat basha labud zulm as.* The man went on, "In the land, there must be security. If not, people would rise against the government." There had been an uprising in Badakhshan Province. One described its bloody suppression calmly. Wherever men fought or were killed for the sake of power, Afghans pictured the scene with the cold eye of the Mughal artist, painting the siege of Kandahar or the beheading of a rebellious vassal. A tyrant, *zalim*, could be accounted a good ruler if he were wise as well as ruthless. Respect for authority, even of the blasphemous kind typified by the Pharaoh in the Qur'an (AM I NOT LORD OF ALL I SURVEY?) had a deep echo in imagination. Abdur Rahman Khan, tyrant *par excellence*, was respected now, even by the descendents of the tribes he vanquished. Nadir, too, had been ruthless. The conversion of the warlike Uzbeks of Maimana into peaceable *bazaaris* was due in large part to this.

We bought two silk *chapans* from this silent, glassy-eyed silk merchant in the bazaar. He had said nothing either to encourage us to buy them or to choose the most costly, and he stated his price in a manner which made bargaining impossible. We were delighted with the hues of these silks, the biblical coat-of-many-colors, the design of which the Uzbeks alter as fashion changes. The older coats we had seen tended to somber, deeper colors—mauve, coffee, gold. The coats of this year were gaily green, crimson, and canary. He did not share our enthusiasm over the designs, but wrapped them in newspapers with string.

Afterward, examining our purchases, Khalil said, "Why did you buy these?"

"Aren't they beautiful?"

"Yes, but they aren't your *maslak* (station in life, role). *Chapans* are for ordinary people. Turks."

We learned of the existence of old graveyards below the sandstone face of the mountains, an hour's walk from the city. This was the closest thing to a historical monument we had, so we felt compelled to see it. Khalil Ullah, in his official capacity, discouraged us because of the danger and inconvenience. In his own person, he told us it wasn't worth it. We were perversely encouraged to go.

Passing the last occupied houses on the main thoroughfare, we saw the foundations of homes, long abandoned, abutting the town: the ruined dwellings of a more prosperous age, now dotting a garden landscape bright with orchards and vineyards. Outside the town, the soil became flinty and bare; from there we climbed up.

The graves lay on the first rise of foothills, which overlooked the town spectacularly. I had never noticed a graveyard with a view on this trip. The great age of the tombs was apparent, for the massive marble *turbas* and scrolls were far beyond the means of the present city's production. Wind swept the skirts of the mountains, burying the graves in sand. In places, only the carved marble turban-stones of the tombs poked above the ground, cocked at an angle because of sandslide. A few, whose inscriptions were exposed to view, we read without much success. The inscriptions, ornamental to begin with, had been ground by the wind and rain, leaving only the flowing pattern of the carver's hand on the soft stone. From their style I guessed they were a couple of centuries old, for the work was not as fine as Timurid stones at Gazurgah or elsewhere in Herat. The one legible monument was crudely carved, of the last century. The contemporary dead were being interred in stone-covered *tumuli* without markers, around the *ziyarats*, the graves of the saints where banners and rams' skulls had been deposited by the faithful. The primitive graves were another reminder of how things had fallen apart in this part of the world.

Here was a picture of decay, not of the body but of the spirit. The town had succumbed to succession crisis in the Khan's house, Russian intrigue, Turkoman raids in the countryside, then Pathan occupation and indifference. The malevolent genie of the town ruled in the stead of the Uzbek Khan. Bad luck, in the stead of grandeur, seemed to hold sway over so much of the East, so much of Afghanistan, but so nakedly in Maimana, the "Auspicious Town."

I asked—and nobody seemed to know—why it was that the *ziyarats* were festooned with ram's skulls and banners. Hunters dedicated the skulls after a successful hunt, but no particular importance was attached to it. However, when I asked if I could have one of the skulls with the fine horns, I was politely refused. Later I read in a learned journal about these skulls, but the author couldn't ascribe any particular significance to them either, although the custom was universal among the Afghans.

At the Ball

Provincial capitals are capitals all the same: they have to have their grand hotels. Ours was almost always empty, a monument of some kind to ambitious planning. Everything about the hotel was big, if bankrupt, in conception. The tariff was eighty to one hundred twenty *rupees* a room, ten *rupees* for a heated bath, five *rupees* for a few sticks of firewood to burn in one's Franklin stove. Food one might buy outside, but cooking it in the small kitchen-house behind the hotel required that one purchase fuel, wood or spirit, which often cost more than the meal itself. All this was to pay for the original outlay of the hotel, which must have been enormous. In Afghanistan, one simply didn't see such things as this furniture, these beds, mirrors, mattresses, toilets. Little had been done to maintain the hotel since it had opened; consequently, much of it had broken down, in a particularly plangent way, and was useless. When something broke down in Maimana, it was invariably from Pakistan or China or Russia and there was just no way to fix it, no way at all. This fact gave every working, manufactured object in the town a rather melancholy aspect. Eventually it, too, would break, never to be replaced. We felt like colonists on the moon.

Of course, we were colonists. The local population frequented the sensible and cheery *samovar*. The derelict hotel became, in effect, a private *sarai* for Surush and Khalil, who entertained themselves every night, making the best of the official allotments of food and fuel, the few heatable rooms in the place, and the threadbare furnishings. The lackey's services they exploited as a matter of course, to brew tea, to cook their meals, to heat the bath water. This latter task involved gathering a good deal of firewood, drawing a dozen leaky buckets of water from the well, filling the tank atop the tub, and feeding the fire diligently for an hour. This the lackey loathed to do, complaining of the lack of firewood, or a leak in the tank, as an excuse. He would go to the bazaar to buy wood and stay there, or he would hide in the garden, when the two called for him, cursing him as a lazy vagrant. In the evening he would sit sullenly inside the hotel—it was too cold to hide outside—resigned to be sent on errands before he could crawl asleep on the sofa in the reception room. He was a Tajik from the hills above Maimana, the Kuh-i-Baba, and spoke a Persian so rough and rude that not even Surush or Khalil could readily make him out. His name, if I understood right, was Abdus Sattar (Slave of the Veiled).

On rare occasions our small séance at the hotel would be interrupted by visitors, welcome if only because they gave us something to talk about after they were miles on their way. One evening, late, cold air draughted through the place. We knew that visitors had arrived. Shivering in the reception room, we stood about and watched curiously the new guests unloaded all manner of equipment from a Land-Rover. They were geologists, come to survey the hills around Maimana for useful rocks and oil. We hosted them for tea, and they spoke readily about their work. The rocks of Maimana were geologically similar to those of Mazar, where a respectable amount of natural gas had been found, so they were hopeful. The possibility of finding oil and joining the ranks of OPEC loomed large in the Afghans' imagination. These young men were acting out the fantasies of the nation as a whole. When I pointed out that the problem was not so much locating oil in the country as being able to cheaply extract and export it, they took quick offense. "We will have roads, pipelines, you'll see, very soon."

Three of the men were in their twenties, still impressed with the excitement of the revolution in Kabul, where people had strewn garlands, they said, over the tanks as they passed through the street to the royal palace. The fourth member of the party was older, slightly paunching, and smiled blankly at the enthusiasm of his younger colleagues. They went on to pour rehearsed scorn on the former monarch, Zahir Shah, calling him incompetent, indifferent, narrow, a pawn of the United States. Of Muhammad Daud they spoke with such admiration one would have thought they'd discovered him themselves, "Ah, if you only knew Muhammad Daud. He has studied in Paris, France, you know, he has a *diplôme*. He is very progressive in his thinking." They pronounced the word "progressive" one syllable at a time.

Muhammad Daud had long been Zahir's Prime Minister, before which he held the all-important portfolio of the Interior. What, we asked, would Daud do now that he had not done before? The three urged us to see that Daud had learned from his past mistakes. "He has read books and considered our country's problems."

The naive way the one had said "He has read books" moved me, in spite of myself, for I thought, *What could a fifty-year-old men learn from a book after thirty years in politics?*

Another one went on, tentative, full of self-deprecation, "Of course, we have had no elections yet, and no constitution, but we cannot come into the modern world in a day." He must have caught the hint of my cynicism, which was not at all directed against Afghanistan's politics, but against politics in general.

The fourth man smiled even more blankly through this, and refilled his teacup. It was a pity to think that, while we certainly didn't like this man, smug, voracious, tongue-tied, we might have approved of his political wisdom more than that of his outgoing, earnest fellows. He knew that politics was an outward play of words and slogans, disguising a pure struggle for power. A dynasty had ruled Afghanistan since 1826, and in the person of Muhammad Daud, still ruled. The press carried stories of the President's tilt to the left and to the right, his purging of the old guard and of his "red guard," while all the old politicians, civil servants, Pathan khans and Tajik *bazaaris* read in Daud's maneuvers a mere pragmatism or, his enemies would say, an opportunism. Especially in Afghanistan, politics came down to opportunism—the pure ability to remain in power being the only sensible goal of a ruler. Political words had no meaning in the language. Political action had no meaning in people's lives. One asked for elections when eighty percent of the people were illiterate. One asked for land reform where water, not land, was the scarce resource and where regulation of water rights could never be assured but by force of custom. One asked for Westernization which would only touch the capital, drawing Kabul into a Never-Never Land apart from the rest of the country, which did not want, which did not understand the aspirations of the *Kabulis*. I wondered, talking to the three, if a handful of sloganeers, earnest, sincere, but rootless, would ever take power someday and try to make reality of their dreams. Power, I observed, soon makes realists of dreamers.

When they left they insisted that we come to see them in Kabul. "We can go to a real hotel, there, the Spinzar, and to the New Town. There are girls there." Winks, handshakes, smiles, exchange of addresses and keepsakes.

Other visitors to the hotel were military officers, dour civil servants, occasional vacationing *Kabulis*, and once even some Western tourists. They were all very private, keeping to their cell-like room all day long, emerging, surreptitiously to answer nature. They took all their meals in their rooms, having brought their own food, and came and went inexplicably from day to day. Surush and Khalil pretended to know what the guests were up to, that this one was a government spy and that one a new policeman or subgovernor—but we never knew. Sometimes our guests could be unpleasant. Army officers appropriated our *sandali* one night and said, when we poked our heads timidly into the room to explain the situation, "Go away, we don't want anything right now." They gambled, they bounced objects against the wall, they broke the furniture. I was out in the hall and bumped into one of them plunging about in the dark. "Where's the bathroom?" he demanded. I pointed him towards the Afghan commode. "No, no, don't they have a *tualet?*" It was broken, I explained. "Barbarians," he grumbled, thinking, for all I could tell, that I was some mountain Tajik working at the hotel. I felt complimented backhandedly.

The Western tourists, too, thought we were locals, or at least Orientals. Weeks of ill-diet and not shaving were beginning to pay off.

Our meals in Maimana were all extremely simple—porridge, bread, raisins, grapes, melons, rarely kebab meat and onions. To vary the diet and escape boredom dominated our conversation. "I would like a fowl," one would say.

"Why don't we have it tonight."

"No, let's have it tomorrow, I'll go to the bazaar and get some *shira* (a sauce concentrate) first."

At the mention of *shira* Khalil's eyes would light up and he boasted, "We really know how to eat in Afghanistan." The poorest country vaunted itself gourmet.

The *shira* proved difficult to obtain, which put the delicious expectation further into the week, enough time for me to develop an appetite even for rooster. They never slaughtered chickens, who furnished eggs, but kept a troop of roosters in the garden of the hotel to be killed for special guests and now for us. They had grown fat on chaff and grass, as none had been killed for a while. My friend and Abdus Sattar sat on the stoop, first sharpening their knives with a whetstone. Blades ready, they sauntered into the troop of birds.

The birds were not unaware. Hearing the sound of scraping steel had brought the gorge to their throats. They began circling wider and wider around the garden, disguising their fears with bravado, inflating themselves, as if in a mating ritual. The one most inflated, though, was doomed: it was the fattest. The lackey grabbed it, and its fellows stopped to watch, not fearing for themselves anymore, but acting as spectators. The rooster flapped its wings and squawked, but Abdus Sattar threw the bird on its back, pinned its wings with his knees and severed the neck at the throat. Muslims, like Jews, were forbidden to wring the neck of animals to be eaten. And they had to say: "In the Name of God the Merciful the Clement . . ." An outstanding *non sequitur* if there ever was one.

My friend sat down to pluck the rooster, making a pile of feathers which blew and scattered across the garden and under the feet of the surviving flock. Abdus Sattar, taking no notice of the feathers, bore the rooster into the sooty cookhouse and began to stoke the fire.

We ate on the floor of the foyer, huddled under blankets, for the night had grown suddenly cold. The bird, well cooked, filled the platter with oil and fat, which we soaked up with our bread. After the bird had disappeared, all but the bones, Surush and Khalil played at wishbone, Surush winning the larger piece. "Do you know this game?" they asked. The innards had been cast out, I noticed, the Afghans eating no tripe of any sort, while meat itself was a prime rarity. "That's only fit for dogs," said Khalil of tripe. We talked of former feasts, of pancakes filled with puddings, of rich-honeyed pastries, delicate cuts of spring lamb, and forgot, briefly, the monotony of our diets in the North.

Surush the clerk had a mania for cleanliness. His pajama always looked starched, his nails filed, his hair combed. He made a strange contrast to the squalorous hotel under his charge, but there was little he could do to keep the place up. He was more interested in learning English, which I begrudged him. I had not been fair to him in this, taking immediate dislike to anyone who studied English, and this in a country where knowledge of English opened all sorts of doors into the ranks of astrakhan-hatted lord-high-poo-bah-ships. When I refused to help him with his English, he looked at me as though I were taking the bread right out of his mouth. Yet I saw myself in the position of a man holding a gun, while a would-be suicide demands it of him. There were enough Turks, Arabs, and Persians illiterate in their own languages. Now Surush plotted cultural suicide for Afghanistan.

I was sitting on the concrete veranda of the hotel, overlooking the tangled garden, when he came to me and sat down beside me. I resented the intrusion on a rare moment of privacy; worse, he had his book in hand. But he didn't ask me to look at the book, instead he told me a story which gave me some sympathy for him.

The road to the north was unpaved, he explained, so foreigners on their way east rarely came through Maimana. This year, though, an adventurous group of young tourists came to town and stayed in the hotel, held over for a week by motor breakdowns. They were four, two men and a young married couple, all of them German. The couple had become estranged over the trip, increasingly so as the husband seemed to become gradually unbent. The woman had explained this in her broken English to Surush with his broken English. Now, as he retold it to me, in subtle, psychologically acute Persian, I wondered what was true and what embellished. Before the four continued on their way to Mazar and Kabul, the woman gave Surush to understand that she loved him and would leave her husband in India. She had given him the book he had.

Now, he went on, a letter had just come to him from the woman in Rawalpindi, saying that her husband had gone insane, committed to a local asylum for lunatics. The woman was debating whether to leave her husband there and return to Afghanistan, or wait for his recovery.. "I want you to do two favors for me," concluded Surush. "I want you to write a letter to her for me, in good English, because I can't explain things very well. And secondly, I want you to tell me what I should say in the letter. Should I tell her to come or to stay?" He pulled the carefully-folded letter out of the book and I read the address, "Helga Winkler, 35 Bharri Chawk Road, Rawalpindi."

I was nonplussed that Surush should consult me on such a question. The last thing I wanted to do was steal someone's spouse for him. He didn't appreciate my moral niceties, as though, in his mind, wife-stealing were an everyday event in my country. It was true, the behavior of the tourist women was frequently notorious, which could have given rise to the bad opinion of them among Afghans. But Surush and the others were mistaken in their judgment: it must be that traveling so far away from home and one's own culture changes fantasy or desire, in women as well as men. To still the latter's desire Afghanistan offered nothing except a few prostitutes and randy *bazaaris'* apprentices, so the men, unexcited by this, passed through the country chaste, provoking the suspicion that Western males were lacking in virility, while their women were insatiable. No wonder Surush should regard stealing this German traveler's bride as a matter of little account.

"What if she should turn around and leave you?" I objected.
"It doesn't matter," he said matter-of-factly. "There's no bride price."

I insisted that he write his letter in Persian and let me translate it, spending a whole day struggling with the subtleties and innuendoes of the letter, translating it into simple enough English for them both to understand. I read the letter back to him, like the traditional *munshi* (amanuensis), and he closed his eyes approvingly. Then, without a word of thanks, he took the letter and sealed it. Stationery being extremely expensive in the town, I was piqued by his high-handedness, but had to overlook this, since lovers were expected to be *majnun* (mad). We had told her, for the actual letter was as much my work as his, that she should do what was best "for both of them." By "both" I had meant husband and wife, though the ambiguity remained.

Later he showed me her picture, a wallet-sized, high school graduation photo of an ordinary-looking auburn-haired *fräulein* with thick glasses.

The evening's entertainment promised to be grand. Tonight the *div's* castle on the hill was showing a film. For this once-monthly occasion the *wali* would make an appearance; the whole official element of the town would be in attendance. This was their moment, their show of solidarity. While banning cards and dog-fighting and dancing boys for the *samovar's* customers, the officials of Maimana had no social life of their own. Isolated in various bureaus, aliens from other towns, and strangers to one another, the officials yet had one thing in common: their alienation from the locals of Maimana. The cinema was an occasion of transitory community for them.

Khalil was embarrassed before us on account of his enthusiasm for the film. "I suppose you go to films all the time, so it's not important to you."

"No, no, it's just that I don't like films," I told him, making matters worse by implying that films were something I'd outgrown. My friend, for his part, was eager to go, until he heard that it was an Iranian film. Usually they showed Bombay films in Herat, movies where one could at least count on the dance scenes for entertainment. Iranian films were bad without exception. But for Khalil's sake my friend put on a brave face.

Khalil shaved, dusted his boots, and even sewed on a few buttons missing from his uniform. We made ourselves presentable. "The *Wali* will be there," Khalil reminded us. Then, in the company of Surush, we set off for the theater. Abdus Sattar crept under the *sandali*, happy to be left alone.

The *div's* castle interior was an area about the size of a

basketball court. Hundreds of folding chairs had been arranged before the stage. The battered condition of the seats recalled the furniture of the hotel, official programs of modernization, elephant graveyards in the wilderness. Almost all the chairs had been taken, by schoolboys in uniform, soldiers, clerks of various offices. They all wore European-style dress—jackets and trousers. In fact, entry was denied to those in Afghan dress, which effectively shut out most of the people of Maimana. Who in the bazaar owned coat and trousers?

Khalil took us up to the balcony reserved for officials of higher rank. They sat row on row in threadbare astrakhan hats, sleepy-eyed, uninterested by the proceeding, making only the political gesture of supporting their chief, the *wali*. I always expected these bureaucrats to look different from the faces in the bazaar, their way of life being so different, but except for the astrakhan hats and the more finely-shaven moustache, these were the same, somnolent, hard faces which one saw anywhere.

A troop of soldiers, looking less motley than those below, stood guard over the *wali's* person. One fellow, posted to act as usher for the arriving dignitaries, was doing nothing of the sort. He stood and stared wide-eyed at the *wali's* daughters, who sat at the edge of the balcony. They were the only females present, and they were unveiled, wearing the Iranian-style *chadri*. This covered the entire figure and was draped over the head and held in one hand, framing the face and showing a bit of the tresses becomingly. One of the girls, an exceptionally pretty, fawn-eyed youngster, peered excitedly over the railing at the crowd below. Her *chadri* slipped down over her neck in dark folds, and I could read the expression on her face: "People, excitement, crowd!" Her eyes darted back and forth from the balcony filling with astrakhan hats to the crush on the floor below. She reminded me of Tolstoy's Natasha Rostova at her first ball. Through her I caught a little of the excitement of the event, this caged-bird's fluttering enthusiasm for the audience around me. An officer with the *wali's* family spotted the gawking soldier and ordered him to be about his business; I realized that I had been staring improvidently at the girl, too.

That the *wali* should bring his family to the public cause like this was a mark of progressivism. Sixty years ago when Aman Ullah Khan had appeared in public with his unveiled queen—we were constantly reminded— religious elements vituperated against him, driving him and his consort into exile. Now times had changed; the *wali* was widely respected. A portly, dignified fellow, he looked like a Turkish pasha from the last century, complete with astrakhan tilted at a genial angle. As we passed by him, Khalil bowed to his superior, who nodded and smiled with self-satisfaction. He seemed pleased by the appearance of the two foreign visitors, under appropriate police protection, as he imagined.

A guest list of the exclusive balcony: chief of police, headmaster of the school, head of the bank, director of the local paper (who smiled to us from across the way), director of the post and the telegraph. Khalil pointed them all out to us; most he knew only by face. "We might be near neighbors in Kabul, but we'd never find out." Each official sat with his entourage, his own sons, I guessed, or else silently, alone.

The film was as bad as any Iranian film I had ever seen; in fact, it was every Iranian film I had ever seen. Whenever they made a spin-off, they used the sets, properties, and precisely the same plot as the original movie. Only the cast was different. This film concerned a young girl from a fishing village in the Persian Gulf who was kidnapped by gangsters and made to sing in a discotheque. When her village sweetheart comes to rescue her, she tells him she likes being a discotheque singer and refuses to return with him to the village. In despair, he goes back to his village and grieves with his aged mother.

The audience was awkwardly quiet during the film. Unlike the easy atmosphere at the concert halls or teahouses, here there was no chatting and cat-calling. What we were seeing—that all Iranians drive fast cars, that the streets of Abadan are all paved, that women sing in cafes, where men drink wine in crystal cups and where the furnishings are silvery chrome—too disquieting. Those who had never been to Iran thought, "So that's what it's like"; those who had been, their pride taking place over accurate recollection, thought, "Yes, that's what it was like." The little daughter of the *wali* was rapt, even Kabul pales before the fictive splendor of Abadan.

The movie ends with a blazing gunfight, the woman's being kidnapped back to her village, reconciliation, and marriage. In the cinema, traditional life is tried and tempted by modern ways; ultimately, the temptation is resisted. Yet the moralizing message scarcely comes across, the audience is so riveted by the temptation itself. The image of the glittering, chrome-plated discotheque sticks in the mind.

I was reminded how old this fascination with Iran was here. Hundreds of years ago, a prince exiled from Persia sought permission to settle in a certain subcontinental domain. The local gentry urged their ruler to welcome him, since he "had been a prince in Iran, which is the finest kingdom in the world." Themselves Persian, or part Persian, the gentry expected everyone more lately arrived from Iran to be more *à la mode*, more saintly, more learned and better bred. Though the Persian of Kabul was "purer" and older than that of Tehran, through the movies people were beginning to pick up Iranianisms, saying *Tehrun* for *Tehran*, saying *ara* for *bali*–"yes."

Khalil and Surush were fitfully excited by the movie. From the visual medium they reduced the film to an oral form, the habit of inveterate storytellers. "And then the three men get into the car and chase the girl."

And Surush, "No, they have the girl and they're running away from the fiancé.

"And they drive down by the waterfront."

"Yes, by the waterfront. It was a big port . . ."

They had never seen Iran, but after a few more years of government service could expect to receive, *gratis*, a passport to travel there. They awaited the moment impatiently: the old Indo-Muslim gentry acknowledging Iran the greatest kingdom in the world.

On the Steppe

The *Kabuli* newspapers always talked of new public works projects for this or that province: hydroelectric works for Baghlan, irrigation pumps for Jalalabad, slaughter houses for Herat. Economic Development was a rage, if not a reality, for most provincial capitals, giving the inhabitants a sense of purpose and change. It may well have been a case of the emperor's new clothes, but the illusion worked. Maimana lacked even the illusion of progress. No great public works lured mountaineers from the backcountry. No factories were built. The road, though improved, would not be paved under the current Plan. Whitewashing the façade of the cinema seemed to be the major urban project.

The cause of this lack of activity was easily grasped. Water was the scarcest resource in the country. The river which might have been used for irrigation or hydroelectric projects was the Murghab, flowing directly into the Soviet Union where it had been long harnessed for agriculture and industry there. Afghan use of its headwaters was bound to upset the Russians, something no Afghan government could afford to do. Instead, the Kabul and the Hilmand rivers saw major development projects, turning Jalalabad and Lashkargah into bustling towns.

For Khalil Ullah and his colleagues almost any post in the country would be preferable to Maimana, except the still more isolated and backward towns of Badghis, Qala-i-Nau, and Bala

Murghab. Civil servants waited transfer while they raised their families to think of distant cities as home. Members of an occupying army a hundred years old and never disbanded, the civil servants of Maimana felt no less foreign than we did; a language barrier isolated them from the native Uzbeks; the divergent histories of Kabul and Central Asia made them unsympathetic. The town's literary men strived to make something familiar out of a foreign place: they wrote Persian poetry under cloying pen names, like "Burnt Moth," "Night Candle," "Broken Heart," while the bazaar yawned with the orderliness of a military parade.

Months later I met a man from Maimana who had lived several years in Herat. "You've been to Maimana!" he said. "What a wonderful place. I'm languishing in Herat." I told him that surprised me. "Why, in Maimana are the finest grapes, aren't they? And the people are the best, they know all the good card games. They really know how to entertain themselves." I offered to play this fellow in cards, *à la* Maimana. We sat down to play in private (card-playing was not something to do in public), and I learned what the special playfulness of the *Maimanis* entailed. The man continually cheated and won every hand. "Oh, only in Maimana do they know how to play the game well," he said wistfully, as I left him.

The grapes were delicious. In size they were as big as apricots, perfectly amber in color, sweet as sugar. Vendors carried them about on great plates balanced on their heads, looking like Caravaggio's *Bacchus*, trailing vines behind them as they went swaying down the street. "If you eat any more grapes you'll be sick," said Khalil, sourly.

"It'll be worth it," we said, cutting ourselves another cluster with a knife.

We had very little money. To buy horses, or otherwise travel into the interior of the country was impossible, until we returned to a city with a major bank. We tried to make the best of being in Maimana, learning as much as we could about the places through which we would later travel. The ethnography of Ghur and Badghis was more complicated than was suggested by our neat patchwork maps of the major linguistic groups. Most of the people we had seen on our way had been Aymaks. Their characteristic villages were sprawling, lane-crossed confusions of black-hair tents and mud houses. They raised one crop of wheat each year (in either winter or spring, depending on the snows) in their *qishlaqs* (winter camps), and migrated to higher altitudes in the summer months to graze animals. In the *yaylaqs* (summer camps) they might have another crop of *lalmi* (cucumbers and melons). The Aymaks spoke a roughhewn dialect of Persian. Historically they were thought to be descended from Turkish and Iranian hillsmen who grew politically powerful during a periodic decline in Herat's authority. They never recovered from the Turkoman raids of the last century, and retreated from a national role to village obscurity.

More isolated and rarer were Tajik villages. An Iranian people with a reputation for industry, Tajiks could be easily recognized by their villages, with their neat networks of irrigation canals, walls and defensively-sited houses. The aboriginal race, the Tajiks had been forced into marginal areas of cultivation by the encroaching Aymaks, Turks and Pathans. Their efficiency in farming was thus a necessity. When even their skills could not scrape a living from the mountains, they came to the towns to work as rag and bone merchants, barbers and druggists.

That does not tell the half of whom we saw, Turkoman exiles from Central Asia, even exotic Kirghiz, and the ubiquitous, socially distinctive Pathan tribesmen. Because Ghur and Badghis were among the poorest of Afghan provinces, visible distinctions between all these peoples were tending to break down, as poverty ground all alike into the same dust. Ghur and Badghis were not high on anyone's list of colorful ethnographic tours, since wars and famines have stripped people of much of their distinctive folk cultures. The animosity between the different groups, invisible to the casual traveler, remained sharply defined.

The Pathans preserved more individual culture, and generated more than their share of the animosity. Their dynasty had ruled in Kabul. Their government settled them on the best land, driving out the Tajiks, Aymaks, and even the warlike Uzbeks, who remained sullenly at hand as subject races. Their language was difficult to master, though it was taught in all the schools. Their distinctive dress and impetuous self-confidence set them apart even in the crush of the bazaar. They were slow of speech with strangers, cagey in conversation.

Pathan nomads lived in the mountains above Maimana. On market days we could find them in the bazaar, bargaining with the Uzbek *bazaaris* for their necessities, and returning to their camps without spending any more time in town. Villagers, in contrast, would pass some time in the *samovar*. Nomad and settled seemed to be mutually relieved by the briefness of their encounters. Yet the nomads provided the town with its milk, meat, dung fuel and wool. Here they bought tea, sugar, kerosene and cloth. Antipathy and symbiosis went hand in hand.

We had come to Afghanistan to meet the nomads. In most of the Middle East ecologically suited to pastoral life, governments found it politically inappropriate to let free, armed tribes roam in the countryside. The struggle against nomads was ancient to the Middle East. The Book of Numbers tells of the wars of Israel with the nomads of Kedar. Now, as in the time of the Judges, settling nomads in the Middle East was preceding apace, a process often cosmetic in execution ('we got rid of those dirty tents and put them in clean houses'), and disasterous in consequences. Settled nomads' livestock would wither on the overgrazed land, while disease ravaged the people unused to sedentary hygiene. Suffering became general as meat and butter would disappear from the markets. All this was the inevitable result of government policy.

That this had not happened in Afghanistan was less a tribute to the good sense of the government than to the power of the nomads. Elsewhere in the Middle East warplanes and bombs had turned the military balance in favor of the central authorities, who then had their will with the tribes. In Afghanistan the tribes periodically revolted against the governments' taxes and conscription, and often won. Moreover, the ruling clique in Kabul was tied by blood and tradition to these nomads, so that diplomatic and moral suasion could be used to secured the place of the nomads. They migrated and grazed as their grandfathers had done, as their great-great grandfathers had done in the time of Abdur Rahman Khan, preserving their haughty insularity.

But how should we ever meet them? The experience of other travelers recently had run the gamut from being invited by the nomads to travel in their tents, to being plundered of all possessions, stripped of clothes, and left to the elements. Our attempts to find some kind of official entreé before coming to Afghanistan had led nowhere through vast amounts of paperwork. My friend corresponded unsuccessfully with the foreign wife of an Afghan aristocrat who might have provided us with a contact. When we reached the end of our resources, an old Afghan hand gave us the advice, "Just go."

But how should we get there? We looked for ways. The lackey in the hotel had many interesting things to say about his village in the mountains above Maimana, near Bandar-i-Mullaha.

"It's just like this, *Meestar*, mountain, water, valley." His Tajik accent was very difficult to make out.

"And are you farmers up there?"

"We live on the land, we sow, we reap." He had not understood my word for farmer, *kishtmand*, which was most common.

"And there are nomads up there?"

"Nomads, they call themselves *maldar*, cattlemen. They have many sheep. Their *qishlaqs* are like stars in the sky among the mountains. On the high *julga*, in *palash* or houses of *shibar* and *tash* and beside sheep they have *tava*, *yapu*, and some of them sow the white crop, or in the *chul* they have the sweetest *paliz*, because the ground in *lalmi*, they have no *kariz*. It is a wonderous life, *kul*, *avriz*, *hur*, *takao*! Do you understand?"

I nodded, doubtfully, only knowing that I wanted to go to Bandar-i-Mullaha. "And what tribes are they, Abdus Sattar?"

"Pathans, Afghans."

"Yes, I know, but I mean, Barakzai, Ghilzai, Afridi," these were just the more famous tribes I could think of.

"Who knows, *Meestar*, they are all one. Pathans."

"How do you get along with them?"

"Get along? They are rich, we are poor. They lend us money for planting, or crops, and when the harvest is poor, we lose our land to them. It was not always so. The Pathans came, not so long ago. I can remember. Now they own the land and we have nothing. That is why I am working in the *otel. Wai*, do you think it is a good life? In a month, I make a thousand *rupees*." He looked at me for his words to take effect. "*Meestar*! I am not married, do you know how much is the *marmar* (bride-price)?"

"They say four or five *lakhs*."

"*Hashallah*! In the city. But for a poor man like me, one *lakh*, two *lakhs*. How does a poor man save so much money? I should have a wife already, my head is white." He wanted to know what the *marmar* in America was, and embarrassed, I had to tell him tens of *lakhs*.

"Abdus Sattar, do you want to go back to Bandar-i-Mullaha?"

"*Meestar*! My heart is constricted." He placed his hand next to his eyelids, to show the tears he had shed. I couldn't reconcile his enthusiastic description of the nomads of Bandar-i-Mullaha and his poverty. He did not complain what was God's will, but merely made a statement of fact.

An afterthought. There was no meritocracy at work in Afghanistan, which had the positive effect of scattering remarkable people at every level of society. I chewed on the fact that my insight into the nomads had come from Abdus Sattar—the lackey of the hotel—and his almost professional anthropological distance.

On a Friday, the day of rest, we induced Khalil to come with us on an outing. Since the idea of simply walking for its own sake was anathema to a city fellow like Khalil, we had to suggest a practical object: to hunt for supper. He had some guns. We went to the bazaar to buy ammunition. The ten-shot cartridges were home-filled, risky, but very expensive. We hope to shoot rabbit, partridge or, *inshallah*, an antelope. I do not like hunting, but still less do I like rooster meat.

So little did Khalil intend to get any exercise that he reserved the front seat of a scheduled *mutar* for us, the morning post to Shibarghan. The front seat was typically reserved for landlords and official sorts, so it gave us an uncomfortable feeling of self-importance to be riding in relative comfort, armed to the teeth, in the company of a powerful official. The driver, who lorded over the other passengers, fawned on my every word as I asked him all sorts of questions about the North. He was a brilliant man, who even knew that music could be written down on lines. Meanwhile he had an idiot brother who rode on the fender saying, "Zooomm, zoomm, zoommm!" After a few minutes of the cloying conversation and the drooling idiot, I wished we were in the back with *hoi polloi.*

We rode the *mutar* past three villages or so, and then had the driver stop and let us off. While the passengers bargained for the front seats, we set off the road towards the hills, due north of Maimana, auspiciously enough, called Kuh-i-Sayyad, the huntsmen's hill. The valley, which had been very narrow, broadened out to a plain here. The *shikargah*, or hunting ground, was a thicket of pistachio trees, a mass of twisting branches where animals took cover. Taller trees of mulberry and walnut grew in the steep ravines, covered with dead, leathery leaves, in ripe and fallen nuts.

In a line twenty paces apart we started up the hill, careful to maintain a field of fire clear from one another, difficult even for three men in the ravines and steep slopes of the mountains. I thought of the hunt scenes in Persian and Mughal painting; this one bore no resemblance. Being only three in the dense thicket, we had little chance of stalking any clever animals. The shahs of old used to completely surround the *shikargah* and have the animals run down by bearers. At the exciting climax, herds of deer, wild onager, lions, and tigers would charge into the huntsmen—only to be picked off at leisure. In a single day, the Mughal Jahangir Shah would shoot 80,000 head of game, which eventually troubled his conscience to the point that he gave up this pastime completely. My conscience was in no such danger. I saw only the tangled thicket of greyish, silky branches, brambles, thorn thicket.

I had wondered if there were any wild boar about—which Khalil wouldn't let us eat even if we should be lucky enough to kill one and escape with our lives. The power of suggestion worked on me to the extent that I spent an agonizing moment stalking a hulking grey rock.

Khalil raised his shotgun to fire into a stirring thicket, but stopped when a child ran out into the field of fire. He had been

Khalil's target. The boy led a tiny donkey, loading brushwood on the toy-sized saddle of the animal. "Where are you from, boy?" asked Khalil. Terrified of the uniform, he gave no answer. "Kuh-i-Sayyad?" He nodded. Kahil waved him behind us, with a casual blow on the boy's shaved skull.

"Isn't it hard work what you're doing?" I smiled at him.

"There's no work without hardship," he said quietly, leading the donkey away.

There is an old story how Sultan Sanjar shot a peasant boy while hunting in the countryside. The boy's mother, weeping, brought the tiny corpse to the sultan's *durbar*. "Who killed him, I'll have his head," said the monarch.

"You did," said the mother.

The monarch threw himself at the woman's feet, saying "If you want my head, it's yours." The bereaved woman demurred.

Khalil Ullah sighed, "What a life these people lead."

Having seen nothing on the slopes we continued to the top of the mountain. The thicket gave out just before the top, and the wind blew. I had thought it much closer to sunset than it actually was. Here on the hilltop the sun shone hotly still.. We could see beyond the mountains onto the open plain, which was the steppe. Light fell on the expanse of sand as rainshower over water—a single fine element everywhere in view. In the sky, delicately interrupting the flat opacity, hung wisps of clouds. Looking at the steppe put us out of breath, more so than the long climb.

"The road to Andkhui," said Khalil, pointing out the single man-made feature in view. He asked my friend for a smoke and perched himself on a rock-outcropping which faced back towards the mountains. "It hurts your eyes," he said.

It did hurt your eyes. The steppe stretched without interruption to the limitless horizon, the Qara Qum desert, yellow and bare, disquieting, as the Russian poetess Anna Akhmatova had written: 'Your lynx-eyes, Asia, spy on my discontent, they lure into the light my hidden self." She had been in exile in Termez, just across the Amu Darya from the Afghan steppe.

For us the exposure to the great outdoors was therapeutic. We had been too guarded from it; we thought ourselves overlarge without it. A little humiliation was in order. The Afghan could never have too little to do with the outdoors, being over exposed to it. His sense of self-importance in the cosmos, consequently, was little inflated. Khalil did not need to be told, "You are a drop in the ocean of existence" by the vast steppe: his every poet told him as much. Besides, it hurt your eyes.

We headed back to the road in expectation of nightfall and the *mutar* from Shiburghan. We flagged it down as it lumbered up, without any room for additional passengers. We underestimated the ingenuity of the driver and his boy. A grumbling rearrangement of passengers in the back, twenty-four became twenty-seven. We had gallantly declined to displace a family of women traveling veiled and fearful in the front seat. The passengers were deferential, we were armed, after all, but expressed an unwonted curiosity to see what was in our game bag. Nothing. A short ride took us home to a late dinner of porridge and potatoes.

Whether the result of the cold night in the steppe or the baths which I took without troubling to heat the water, I became very ill, suddenly, overnight. I woke up in the morning, shivering; no amount of bedclothes could keep me warm. My friend rose, dressed, and heaped his bedclothes over mine. In a minute I felt so hot that I pulled all the covers off, sweating seas of sweat, so that my hair hung down dripping over my eyes. I don't know how long I lay there, alternately steaming and turning to ice.

My friend fetched a doctor. He stuck his petulant, Roman face into mine and examined me perfunctorily. Then he consulted with my friend, speaking in French, which I overheard, disbelieving as a delirium. Instruments and sticks were stuck in my throat, wrapped around my arm, shined in my eye. I heard dimly, garbled, "*Il faut partir pour Kaboul immédiatement. S'il ne reçoit pas . . . c'est possible qu'il doive quitter l'Afghanistan pour un lieu plus salubrieux . . . l'Iran ou l'Inde.*"

In my delirium I had a dream. I suddenly understood just why I had come to Afghanistan, something about impure motives, willingness to suffer, and I wept at the thought of it. Shivering and weeping at the same time, I forgot my grief. The day passed without my taking any food. I woke up in the middle of the night, hungry, freezing. Towards morning I fell asleep.

Some hours later I woke, now feverish, to see two unfamiliar figures in the room. Neither was my friend, but one looked like Abdus Sattar. He squatted by the bed, impatient and curious. Why had he awakened me? The other man had a long, white, wispy beard, like a dragon cloud over the steppe. He stared in my face. His was covered with wrinkles, his eyes drawn into almond-corners. Were they the two recording angels who come to catechize the departing soul of the Muslim dead? No, one of them was Abdus Sattar; who was the other one? To my surprise, I had asked the last question out loud.

"*Meestar,*" said the lackey, "he is *hakim*. Give him your wrist." Without considering the purport of this, I put my weak hand out from under the bedclothes. My hand was sticky with sweat, and I was loathe the *hakim* should notice, but he took the wrist gravely, silently, in his wrinkled hands—it felt as though he were wearing a glove. The examination proceeded.

"He's *dagh*," said the *hakim*.

"Yes, *dagh*," repeatedt he lackey. Did he catch cold?"

The lackey said, almost as an accusation, "He took cold baths, *Sahib*, and ate yoghurt together with grapes. I warned him."

I thought I was on trial. I said, horsely, "Hunting . . ."

The *hakim* said, "Quiet," and put my hand aside. "He must have *gush-i-kharak*, do you know?"

"Yes, yes, of course I know. They have that in the bazaar." They both got up and went out without a word to me. I wanted to call them in, call my friend, call Khalil, but had no energy for it. I lost interest in the whole examination proceeding.

My friend and Abdus Sattar returned with tea. "*Meestar*," he addressed himself to my friend, "this is *gush-i-kharak* ('little donkey's ear') It's like this, you roll it in your hands, around, around, and throw it into the tea. He must drink tea. It is medicine." I sipped a few mouthfuls, the tea was strangely aromatic. "*Meestar*, for the *hakim*, for the medicine, I need money. Fifty *rupees*."

The lackey went out. My friend said, "The thing is, I had to give the real doctor a lot of money. We have to go to Mazar-i-Sharif, because there's a bank there, and a hospital as well. We don't have the cash to get to Kabul."

"I'm not riding in a *mutar*," was the only thing I could say.

My fever subsided a little, my friend judged it time to leave. The lackey, taking credit for my recovery, asked for a private audience. "*Meestars!* You are leaving. Look you, I am a poor man. I work here. Why? To raise the *marmar* for a wife. So far, I have paid the father three-quarters *lakh* of *rupees*."

"You have a bride already?"

"Three-quarters, *Meestar*. I need five thousand *rupees* more. What is that to you. Give me the money."

Five thousand *rupees* was about one hundred dollars, not a great sum of money, but we explained that we had spent all our cash on the doctor. "Ah, the *duktur*. What did he do for you? And what did I do for you? Who summoned the *hakim?*" Explanations were impossible, but he insisted it made no difference in the end. "God will be provident."

"Abdus Sattar, if we go to Mazar and get money, will you take us to *Bandar-i-Mullaha*?"

"*Inshallah, inshallah*, you will return from Mazar and we will go to Bandar-i-Mullaha together."

Khalil was lukewarm in farewells, half-expecting us to come

back in a week, half-distrusting us to come back at all. "We make so many obligations for ourselves," observed my friend. "We have to go back to Maimana, Herat, to so many different people." One wished one could run the movie in reverse, turning good-byes into hellos.

The *mutar* set off for Shibarghan and Mazar later in the morning. I was still sick, but knew not to expect the sympathy of my fellow passengers. Bundled up, with a headband around my feverish face, I resigned myself to the torture of the *mutar* again. "But never again, after this," I told myself. My only outward acknowledgment to fever was a canteen of tea which I carried outside the bags.

The ride was unpleasant as usual, stuffy this time, choked with dust from the approaching steppe. Although I had not taken a drink, which would have been a breach of courtesy, my canteen did not long go unnoticed. Hands seized at it; passengers asked how much it cost; "Give it to me, give it to me as a keepsake," repeated some voice. I ignored all this behavior; it was normal enough.

When we had driven far enough upon the sandy road for the men to become thirsty, they grumbled more persistently about the canteen. "There's water in that *quti*," said one man.

"He's not very polite not to offer us any."

I wanted to say that since I was not drinking it myself, I was under no obligation to offer it around. But explanations were worse than silence, always, in Afghanistan. I said nothing, my friend likewise, while the passengers grew more sullen in their conversation. To be too weak and sick to care was a blessing now.

The long road to Shibarghan led through Andkhui; the short road led across a sand marsh. The character of the Afghans showed through. They chose the shorter, more dangerous route. The track ran through sands, which obscured the roadway altogether. The danger was that, if we lost our direction, we might drive into the marsh and be lost. From time to time the driver would stop and dismount from the cab, stand in what seemed to us a completely trackless waste, determine our course by some mysterious manner, and set off again. He never veered from his cardinal direction by more than 45 degrees. At one halt my friend asked the boy how the driver managed. "There are signs in the desert. Do you see that out there? It's a ruin."

We saw nothing. The boy insisted that the haze dead ahead of us contained a landmark. When the *mutar* drove on for fifteen minutes, we came upon the sand-covered walls of a ruined caravansary, and after that, a high steppe watchtower, part of the *limes* against the Turkoman raiders.

In the tenseness of our moments of stopping, the passengers were cowed by the steppe. The matter of the canteen was forgotten. When the *mutar* became stuck in the sand, all the baggage had to come down. My friend and I pitched in to unload, I with feverish energy, while some of the passengers leaned slackly against the *mutar*.

Shibarghan. The single street was even emptier than Maimana's, while the steppe town had none of the greenery of the mountain valley. Steppe showed down the end of every lane. A single machine generator, serving some small mill, filled the air with incessant mechanical explosion. The flimsy facades of the buildings on the main thoroughfare reminded me of the Old West, of Silver City, Colorado. We stopped here only for a meal, my first in two days. In the chatty atmosphere of the *samovar* I discovered I had lost my voice. The doctors later diagnosed laryngitis, resulting from extreme nervous exhaustion.

3.

ON PILGRIMAGE

Mazar-i-Sharif

There was nothing that could be done for it: it looked like a circus tent. Mustering all the understanding I had for the greatest shrine in Afghanistan, searching myself for appropriate awe and humility, still I could not help thinking: *It looks like a circus tent.* Pretty, insubstantial, temporary. The turquoise domes loomed over the vaults like big balloons, threatening to blow away with the wind. Wild, canary pentangles lashed them to the walls, but these were visibly stretching, jangling. An arabesque in green, lapis lazuli, and yellow fluttered on the porcelain skin of the facade, but the colors faded whenever the sun passed behind the clouds. High up on the minarets twin, gaudy, babyblue cupolas gave the impression of bobbing on invisible strings, like Chinese lanterns in a garden. Nowhere was there a solid shape, a somber arch, a reposeful wall. The spectator's eye had to look everywhere at once, ceaselessly, each corner of the shrine calling out like a carnival barker for attention, pleading that tonight is the only show, that at dawn the roustabouts will come and disassemble the whole place. The vaults need only a push. One had only to find the big top's main stake, the principal winch, and the whole shrine would come crashing down in a heap of canvas and guidewires. I shrank back, instinctively, from the catastrophe.

A shrine, a grave such as this, should be a reminder of our transitory journeying through this world. The spectator, the pilgrim, should scan the stones of the ancient shrine, reflecting on the many who have preceeded him to this spot, and are no more. The shrine itself in its permanence, should cause the viewer to consider the temporality of worldly things. Here, I met with the reverse. The shrine seemed fragile, the most temporal landmark in the city. It looked as though it had been built yesterday, and

should be razed tomorrow. On several such morrows, I went back
to check; it was still standing, as unconvincingly as before.

Mazar-i-Sharif (The Noble Shrine) is the most prestigious
holy place in this land covered with shrines. Compared to the
Timurid ruins in Herat, its condition is pristine, its maintenance
exceptional, thanks to the throng of pilgrims who are in constant
attendance, but particularly at the vernal equinox for the New
Year's festival.

Beside the shrine stands the modern city, which takes its
name from the holy precincts. The city orients itself around the
shrine, with large avenues leading off from its central square,
the result of extensive demolition and renewal carried out ten
years ago. The public buildings which used to abut directly on
the shrine have been set back for the sterile view, yet the tight
ring of modern structures around the shrine represents a jarring
contrast. There are four- and five-storied buildings in Mazar today, for although it is only the fifth-largest city (behind Kabul,
Kandahar, Herat, and Jalaabad), it is Afghanistan's most heavily industrialized. Astride the notorious flow of traffic north and
south, it exports natural gas, karakul skins, fruit, and cottage
manufactures. Through Mazar the Soviet Union floods the country with everything from plastic shoes to hydroelectric plants.
An observer notes the palpable result of this activity in the street:
Soviet businessmen and technicians jostling one another in lines
at the big hotels, their squat wives poking through bargains in
the bazaar; Volga taxicabs and Pakistani hansom carriages vy-
ing with one another in embryonic traffic jams. The city grows,
rural flight fills lane after lane with depressing slums, while a
burgeoning middle class expands into neat stucco bungalows
which lead down the broad avenues into the suburbs. Some *Mazaris* have to take buses to work. A day's factory smoke, if it settles
on the town center, leaves the shrine difficult to make out from
afar. Its central location not withstanding, the shrine strikes one
as a pretext for city planners, intent on building a modern city,
like any other white-stucco-and-mud metropolis of Asia.

To repeat: I thought I had given the shrine every chance.
I had plenty of time to spend there, convalescing from illness in
the hospital of the city, unconfined and unoccupied by day. My
friend had gone off to Juzjan, the mountain country south of
Mazar, leaving me in the friendly care of some young Afghan
interns, who mostly wanted to talk about *buzkashi* (the "goat
game")—a sport resembling rugby but played on horseback with
a beheaded goat as the football. Notwithstanding their own orders
that I should speak as little as possible, they used to exhaust me

with their talk, so that the few moments of rest I had were those spent visiting the shrine, down the main avenue from the hospital. The interns, all self-proclaimed Marxists, professed to have little interest in the shrine.

One day I felt more well than usual; in spite of constant strain my voice was stronger again, and I was eager to talk to somebody other than the voluable *dukturs*. I went to the shrine with the firm determination to speak to somebody about the place. The shrine of course was jammed with tourists, pilgrims, and petitioners, from as far away as India and America.

I walked in under the low lintel inscribed with Qur'anic verses. Women milled about in the courtyard with the bird-like flapping of veils, each surrounded by a troop of doll-like children, clinging onto the pleats of the mother's *chadri*. Their men walked ahead pausing now and then, admiring the mosque. A festive atmosphere prevailed. I couldn't bring myself to interrupt anyone here. Not that they were all involved in the mysterium of the shrine—on the contrary, they looked like they were on tour. Chocolate-skinned Indian Muslims strolled about in flapping pajamas, snapping pictures of the place, with the children, with the wife, just as they had done visiting Bagh-i-Shalimar and the Red Fort. There were *Kabulis* in worn business suits and karakul hats, strolling with their hands folded behind their backs, talking among themselves. I decided not to speak to anyone here today.

Not ready to go back to the hospital yet, I walked out along the corridors of the shrine, where I saw a sight for sore, would-be spiritualized eyes: a row of dervishes sitting against the wall with their begging bowls. Behind them, protruding from the wall, were a series of graves with marble plaques. The dervishes seemed to be keeping vigil over these tombs; they stared heavily at the ground, buried in their dark robes, unconscious of the crowds and traffic that circled around them. I approached timidly, stood at the side of their crowd until one of them should notice me.

One looked up. "Give alms," he commanded me. I did. He resumed his concentration upon the space in front of him, in spite of the fact that I stood where I had been, motionless, watching him.

No one looked up. "Who's buried here?" I asked. "M-m-m..." the same one muttered, as though I deserved no answer. I asked him again. "M-M-M-..." he repeated loudly, through his teeth, so I still didn't understand him. I asked him a third time and got the shouted, contemptuous reply, "*M-S-S-S-*," a name which could be interpreted in many ways, including Mir Shah-i-Shahid, Muhammad Sayyid Shah, Mirza Sultan Sa'ib, etc.

"Mir Sayyid Shahid?" I asked, persistantly. He nodded. "And

the others?" There were about six of these tombs. He said nothing. Apparently all six belonged to Prince Sayyid the Martyr.

"*Meestar* is American?" said a voice, in English. It seemed to have been emited, disembodied, just by the dervishes. Not one of them was looking at me. "If you please, sir, I very much enjoy to talk with Americans," the voice continued. Was it a *hatif*, a voice from the unseen? Mir Sayyid Shahid himself? I looked into the dervishes' faces; not one of them seemed aware of the voice.

"Who's speaking?" I demanded, in English, feeling like a fool.

One of the dervishes swayed on his haunches and made a vague gesture in the air. He continued to look at the ground. I stepped over to him.

"*Meestar* is well, I hope."

"Yes, thank you. Excuse me, but I'm very surprised. In fact . . ."

"You are surprised. That is not surprising. You are wondering how I am speaking English? The Americans taught me English. I like Americans very much."

"Why did you learn English?" I asked, wondering rather more why, if he spoke English, did he sit in the lane of a cemetery.

"When I learned to read braille . . ." I waved my hand in front of his downcast face; he went on, without looking up, "I did not know any English, but the Americans were very clever. There was no braille in *Farsi*, so they taught me English."

"But, what do you do now?"

"I am a *hafiz*. We are all *hafizes*, here." A *hafiz* was one who memorized the entire Qur'an for recitation, usually a mendicant, who recited at public occasions for a small fee. Blindness, traditionally, was an aid to memory. I wondered if he had any braille to read. "No, *Meestar*, when the Americans left, they took all their braille with them."

I asked him about the shrines. "Oh, you are interested in Islam, that is very good. This is the shrine of Amir Sher Ali Khan." I had certainly misheard the first dervish.

"Who was he?"

"Who was he? What do you mean? He is our saint. Our *shahid*. Do you know what is *shahid*?"

"Martyr," I prompted him.

"Martyr. Hm. Yes, martyr."

"But who martyred him, what did he do?"

Silence.

"When did he live?"

"I like Americans very much." He repeated this final pronouncement with a strong accent on the word *very*, so I had to put something substantial in his almsbowl.

The tombstones behind the dervishes were of white marble, slightly cloudy, half-effaced by the actions of pious hands. Since the dervishes now paid me no attention, I leaned over them to peer at the inscriptions. Difficult to read in the swirl of ornamental patterns, yet they were mostly new enough to be made out. The style and workmanship were the same as those on Gazurgah's recent graves in Herat. Here were one Kansh, daughter of Kilich Khan (1543), Shafira Sultana (1619), and two Uzbek princes whose names I didn't record. Amir Ali Sher Khan proved, by date, to be the infamous Sher Khan, the villain, I noted, of numerous Bengal Lancer matinees. Why he was considered a martyr by these dervishes, and why he was buried with two Uzbek princesses from two centuries previous, I could only speculate.

Without another word to the dervishes I made my way back, my picture of the shrine at Mazar-i-Sharif completed: a traffic circle, subcontinent tourists with chocolate-colored skin and Kodak cameras, gaudily restored tiling, and dervishes, bemoaning a handful of unknown Uzbek princesses, and regarding the crafty Sher Khan as a martyr.

Nothing that I subsequently learned distorted my initial impression. The first, striking point is how new, by Afghan standards, the shrine at Mazar-i-Sharif really is. In the fifteenth century it didn't exist. A cluster of villages on the fertile fringe of the Uzbek steppe was all you would have seen passing this way. You would have been on the road to Balkh, several hours ahead (fifteen minutes by taxi, today). The capital of the Bactrian Greeks, Balkh was known to the Arab geographers as "The Mother of Cities" because of its great size and antiquity. It served as a showplace for Greek, Buddhist, Hindu, and Muslim dynastic architecture. Though sacked by the Mongols in 1245 with the loss of half a million lives, the city was subsequently rebuilt. The architecturally manic Timurid dynasty lavished its peerless artistic patronage on the city, leaving it a dazzling assemblage of mosques, palaces, baths, and gardens, making it the northern rival of Herat. Foremost among Balkh's monuments, and possibly the finest Timurid work in Central Asia, was the tomb of the holy man Pir-i-Parsa. A daring, yet delicate dome rose twenty-five meters in the air, the thrust of its pinnacle mollified by the delicate crenelations of its surface. The dome worked its way gently into the supporting arches, with a series of jewel-like polygons filling the infinite space between the circle and the square. Color was entirely matched to structure; that which rose violently was softened with the most weightless turquoise, while that which remained immobile on the ground was animated with lively floral patterns. The porcelain mosaic tiles caught the last drop of sunlight off the sky in the hard, glassy crevice between colors, remaining irridescent blue until after nightfall.

All of this is apparent today, though the high dome teeters over the ruined facade. The tomb of Pir-i-Parsa retains its magic; Balkh, by and large, does not. Except for a few vagrants the city is uninhabited. There is refuse in the streets, all the same, because the brick houses are slowly resuming the state of mud. The tape lines of archaeological expeditions reflect the principal industry of the city today, and the traffic you see is only the caravan of taxicabs bringing tourists from Mazar-i-Sharif. They come in, admire the tomb of Pir-i-Parsa, and wonder, some of them, why this city of three millenia's history should be an emptying lot today. The guide will tell them with artless ignorance that Mongols destroyed the city as it is today; as far as this paper patriot is concerned the Mongols and the British are jointly to blame for everything wrong with Afghanistan today.

In truth, a simple party of peasants destroyed the Mother of Cities by digging a ditch many miles away. The cause and effect relationship may be hard to discern at first, but the following story makes it clear.

Ditch-digging is the relentless necessity of spring irrigation in the flood-prone mountain skirts above Balkh. A few peasants are engaged at the work; corvée for the local landlord, the practice persists today. Someone's spade turns, breaks on a rock. Clearing the earth away, they come across an old sarcophagus. An unidentified body! Imagine the consternation of the village headman confronted by this news. To begin with the burial ground renders impure their own farm land. Worse, the body might present some special curse; it might be the body of some ancient idolator, or of some liquidated enemy of the local princes. The greybeard would prefer to hush the whole matter up. That night, he goes to sleep, troubled by the affair of the unwanted body. The rest of the village sleeps, too, uneasily awaiting his decision. The next morning he gets up, very excited, and calls the villagers together. He has just had a dream, he tells them, explaining the whole wonderful affair. In his dream, Ali ibn Abi Talib, the Prophet's Heir (a long string of Arabic benedictions always follows both names, to wit, *sallalah alayhim wassalam*) appeared before the headman to explain that the mysterious body was none other than his own very blessed one. *Hazrat* Ali (upon whom be blessings and peace) revealed that he had died here, doing battle with an ancient race of idol-worshippers, and that to this day the secret of the glorious tomb remained hidden from the world.

When the headman finishes his story, restrained pandemonium erupts. The local *mulla* confesses that he has had exactly the same dream last night. Wait, the village greybeards, by pious coincidence, have all had the same dream. The young men, modestly silent and withdrawn to the fringes of the conference, are awestruck at the shared sanctity of the elders. They put their hands to the mouth of astonishment at the momentousness of the event. The village has become transformed overnight. Now, although it has no market like Murghir, no *kariz* like Panjadukhtar, forces greater than the material needs of men have conspired to make this village the epicenter of divinity. The elders, contemplating the future destiny of their village, must have felt something like Sutter at his mill.

With unaccustomed speed the news makes its way to neighboring villages, and even to Balkh itself. Pious enthusiasts begin to throng at the grave. Cripples, it becomes known, go home without their crutches; the blind see their first sunlight shining over the grave. Finally, his August Presence Husayn Bayqara, the great-grandson of Timur, arrives with his courtiers and sages in train, curious but cautious. They know very well, as the villagers do not, that the Prophet's Heir is buried in distant Iraq, in a town called Najaf. But the evidence of the miracles does seem unmistakable. Besides, the Prince reasons that his cousin—the amir of Iraq—makes a handsome income off taxing pilgrims to *Hazrat* Ali's tombs. More importantly, the honor of Ali is vigorously upheld by the Shi'ites, and their power is growing everywhere in the lands of Iran. Perhaps by patronizing the tomb, the Prince might court the favors of the burgeoning schismatics.

Husayn commanded a fitting tomb to be made. His successors have adorned that construction and today it is of magnificent scale. Mazar has all the vivacity and childish grandeur of the Brighton Pavilion, of a circus, as it first seemed to me. It is as though the architects employed in the task knew that the real tomb of Ali was in Iraq, but it made good business to build one here anyway. They have not built a tomb, but a pleasure palace for a secular monarch. There is not a whit of religion in the whole place. Yet it appeals to the tourists because of its gay decoration and good condition. While the gem-like monuments of Balkh languished under earthquakes and Turkoman attacks, the tomb of Ali had been lovingly restored and expanded. Husayn Bayqara was right: the Shi'ites did grow more powerful in the land, and their patronage of the shrine transferred the seat of power from the city to the one-time village. Settled pilgrims, entrepreneurs, wealthy families, and *bast* fugitives have chosen to settle in around the shrine, joined by the snowballing effect and rural flight, so that in a few years the stucco bungalows of Mazar-i-Sharif will reach right up to the old triple walls of Balkh, and if the headman of the village should see Mazar today he would be well assured that he had identified a true miracle.

In the end, that is what makes a city holy: recognition, crowds of pilgrims, pious endowments. When the palpable miracles dwindle out, the miraculous nature of everyday life makes the city a marvel. The transubstantiation of puny individuals into a powerful unity is the chief miracle of a town like Mazar, surrounded as it is by dead, sleepy villages and ghost towns. The energy of the city is miraculous beside the entropy of the countryside. The *Mazaris* feel justified to rate their town with Mecca, Medina, Quds, Sham, and Najaf, the holy places of Islam.

Graves of Giants

In Afghanistan nearly every graveyard has a shrine, and every shrine attracts its graveyard. The land is covered with holy places without name and without the fortune of a site like Mazar-i-Sharif. We travellers are curious about their origins. Afghanistan is a sargasso of wrecks from earlier civilizations; buried in its earth are hordes of Greek coins, Aramaic inscriptions, Saljuq mosques, and Mazdakite fire temples, flaking away in their own dust, forgotten in valleys where the local villagers carry away their bricks for cattle folds. Archaeologists have crisscrossed the country, by foot, by Land Rover, and exhaustively by air, trying to turn up the pieces of the past. They come from all over the world. Japanese scholars dig, funded by Buddhist monasteries in Kyoto which are curious to learn about their Central Asian traditions. Europeans seek the fate of the Greek kingdoms of Bactria and Parthia, scouring for ruins in the wastes of Ghur and Badghis. Indian archaeologists are at work in the oasis of Jalalabad, which was a flourishing outpost of Gandharan culture three millenia ago. It is as though every nation can trace its roots toward Central Asia and uncover their new sources of its origins.

But not the Afghans themselves; for the most part, they look on these investigations with skepticism, suspecting espionage, subversion, or prospecting for gold as the more immediate end of the so-called archaeologists. Even in the Capital one hears the Archaeological Museum (where the magnificent frescoes of Bamian are on exhibit) referred to contemptuously as *butkhana* (idol temple).

The Afghans do not romanticize the relics of their ancient past. They have no interest in these ruins, as Iranians have come to have in Achaemenid ruins, because they attribute them not to their own ancestors, but to alien tyrants, Hindus and idol-worshippers. Their provenance, the Afghans imagine, is that of a dark age, where the only light was the glinting of gems in the eye of the graven image and the smouldering light of the sooty fire temples. The land was ruled by Hindus, black their skins, black the history of their reigns, with treachery and bloody massacres, incestuous sins. The twin Buddhas of Bamian, they say, are two tyrannical monarch consorts of old whom God turned into stone for their blasphemies. Such was the age before Islam.

The tribes of the Sulaymaniya Mountains claim that one of the earliest followers of the Prophet Muhammad, one Qays, journeyed hence from Hijaz and became the founder of the Afghans. Thus they obtain their precedence in Islam, the patent of nobility. Most Persians and Sayyids are content to trace their descent from heroes in the conquering armies of the Arabs who overran Afghanistan in the year 64 of the Flight. These were troops of the Tamim tribe and the Bakr, later joined by the Azd of Yemen. They overthrew the Hindu kings, drove out the idol-worshippers, and established themselves in the then ancient towns of Kandahar and Herat. But pagandom was tenacious; as late as 343 of the Flight the Hindus threatened the very walls of Herat, the countryside by and large remaining beyond the pale of Islam. In the long centuries of battle, those who fell on the Muslim side were entitled *shahids* (martyrs) and their tombs were venerated as those of saints. The men of the first generation of Islam were called the *kalan* (giants), for they were great in all that they did. Their graves are now thirty to forty feet long, a literalization of the expression "The men of bygone years were as giants." These are the graves pinioned under horsehair banners and offerings of antelope horns, plots of earth which can be seen in every village, in the middle of busy city streets, and in valleys far from present habitation. These are the monuments Afghans show interest in. The first century of Islam was history, and all else before is an empty tale.

The tombs of these *shahids* themselves perpetuate the pre-Islamic past. The many which are known as *"shah"* preserve a memory of Buddhist priest-kings, or the aristocratic clergy of the Manichaes. *Hazrat* Ali, worshipped by the Shi'ites of Hazarajat, may be the palimpsest of the Bamian Buddha. The Islamic shrines are very often sited by the ancient ones—temples and *stupas*. Skeptics would say that the shrines *are* Buddhist or Hindu, whitewashed with an Islamic history. I think rather that Islam's holy men were drawn to martyrdom or miracle-working at the site of pagan places just to fly in the face of the old religion. When a village changed religion, it did not change burial grounds, but reconsecrated it to the One God and buried their new saint beside the pagan dead.

Afghans build their lives around these shrines. Often, as spectacularly exemplified by Mazar, a village springs out of pilgrims' settlements about the shrine. In a large city with many shrines—Herat, for example, with its population of 80,000 people, has over 2,000 recorded shrines—families will patronize traditional favorites. They may go to a particular shrine on certain days of the week or in the case of a particular physical infirmity. Very famous are the shrines where women go to petition for offspring. If the shrine is a popular one, it will support its own attendants, dervishes, and a *mir* or *turbadar*, who supervises the workings of the shrine, its land, its revenues, which are sometimes among the largest in a province. I have heard it said, "Sometimes the graves are the liveliest places of all." That is certainly true of Mazar.

In a land covered with shrines one can always get into a discussion over the powers and properties of a given shrine, with one caveat: one must never question the efficacy of a shrine in a stranger's native town. Talking to a *Herati* one might say, "Verily, Shah Abdullah Walid is a good place to pray for the teeth, but where does one go for the gout?" Your *Herati* knows where to go for a bad cold and where for marital problems. "I'm not married," one replies.

"In that case you have no problems."

One free-thinking fellow explained to me the mystery of Ali's troubling multiple burials. He had been on the *hajj*, had passed through Iraq and Najaf. "Some say he is buried in Najaf. Others say, Mazar-i-Sharif. Still others say this place or that. But *Hazrat* Ali has said, 'I am everywhere, look for me in your hearts'. This means that the tomb of Ali is hidden from us, so that we can discover him anywhere, even within ourselves."

I asked him if he considered it a blessing to have made the pilgrimage to Mazar, even if it were not truly Ali's grave. "Certainly," he said. "The impulse to make a pilgrimage, the prompting, this is the blessing itself."

I didn't tell him that I'd come to Mazar only to be hospitalized.

My time spent in Mazar had been inactive and depressing on account of the gloomy, camphorized atmosphere of the hospital.

In some weeks' time I was to meet my friend. I don't remember how the idea came to me, to go on a pilgrimage. I had no special prayer, no wife who was trying to poison me, no deceased relations who would have appreciated the intercession of a Muslim saint. Whimsy alone guided my choice of shrine. Since the impulse to travel had been commended to me, I wanted to prolong the impulse as much as possible, to make it a long journey. To avoid the Indians with their Kodaks and the astrakhan-hatted *Kabulis*, I looked for a little-visited shrine, in an inaccessible, if possible, part of the country. There were many hundreds of anonymous country graveyard places for such a pilgrimage; I chose a shrine which had struck me, at once, as the right one: the cave where the Seven Wise Men of ancient times went to sleep for a fabulous number of years. The Qur'an mentioned it in the chapter THE CAVE, and the place was known as Ashab-i-Kahf, "The Companions of the Cave." Distant as it was from Mazar, all my acquaintances knew of it, even my Marxist sawbones. Everyone had a different version of the story of the shrine to relate to me, which quickened my interest in going. They gave me directions for the road, prayers for my safe return—and again I felt the resentment of those who stay for those (foreigners) who can leave. "There goes a *farefelu* to a well-deserved perdition" may have been their true sentiment, and I did not blame them.

The Cave of the Sleepers

In my eagerness I forgot the discomfort of the *mutar*, going back over the same road, across the sandy Uzbek steppe, where the road was lost more than once and where we had to get out of the *mutar* and push it out of the sand over and over. That increased the *barakat* (blessing) of pilgrimage, if nothing else.

Shibarghan, the same sleepy town where the noise of the diesel generator rattles the air. Nothing human moves because of the heat.

Maimana. I knew that Khalil would try to stop me from going and hadn't the nerve to face him. It seemed better, to slip through town without seeing Khalil, Surush, and Abus Sattar. I stayed with the *mutar* as it stopped at the *samovar*, then went on, thoroughly exhausted, through the night.

Qaisar, a feeder town for the markets of Maimana. Inexplicably large hotel, here. Sent there by the local gendarmerie I found all sixty rooms vacant, ivy and crawlers spreading through the corridors, empty as a *mazar*, a tomb. An eggplant-bellied fellow popped out of nowhere with a ewer, having stepped out to answer necessity; he stared at me as though I were a ghost. When he realized that I was a prospective paying guest he regained his composure and tried to show me to a room. I could take my pick of sixty unheated, unfurnished rooms, mandatory government tariff, 160 *rupees* a night. I declined this outrageous offer. He insisted, such was the government rate. I said no. 150? 140? 100 *rupees*, bottom price. When I foolishly let it slip out that I intended to visit Ashab-i-Kahf, the fellow took it upon himself to stop me. A foreigner traveling in the countryside? The wild natives are predatory! No less, I told him, than the hotel clerks. He said something to me about arranging an official escort, which would have been the end of my pilgrimage. I slipped out on a pretext and caught the next *mutar*, riding all night to a town called Chikchakto, at the foot of the valley where the shrine lay.

It was market day in the morning, and the whole valley of the riverlet was aswarm with travelers and traders, bringing goods back and forth from the third-class market at Chikchakto. Merchants from Qaisar were here, for Chikchakto was a feeder town for Qaisar, just as the latter fed the market of Maimana. This web of regional markets covered the whole North, and explained why there were always travelers and traffic upon the smallest roads. I knew that the countryside would not be the empty, hostile place the cityfolk imagined it; as long as I got along with my traveling companions, I would be safe. Some of the *bazaaris* from Qaisar recognized me, having been on the *mutar* the day before.

"So, *Meestar*, you are still set on your pilgrimage? How are you going to go? By *mutar*, surely, or Land Rover? No? On foot! *Mash'allah*, indeed, you're too frail for that . . ." Afghans never saw foreigners walking, so they imagined them to be incapable.

I explained in somber piety: "The great men of old used to walk barefoot for the *barakat* of pilgrimage. Am I not to walk a few miles in my boots?" They accepted this answer gravely.

Actually, after the hospital and the cramped days in the *mutar*, it was a relief to walk out on the solid earth. The clay was rutted but firm. August heat had bronzed the grass beside the road to dust, while the thirsty watercourse, like a wild horse, bolted alongside the road. On the way, passersby were many, trafficking from the bazaar. I began to walk with a mule train, but these folk were too slow, and their conversation too banal. I walked faster, and passed several camels, which said something about the value of that animal as a mount. I couldn't have paced myself too quickly, though, since the sun was setting with unwelcome speed. After a full summer of light evenings, I misjudged the length of day.

At a certain point I was to turn off the road, past a large grave, one of those stretching forty feet beside the road. This was a *kalan*.

My path skirted by the edge of a village. It stood away from the roadside for fear of strangers; the strangers stayed back from the village for fear of the dogs. Several of these man-killing mastiffs could be heard now, growling discontentedly. I had received varying advice about dealing with these animals, all contradictory, none of it psychologically reassuring enough to risk having one's foot swallowed whole. The silliest one was "Don't show fear; they can *smell* fear." When I spied the web of water ditches and flood barriers between me and the growling noises, I felt better.

I was in the mountains now. What had seemed like a mass of brown and goldish dust from the valley was actually an intricate pattern of matter; I passed another village, walled behind its silver poplar trees, black irrigation ditches churning up its enceinte, wind-protected behind heaps of yellowish clay. Goat paths led everywhere, confusing the road, like a silver lace on the mountain side. Shadows fell across my path, and I began to fret.

Providentially, a man with a crook was making his way down the path. I had always been afraid of asking strangers for directions when I was lost, say, and trying to find Orchard Street in Manhattan. Here, shyness was out of place. I approached him with a loud, "*Salaam alaykum*, is your soul in harmony?" I smiled weakly, wishing he did not have the crook. The man, terrified of my odd appearance, accent, and general air of the extraordinary, could not bring himself to answer. "Which one of these paths lead to Ashab-i-Kahf?" No response. "Look, I'm a pilgrim." Undecided as to whether I were a pilgrim or a bandit, he sullenly pointed out the way and hurried off. I followed the path in the distressingly long shadows, and before light failed I spied the shrine, hiked up a bit above it to plot my entry and catch my breath before going down.

Ashab-i-Kahf is a small group of houses with a common wall, indistinguishable, but for the shrine, from the other villages in the valley. Water flows beside it, muddying in the sun of dusk, irrigating the long, bony poplars and stunted-looking wheat. Fruit trees, quinces, grow within the enceinte of the village proper, protected there from the wind. Built into the wall are mud-and-plaster houses, and a great pool of water, where a large cow stands lapping. Beside the pool, a neatly built and newly roofed edifice, clearly the headman's *mihman khana* (guest house). Just above the village on the slope of the mountain stands the only other real edifice to be seen: a ruined arch of proportions too grand to have been recently built. This is the entrance to the shrine, which is but a cave set into the mountain's face. The brick arch is high, with a Chaghatai cupola atop. Issuing from the mouth of the cave, and spreading on all the slopes above the village lie white tombstones, quarried at great expense and brought from many miles away to mark the resting place of a thousand petitioners of the shrine. The village is outnumbered by the dead. The size of the cemetery, the good construction of the fifteenth century arch, all point to a once greater, more important cult here than is presently to be found, given the small size of the actual village.

I went down from my roost in order to be received before nightfall, when no traveler was welcome. When the sun set in the mountains, though, it set slowly, fold by fold, so darting rays of light lit my way to the village where the man watering the cow gave me my due hospitality. I was led into the foyer of the headman's lodge and left to rest awhile (an important Afghan courtesy) before anyone questioned me as to my business or my parts. The light having failed now, I had to sit in the pitch dark, trying to comfort myself with having made it here, without knowing exactly where I was and who was receiving me. A silent person entered, lit a kerosene lamp, and withdrew. I could look around the room. It was covered with fresh *gach*, that pleasant-smelling clay plaster which replaced brick, stone or wood in Afghanistan, its own drawback being that it flaked into dust constantly, and had to be swept up all the time. My room was very well swept. There was one window papered shut, and a single, very grand beam holding up the roof. In this deforested land, the principal outlay necessary to build a new house had always been this center beam. In troubled times, a common practice was to throw down one's neighbor's house and steal his beams. I felt this one had been honestly acquired. The whole room was about 7 by 15 feet, or big enough for six Anglo-Saxons or thirty-six Afghans. At the news of my arrival the villagers were greatly interested, and all thirty-six places were promptly taken. The young men stood modestly, as always, in the rear. The greybeards made no effort to mask their curiosity about me, staring from a few feet away, and fondling a grandchild or two. The infants were not interested in the foreigner.

The master of the house, a *sayyid*, was momentarily expected, they told me. I had read that the shrine was in the caretaking of a *sayyid*, and found it curious to hear him described as an Arab, though of course, all *sayyids*, by virtue of their descent from the Prophet could theoretically claim Arab heritage. I had met in Mazar people claiming to be Arabs, but they were vague on this, speaking Persian or Turkish, and looking a mixture of both. The *sayyid*, they claimed, was a real Arab, a true aristocrat of Islam.

He strode in, almost brusquely traversed from the bottom of the room to the top, taking no notice of the gathered crowd. He led me up, wordlessly, to a grander, higher position in the room, and then seated himself with an astute combination of gravity and nonchalance. Readers of the Gospel will remember, as I did, the advice, "Seat yourself at the bottom of the room, lest the host ask you to move down, shaming you." It was a good sign. My host sat as close to me as possible to indicate his courtesy, and yet not intimacy. We exchanged formal greetings and basic explanations. "Oh, yes, many foreigners come here. Often." I was crestfallen, but asked how often. "Why, a man and his wife came here from, where was it, *Alman*, about eight or nine years ago. They took many photographs. Do you have a camera?" I told him no. Now it was his turn to be disappointed.

A meal was presently brought, at which only he and I ate. The rest merely watched. They had eaten already and the *sayyid*, too, possibly had dined, but accompanied me as part of his duties as host. The meal was silent, but as soon as it was finished we began discussing the twenty basic questions which the Afghans invariably posed to foreign people. I had to hasten to explain that we were neither incestuous, nor anthropophagous, nor atheists, nor any like abomination. Then they asked if we prayed five times daily, bathed after sexual intercourse, buried our dead in the direction of the Holy Land. I answered yes on all counts, with some equanimity, as I had a great-grandmother who did pray five times a day, if not more often, and there were tenuous justifications for the rest of my answers as well. Finally they asked, do you recognize His Excellency the Prophet Muhammad as a true prophet? Having had much practice at this question I answered that men of conscience in the West recognized in Muhammad the qualities of a great, prophetic voice. The *sayyid*, acting as the moderator in these discussions, perceived that the polite limit of time and profundity had been reached, and signified that the assembly was at an end. His guests, disappointed at not hearing of guns and horses, or cannibalism and other wonderful abominations, went speedily home, and I fell as fast asleep, wrapped in the blankets my host set aside for me.

In the morning my feet ached terribly; a blister made it difficult for me to stand. One of the household led me outside to the facilities, then brought me water to wash with, bread, and some raisins for breakfast. With tea my host returned. It would be giving a misleading picture of the *sayyid* not to point out his modest circumstances. His household was composed of poor relations, I was sure, living off this relatively more prosperous connection. The children and grandchildren of the house went about in the same patched clothes and snot-dirty turbans as the other youngsters. But the *sayyid* retained a tutor for them, to teach them Arabic and letters, and they had a certain gravity, even for their age, on account of their high lineage. The *sayyid* himself was difficult to describe, having a young, old face, a decayed face, yet graced with an aristocratic manner. The subtlety of his expression was that of an actor. On his head he wore a pure white silk turban, set off with fancy plastic shoes from the Soviet Union and an ancient grey waistcoat gathered around his flowing pajamas. Everything he handled gingerly, so as not to dirty himself needlessly, but his movements were athletic, direct, there was nothing soft about him.

When the indefatigable Yate visited the shrine in 1887 he reported a family of *sayyids* with considerable local wealth and power occupying the sinecure at Ashab-i-Kahf. In those days the North was thoroughly Turkish, and the *sayyids* were known by the Central Asian title of *ishan* (literally, "they" as in Italian, "*loro*"). Yate's *ishans* were of Tatar and Arabic descent, and extremely ambitious in their enthusiasm for their shrine. Due to their efforts at propagandizing, Indian Muslims from Yate's own detachment had heard of the place and sought leave to make the pilgrimage there. The *ishans*, according to Yate, were crafty, greedy, and proud. Did any of this, I wondered, lurk in the background of my host?

Yes, said the *sayyid*, his family was long on this land, more than a hundred years if the truth be told. He continued to insist on his Arab descent, while admitting that he knew Turkish (as well as Persian, of course): "These are the languages of men, after all." If the *sayyid* were the great-grandson of the *ishans*, as I now assumed, it remained to be known what accounted for the impoverishment of the shrine since the time of Yate's travels. The *sayyid* only owned the one village, now, not the whole valley, as had the *ishans*. I wondered about the villages in the valley, if some recently arrived Pathan clan had usurped the headlands of the stream, placing the village/shrine in the position of vassalage. The *sayyid* waved aside my questions with unemphatic answers, uninterested in my curiosity, thinking that this was hardly the sort of conversation a pilgrim should carry on. Abruptly, he changed the topic of conversation. Did I want to see the shrine? We got to our feet.

I followed him out of the *mihman khana* into sunlight that blinded my eyes. Still curious about the Pathans and their progress in the neighborhood, I kept silent; as my eyes adjusted, focused on the scene of graves and the great arch of the cave, I reflected, *No, this was not the sort of questioning a pilgrim would do.* Guiltily, the original impulse of the journey recalled itself. To reinstate myself in the good graces of the *sayyid,* I began to ask him about the shrine, and the legend of the cave; these seemed like reasonable questions to me. I had read, I told him, many conflicting versions of the story. It appeared in the Talmud, and in Gibbon's *Decline and Fall,* the second being the received Christian version, known as the Seven Sleepers of Ephesus. The Qur'an, too, hinted at details of the story (this I discussed with the *sayyid*) while Amir Ali Sher of Herat wrote the fullest local recension in his Chaghatai Turkish version of the story.

According to Ali Sher, in the land of Rum, the Greek kingdom, there ruled a tyrant, Daqyanus (Decianus) by name, who had a number of servants who were Muslims and who worshipped God Most High (remember, the first Muslim was not Muhammad, but Father Ibrahim). The tyrant having gotten wind of their devotion to God grew angry and intended to slay them, but an angel alerted them to their peril and they hid themselves in a cave. There they slept for three hundred years. During this time, Daqyanus and his unbelieving passed away, and a monarch, Muslim and God-fearing, sat on the throne (Constantine the Great, in Christian versions). God Most High awakened the companions from their sleep. They sent one of their number to the bazaar to buy bread, for they were hungry. When he paid the baker for his purchase with a 300-year-old coin, the baker, and then the rest of the bazaar, got into commotion over the coin of Daqyanus; questioning the stranger, they brought history to light. The monarch of the faithful was informed of this event, and consulted his wise men. "It is in the scriptures," they advised, "such and such took place in the reign of Daqyanus." The monarch reunited the stranger with his companions in the cave, feasted them, and gave thanks to God Most High.

Confusions abounded. Ali Sher, writing in the 1490's, confidently placed the miracle in the Kingdom of Rum, the realm of his cousin Turks, the Ottomans. Yet his own patrons, the Timurids, built this arch in honor of the event, in this obscure valley of Northern Afghanistan. Other aspects of the story had been localized as well, for they said that the two monumental Buddhas of Bamian were in fact Daqyanus and his consort, turned to stone as divine punishment. Or weren't they giants vanquished by *Hazrat* Ali? I had already noticed the Timurid willingness to patronize any promising place of pilgrimage. Perhaps Husayn Bayqara had visited Ashab-i-Kahf, too, with Ali Sher complaining all the while that the Seven Sleepers were off in Ephesus.

I asked the *sayyid* about the many hazy parts of the story. Were the sleepers awakened by the birth of the Prophet (at which time celestial music was said to have rocked the globe)? Did they awake at the birth of Christ and return to sleep afterward? Why were they still there? And how many were there, six or seven? Was one a shepherd, and was his dog the sixth or seventh? The *sayyid* deferred all these questions with a simple statement from the Qur'an: "THEY WILL SAY THREE, THE FOURTH WAS THEIR DOG; OTHERS SAY FIVE, THEIR DOG THE SIXTH, SEEKING WHAT IS HIDDEN. SOME WILL SAY SEVEN, EIGHT THEIR DOG, BUT YOUR LORD KNOWS THEIR NUMBER, AND NONE BESIDE, BUT A FEW."

We went in under the arch, entering an antechamber to the cave. Here, hundreds of visitors to the shrine had etched their palm-prints in chalk, or scratched their names into the clay walls, and we read countless names, Hasans, Ahmads, Abdul Karims, in mad jumble from ceiling to floor. Beyond the antechamber it was dark, so we paused to light our hurricane lamp. I had reached another limit in my dialogue with the *sayyid*. He was not curious about the story of the sleepers, at least, not as I was, for information or analysis. Everything about the man was contradictions, his old, young face, his shabby, genteel manner. He could live with contradictions, obviously.

Following the vague glow of the lantern, I stepped into the dark passageway of the cave. Yate must have had an electric torch, since his description of the cave was very clear, while I could scarcely see at all. The long, deep natural cave snaked into the mountainside about thirty feet. Midway through the passage an air-hole had been cut through from above; a tiny shaft of light with dust motes danced before us briefly. The *sayyid* stopped and pointed this out. "Was that how the sleepers could breathe?" I asked.

"Perhaps, perhaps."

We reached the end of the passage and stood in a rock-cut chamber, confronting, through the dim light of the lamp, a well-wrought wooden cage, or screen, such as usually protects the tombs of the famous. Here were seven (or eight?) shadowed figures laid out beyond the bier, in what looked like linen shrouds. Were they asleep again, or dead? That was another of the mysteries. Yate, with typical Anglo-Indian bravado, had asked permission to go behind the screen and examine the shadowy bier/beds. Permission was refused him on the grounds that it would lead to sudden blindness. I didn't ask any such thing. Yate perceived, with his torch no doubt, the body of an animal, possibly the shepherd's dog, crouched in a corner. "Its leg had rotted off, which rather told against its being asleep," he noted. I peered and peered into the gloom beyond the screen, and could make out nothing. My curiosity obviously bothered my host, who seemed quite bored. Meanwhile, the chamber filled with the soot of the lamp and stank of kerosene. Feeling that I had again hit a dead end, both in a spiritual search and an intellectual one, I signalled my willingness to go.

Outside the light seemed warm and pleasant, the white tombstones reassuring in their quiet numbers. The *sayyid*, perhaps sensing my disappointment, became talkative. "You ask whether I believe in this or that retelling of the story of the cave. I do not know. The Holy Qur'an tells many parables, which, to the untutored reader, must appear contradictory. But there is no contradiction. We are not meant to know everything. Is there life after death? Will these dead, these many, really rise from their graves at the end of the world? What does your religion say?"

"My faith says they will rise, but many people dispute it."

"So it is here." This admission of doubt was like an intimacy between us. It was achieved; now there could be no more talk. We returned to the village.

I decided it was time to go. The busy man, with his fields, his chattel, his farmers, and dependents, had spent a morning of leisure with me, and it was obviously a rare holiday. Activity in the village had grown brisk, with oxen to be watered and winter wheat to be sown. The villagers gathered to watch my leavetaking. Previously I had offered the *sayyid* a gift of money, not for his trouble, but for the upkeep of the shrine. He firmly refused it. Now in honor of my departure, he summoned a servant with great bags of walnuts and almonds. These he drew forth with sweeping gestures, and placed them, even as precious gems, into the skirts of my coat. If I had been John Roe, Stuart ambassador to the court of the Great Mughals, my send-off could not have been more grand. Having overloaded me, he turned to each of his villagers, honoring me with his liberality towards them, giving each of them his due according to rank and age. Children scrambled to pick up what had fallen.

I hurried to be out of sight, and was probably soon out of mind. I rehearsed again my conversation with the *sayyid* so as not to forget a single detail. The dusty trail led me down the mountain back to the valley, and I had much time to think. What was clear to me was that the *sayyid* had inherited an important shrine, but had seen it decay. The testimony of the graffiti in the anteroom, the fame of the shrine among Yate's sepoys, and even in Mazar, was testimony to its past greatness. Now the shrine was quieter, the *bazaaris* of Chikchakto had smiled at the thought of my going there.

The doubting *sayyid* could have been the cause for this decline. The man was too intelligent, too deeply feeling about religious matters to keep the spiritual reputation of the shrine at the level he had found it. His ancestors might have been swashbuckling Turks, greedy to exploit the place, almost as a tourist attraction to finance their power. Now when pilgrims came, their heir made no claims. Important visitors arrived, he treated them with simple dignity. Benefices were offered, he turned them down. A shrine needs a Bernini, even a Barnum, just to give it the mystique, the reputation which generates religious hysteria, and which in turn produces miracles and revelations. I had found none of this, but I had found much more: in a way that I could understand, a sincerely religious man.

The *bazaaris* of Chikchakto were glad to see me, having worried that, if I had fallen on my face and died there would be an official inquiry and an always unwelcome run-in with the provincial government. They asked me about the *sayyid*; I told them I found him a genial, good host. They smiled at this, clearly keeping their poor opinion of the man, for which I now scorned them. A *mutar* arrived, heading to Bala Murghab, and I sped off in it.

I recalled a characteristic story about holy men in Afghanistan. Wandering around the mountainous countryside working miracles, a holy man came to a small village. Here the peasants were so benighted, they had no one to lead them in the Arabic prayers, no one to circumcise their children, nor to bury their dead. They greeted the arrival of the saint with great relief and excitement. They opportuned him to stay a week, circumcise their children and organize hasty primers in ritual. They feasted him and dined him to the extent of their poor resources. At week's end the greybeards of the village gathered to plan his farewell party, and came to a momentous decision: they killed him in his sleep and buried him just outside the village, blaming his death on wild animals. News of the saint's demise spread throughout the kingdom; disciples flocked tearfully to the village to pay their respects. Some stayed to teach and preserve the memory of the great man; they built mosques, schools, hospitals, and in short, fulfilled the wildest prayers of the greybeards of the village.

The real miracle is faith itself. Shrines, the many hundreds one sees in Afghanistan, are mere *faits accomplis*, a question of real-estate speculation, of pure hokum. Some shrines would be built on the sites of older ones, priests of one religion trying to preserve their investment as they converted to another, in which case the energy focused on a single plot of land remained for centuries. And yet other shrines gave out, the mountain fire-temples of Iran, the *stupas* of Taxila, when the faith that inspired those places was lost. Perhaps not too far away, a new shrine and a new faith attracted pilgrims, and the same human energy was transferred at a stroke to the new. At the old shrine, columns and arches fell producing an archaeological site.

What will become of the *sayyid* and his cave? I am afraid his lack of enterprise and agnosticism will doom the shrine to oblivion. After fifty years his family will sell out of the village and move to Mazar and Kabul to become petty bourgeois, or proletarianized by a new, industrial Afghanistan. Then the cave will be the provenance of the archaeologists; they will open the cage, examine the bodies, carry out carbon testing and answer all the questions I had once asked. But they will never know; they will know neither the men of faith who lived here, nor the men of little faith who went there because it was holy.

4.
HEART OF AN OASIS

The Old City

In the cafe where I once passed a *Ramazan* night with Gul Ahmad and my friend, I felt quite at home on the first evening of my return to the city. On this certain day in November my friend and I had arranged to meet. Time, that is, the season of the year, was getting on; the nights were growing especially cold now, the sun set early, though the city lights still didn't come on until after six. A Franklin stove smoked in a corner of the cafe, the windows lay shuttered for warmth. Whenever the door banged open a cold draught blew in, shivering the old *bazaaris* who huddled by the stove. They sat away from the windows and doors, sipping tea for warmth, with wool blankets thrown over their shoulders. I was cold, too, and shivered, but perhaps it was with expectation, so glad was I to be back in the city.

The door swung open and my friend strode in, wearing a heavy, brown *barak*. I stood up, greeting him in mock Eastern etiquette, "Is your soul in harmony?"

"May you not be tired." He sat down heavily, exhausted. More tea, a barrage of questions, a reticence to describe what had happened to each of us, for fear that the telling might not be up to the experience.

I asked, "Was the temptation to no-show very great?"

"Very," he admitted, and told me how he had traveled from Mazar to Sar-i-Pul, in search of a monumental inscription which fable had placed somewhere in that region, though none had seen it. In Sar-i-Pul he met an Uzbek singer who commemorated his travels in song. Later he showed me the cassette, and we played it. Neither of us could understand the Uzbeki, except for the repeated outbursts of *"Wa wa, Walijan, bravo!"*

I had to hear the story of his travels piecemeal, from his own reluctant telling. I could see that traveling alone had been a great satisfaction to him. His style of dealing with people was so different from mine. He might be tempted to remain on his own now. Whatever happened I would have to accept, though the sense of loss would be greater than the inconvenience.

"I went to Qadis, and a place called Darzak, by *mutar*. It was very interesting. There were nomad *qishlaqs* there. In the winter the nomads will be coming back from the high mountains and we can find them. The people I was with told me to come back with a camera and take pictures of what I saw. We should get one and go there."

It was a relief to hear my friend say "we."

Out of a sense of inevitability we went to Abdul Wahid's hotel. It was closed, shuttered, bereft of its sign, and no one answered at the gate however long we banged at it. His shop was not far away, and there we found him. He was glad to see us; he said he just praying that we would soon return. I asked him about the hotel. "Alas, the *otel* is no more. I had to give it up. After you left I had no more guests at all. A thousand pities, since now I have nothing to put at your disposal."

"I'm sure we can find something convenient, perhaps in the Old City."

"You would live in the Old City? In a *sarai*?" The idea amused him. "Tonight, please, *Sahibs*, you will be my guests. You must be tired from the road, and it is too late to make other arrangements. Here is my address." He scrawled it out for us on a box of cookies.

When we left him my friend asked, "Do you really think Abdul Wahid wants to put us up tonight?" He was unsure of his welcome. "Why didn't he just take us along home, instead of giving us his address?" I reasoned that, if we went, we would be welcome. If we didn't go, that would be fine too.

In the night the lightless street was only a pool of shadows, but the droshky driver seemed to have a sixth sense for making his way through the narrow lanes. He talked incessantly to his horse to reassure the animal, but would not speak to us. He was mystified that two *meestars* should be visiting the Old City at this time of night. He drove us only reluctantly, in hopes of a big fare, but fearful that terrible things would come of it; and thanks to him, they did.

As we passed through one of the big, empty squares of the bazaar, the ghostly light of an electric bulb appeared in front of us. A sentry, one of those soldiers stationed in the city to police the streets by night, called the droshky to stop. There was no cur-few in Herat, only bored soldiery.

The soldier approached the cab with a furious look. "Where are you going, who are you?" he bellowed, in the half-intelligible accents of a Turk, fixing on the driver suspiciously. He was young, younger than we, but carrying an oversized rifle and fixed bayonet. The driver decided to throw us to the dogs.

"By God, I have done nothing. These two *meestars* . . ."

And I thought, *Oh, Christ, why did he have to open his trap?*

The soldier turned on us in a vengeance, gratified to find something amiss. "Foreigners, down, down." We had nothing to do but climb down from the droshky and stand in the street, feel-ing very foolish and angry, while the sentry scrutinized us at his leisure.

"Hey, what about my fare?" asked the treacherous droshky driver. The soldier told him to clear out; we watched him leave with mixed emotions. Now we had no way out of the Old City. I said as much to the soldier.

"Quiet!" he ordered, and then thought about what I had just said. He dismissed this thought from his mind, once he convinced himself that we were speaking a foreign language. He had never seen foreigners before, at least not this closely, and he stared at us as though at exhibits in the zoo.

I shivered in the cold, and then, thinking of the fellow's ugly bayonet, decided not to shiver again, lest he think I was afraid. I was definitely not afraid, but I was angry.

Finally the soldier decided to imprison us in his sentry box while he went for instructions. "Stay here," he said, and van-ished into the shadows. We might have walked out just then, ex-cept that we could never have made it out of the darkened bazaar. So we sat in the sentry box. My friend had a smoke. The unforeseen, unpleasant mishap in the middle of the night tar-nished my enthusiasm for being back in "civilization." Well, many an Afghan friend had said that they needed an army to protect them from the soldiers.

The soldier returned.

"Light?" asked my friend, handing him an American cig-arette. He took it readily, let my friend light it, then retreated suspiciously.

"Where are you from," my friend asked gently, when the soldier had begun to relax on the thick, rich smoke.

"Juzjan. Sar-i-Pul." He spat out the words blankly.

I could see my friend react; he capitalized on his polite offer of this cigarette: "I've been to Juzjan," he said. "I was the guest of Hajji Akbar Khan." It was a shot in the dark.

"You were the guest of Hajji Akbar Khan?" The soldier was impressed. We began to talk a bit, in broken Persian, which is all the soldier understood. In the army, the language of commands was Pashto, the Pathan tongue.

"How do you like Herat?"

"Juzjan is good. Home. Family. Do you know what is family?" We assured him we did. "My mother . . . do you know what is mother? My mother misses me very much. She sends me food, clothes. The army life is very hard. Do you know how much they give us a month? You can't live on it." He pulled a crumpled forty *rupee* note out of his pocket, his monthly pay. "So mother helps me. I would like to go back to Juzjan soon." His tour was fourteen more months; he had been in the army a little over a year. "In a year I lost a stone's weight."

We talked freely now, and joked, and he went so far as to put his rifle away and break out a pot of tea, which he warmed by disconnecting the electric light of his sentry box and plugging in a heater instead. So we sat on in pitch blackness, drinking tea and smoking.

I grew uneasy. "Does anyone know we're here?"

"Yes, I telephoned to the *Gendarmerie*. They are coming to take you away," he said, without attaching any importance to having had us arrested.

"In that case, don't you think we should turn on the lights and put away the cigarettes?"

"You're right. You are good *qaradash*." The lights came back on, tea and cigarettes disappeared. We waited and waited. I was tired, and only wanted to go to sleep, but wondered what the jails of Herat looked like. *Another adventure,* I thought weakly, everything for the best.

A droshky clopped up with an officer sitting in back. Our soldier saluted and presented his captives. A few words of Pashto were snapped back and forth, while the officer eyed us coldly, motioned us to get into the carriage. We set off.

"It's the greatest kindness of you to provide us the means for leaving the Old City," I said, in the most mincing Persian I could manage at that hour.

"Not at all. What were you doing there in the first place?"

I came up with a good story, explaining how we were on our way to the Hotel Parc, when a dishonest droshky drover kidnapped us and threatened to leave us in the bazaars.

"Good Lord. These people. Driver, the Hotel Parc." He turned to us cordially and said, "These people are like savages. It must be very difficult for such gentlemen as you to deal with them, but imagine how I, an academy graduate and a *Kabuli,* must feel when I have to face them every day. They are like brutes. In the army, all we can do is thrash them into discipline. When the war comes, America has a *carte blanche* for taking over the whole world. By the way, where did you say you came from?"

"France."

"Well, you see, then, we're in the same boat."

Under repeated encouragement from the officer the driver whipped his horse into a canter, and we went bowling out of the Old City by the Khaki Gate and on to the Parc. At the doorstep the officer gallantly took his leave from us and returned to town.

Too late to do anything but spend the night, we paid the huge tariff at the Hotel Parc and enjoyed its false luxury. This was the last place I hoped to end up, sleeping on rusty metal beds surrounded by shabby, decayed decor. A rock concert, of all things, played in the salon for assembled local notables; it might have been a wedding, but all we cared was that the noise kept us awake, though only for a little while.

Apologies were never required here, nor were explanations ever believed. "We just couldn't get to your house last night; the course of our pilgrimage to your side was interrupted by the intervention of mischance."

Abdul Wahid waved all these explanations away as though swattting gnats. "No matter, no matter. You are here, it is a great occasion for eye-brightening. Please make yourselves comfortable. This house, poor as it is, is your own."

We sat in the small *mihman khana* (guest chamber), a windowless box with a single slash in the roof for a vent. The walls had been freshly coated with *gach,* and some thin but clean carpets laid on the floor. A stove with a tube of pipes leading from the vent stood cold, its belly open. There was no firewood. The room was one flight up off a courtyard around a communal *sarai.* Each of the four walls of the courtyard belonged to a different family, with the yard and a well in common. The guest room had its own staircase, for the rest of Abdul Wahid's house was the harem, the family quarters. Abdul Wahid had repeatedly said that he had only his nephew as heir. I presumed that he was widowed and childless, though I thought it better not ask. From the constant activity we could hear behind the thin walls of the *mihman khana* it seemed likely that he had a number of daughters. But the room was divorced from the rest of the house just for the reason that domestic life might go on without disturbing or being disturbed by the guests of the house. We saw no one, but came into the *mihman khana.*

When the uncle excused himself the nephew replaced him as

host. Abdul Wasi greeted eagerly. *"Sahibs,* tell me, where did you go? Surely you went to India, to Pakistan, no?" He was disappointed to hear of the small towns and villages which so interested us. *"Sahibs,* were not the people of those places savage?"

"You know what they say, the men of the countryside are old-fashioned, they are hospitable." He chewed on that. There was a certain ambivalence of attitude towards the countryside.

For a long while we fell silent, having nothing more to say. Abdul Wasi knelt and kept his smiling face, looking distractedly into the air.

I said, "The *gach* in this room is fresh."

"It is fresh," replied Abdul Wasi, as though to prove the inutility of speech.

The door of the guest room sounded with a knock; Abdul Wasi opened it and took a tray of food inside to set before us.

"Who brought that?" my friend asked, surprised at this Arabian Night invisibility.

"The women." That was the first and last we ever heard of them.

Dinner was simple, fresh bread from the bakery across the street, still warm, and a mash of yoghurt and pumpkin squash which was very tasty and delicate. It struck me as an appropriate November dish, as close as one could get to pumpkin pie with cream.

After dinner, tea with sweets from Abdul Wahid's store. "Where is your uncle?" asked my friend.

"Bazaar."

Having finished our tea, my friend and I must have seemed a little restless. We couldn't go out, we couldn't read—there was hardly any light except from a lantern. Abdul Wasi noticed our restlessness and suggested a call of nature. At least it was a chance to go outside. The privy was on the roof, where it was so cold we were happy to get back and snuggle under the blankets in the *mihman khana.* In Afghan style, we went to sleep very early, there being nothing else to do on this cold November night.

To be closer to the heart of Afghan life was exactly what we wanted. We could not, of course, stay long in the hospitality of Abdul Wahid, the imposition on his modest household being too great, however he protested to the contrary. In the end we wound up insisting that he help us take a room in a *sarai* of the Old City, where we would live exactly as the Afghans. We would buy horses, as we should have done months ago, and stable them in the *sarai.* "Horses?" puzzled our friend. "That is not like you. You should have a Land Rover." We convinced him that horses were an important part of our willingness to live like Afghans.

Horses would be a responsibility; it would not be so easy to wander off from them. What distinguished us from Afghans in one important respect was just this freedom of movement. "And with horses," mused Abdul Wahid, warming to our project, "you can ride anywhere, to Kandahar, to Mashhad!" He didn't understand that we sought horses, not for the possibility of movement, but for the possibility of staying put.

"I know a *saraidar* (stable-keeper), an honest man. In general, one cannot mistrust their lot too much, they cheat one on hay and fuel, and there is much stealing in these *sarais*, but you will be well in his *sarai*. It's near the Malik Gate. I'll write a note." We said he needn't bother, but the sweetseller insisted, and went off for pen and paper. Good old man, he still hoped that after we had mastered the way of life we would embrace his religion, or still hoped we would bring Abdul Wasi to *Urupa* with us. Our tales of the North and of Badghis touched him, because we did not carp at the natives or allow criticism of their humanity. "That is true *musalmani*," admitted the sweetseller. He had a good heart.

For two more nights he insisted we remain under his roof, helping Abdul Wasi with next year's school work, struggling with and eventually giving up on a Pashto grammar book, feeling increasingly restive and underfoot. My friend kept hitting his head on the low lintel of the *mihman khana*. Presently, Abdul Wahid hinted that we were free to go, the honor of his hosting us being complete.

The *saraidar* read Abdul Wahid's note of introduction though and looked up with the same, affable, curious face as when he had first greeted us. We sat in the *samovar* adjacent to the *sarai* and took tea while satisfying his curiosity about why two foreigners should want to take a room in his *serai*. A ready excuse was that the rent was only 400 *rupees* a month. We talked and I got to like the man, whose name was Amin Ullah (Trust of God). Amin (Trust) seemed precisely right for this strong-jawed, blue-eyed young man with a perpetual half-smile on his face. "As you like, you can have a room right away, but it says here something about horses. If it's horses you have, I'll have my stables ready later, but now they're full." That was no obstacle, since we didn't yet have horses.

The *samovar* belonged to Amin Ullah's brother. Through the back door, or through twin metal-plated gates alongside the *samovar*, one entered the dusty courtyard of the *sarai*. In the center of the courtyard stood a small well, with a weathered wooden frame and a bucket. Around the court were the rooms, *utaqs*, single, cubicle-plaster units, each closed with a small wooden hatch and a padlock. In one corner, a long trough gave off a foul smell—the latrine. Another long-roofed structure in the opposite corner reeked of horses. The water in the well, not surprisingly, had the odor of urine, for the ground water was badly contaminated. But the good, clean smell of mud and plaster filtered out unpleasant odors in the rooms. Amin Ullah showed us an *utaq*, raised off the ground for warmth, small as a closet, but big enough for two sleeping rolls. He lent us s omematting and an old rug, while we agreed to rent it for two r nonhs, with the provision that stables would soon be available. "Do you want a *mulla* as a witness?" he asked. We said we trusted him well enough.

With our belongings in the back of a droshky we returned from Abdul Wahid's house. It was near sunset, and I worried about a repetition of our run-in with the soldier. The sight of foreigners visiting in the Old City after dusk begged trouble, a thought we had to consider whenever we had to go to our *sarai*. I hurried the driver on, who kept mumbling, *"Meestar* wants to go to the Malik Gate? You must be mistaken. You want to go to the Tanks," naming the petrol station just outside the Malik Gate.

We discharged him, so as not to arouse suspicion, nearer the Tanks than the *sarai*. The sun was setting behind us, splashing the whole mud-red panorama of the Old City with light. From the Malik Gate, which was a high point in the flat city, we could look down over the domed rooftops, plane trees, pines, square-topped pigeon towers, the arches of tombs black with lamp-soot and shadow. People were returning from work at the hour of five, with warm loaves of bread wrapped in cloth, or dangling a clump of grapes from their hands. In the bad light no one paid any attention to us, as though we'd lived here for years.

We banged on the metal gates of the *sarai*, for they stood shut. A smaller trap in the gates opened up and a voice called us inside. The trap was child-sized. We threw our bundles through and crawled inside. A man waited for us, Amin Ullah's brother, Hamid Ullah (Praise of God), whose dark complexion and droopy moustache made him utterly unlike his brother, though he seemed to have the same genial manner. He helped us carry our bags to the *utaq*, where Amin had already spread his rugs and mats. We rolled our bags into bolsters along the wall, stuck a few old photographs we had found along the wall niches, and spread our books beside them, covering them with old newspapers to keep the dust off. Dust was the perpetual problem, since all six surfaces of the *utaq* were of mud. We resisted the homesick temptation to clutter up the room any further than this. We were moved in. One more gift from the *saraidar*, though.

Hamid Ullah hung his lamp on a nail in the wall and said we could keep it for the season.

Our arrival excited the curiosity of the tenants of the *sarai;* doubtless Hamid Ullah told all in the *samovar* that evening about these wonderful *meestars* who had just taken a room for two months. In the morning they came by to see for themselves, appearing at the door of our *utaq*, disinterestedly curious, as though our privacy were no more an issue than that of zoo animals. Well, we had not come here for privacy, on the contrary. Inviting each one in for tea, we met with different reactions. A heavy-set droshky driver in an olive sport-coat and olive silk turban took one look at our arrangements, saw they were no better than his, snorted and left. Next came a cadaverous-looking schoolteacher in full Western dress capped with a flea-bitten astrakhan. He pointed out that the rest of the tenants of the *sarai* were ill-bred scoundrels and that we must trust no one, except men of education. He commended his services to us whenever we should need them, and we thanked him for his advice. After the teacher appeared a man who had no business at all, a perpetual litigant at some lawsuit who had been reduced to living in penury in expectation of a favorable resolution of his case. All he did was complain to us of his stomach pains and inquire if we had any medicine. We gave him some mild tablets, and he rewarded us with the details of his lawsuit, which had already dragged on five years.

The *sarai's* tenants were all unmarried men, without patrimonial houses in the city. For the most part they were poor and foreign to Herat. Men like the schoolteacher were stationed here by the government, coming from far-off villages of the province. Others were transients, truckdrivers and merchants from Lashkargah and Kandahar to the south. The fact that we were all strangers to the city, or at least isolated in it, gave the *sarai* the quality of being a world of its own.

Three tenants did not show up to inspect us; we learned of them later. They were a musical troupe, a *dutar* player, a drummer, and a third member who seemed to play only the castanets. All three were Tajiks from Panjshir, darker by far than *Heratis*, although they spent all day in their *utaq*, without any light, behind shuttered windows. There they practiced their doleful music. The castanetist sometimes appeared out on the stoop, blinking in the sunlight, sewing sequins onto cloth, or polishing little brass bells. Everyone in the *sarai* gave the three a wide berth, and the schoolteacher warned us of them repeatedly; these professional music makers were considered a little better than gypsies (Hamahang, though, was in a different class altogether, being a *radio* singer). I asked Hamid Ullah about the sequins and the bells, and he whispered, "That one is a dancer," in other words, a female impersonator.

If we were going to move freely back and forth from our *sarai*, we would have to countenance impersonation as well. My friend balked at the idea of "wearing costumes"; people might take offense or take us for pretended Muslims. But the liability of wearing our own clothes in the Old City was too great; there were the sentries, the nagging children, suspicious neighbors. We agreed to get Afghan clothes as soon as possible.

During the first day we had a surprise visit. Daud, whom we had long expected to have gone to Kabul, if not Europe, turned up at the *sarai*. "*Daudjan, Walijan*, why didn't you let me know you had come back to town? I had to hear the news from strangers, from that sweetseller with the pockmarks."

"How were we to let you know? We thought you'd be out of the country by now!"

"What made you think that?" This suggested that the subject of Kabul and the passport was not to be discussed.

Daud inspected our new quarters with an ironic expression, and asked, "Why don't you stay at an *otel*; isn't that much better than this?" We protested, a hundred times, no, and told him about our one night in the Parc. "Well, may it be *mubarak* (fortunate)." We ordered tea to be brought; Hamid Ullah's *samovar* kept brewing all day long for the tenants of the *sarai*. A cup was two *rupees*. We sipped tea with Daud and practiced all the "Orientalisms" we could muster. These heavy courtesies were a game, which everyone knew as such, enjoyable to play, if one were good at it.

"*I'm the dust of your door.*"

"*I'm your servant.*"

"*My eyelashes shall be the
      broom of your
            gutter.*"

When we ran out of ceremony we told Daud we were going to the bazaar to buy pajamas.

"Why do you want to buy *kala*?"

I told him about the sentry and being tired of hearing the children calling insults behind us as we walked down the street.

"Ah, I know what you mean. We say, 'It itches back here'," and he scratched his neck.

"So will you come with us to the bazaar?"

"Today, no, sorry. I have to visit a sick relative."

Since Daud's relative wouldn't recover until we had gone to the bazaar and bought the clothes ourselves, after he left we went straightway to the clothsellers lane. "We want to buy *kala*," we told the merchants. Gaudy synthetics were unrolled before us like precious scrolls; these were from Taiwan and Japan, said the merchant, pronouncing the names as we might say "Samarkand and Bukhara." They urged on us the importance of being grand. "Fine young men like you must wear something *kharabati*, (extravagant, tavernesque)," they said expansively. I looked at the local Afghan cloth, cheaper, somber-colored material. "No, no," they said, showing us their imported electric blues and aquamarine and peach.

I rubbed a bit of cloth. "Are these warm, though?"

"Warm? They are *luk* (very warm)."

For my friend they urged nine meters of fabric, and seven meters for me. As they measured out the cloth it seemed like miles to me. "Are you sure we need so much cloth?"

The merchant leapt on a stool and spread his knees wide a-part; the pleats of his voluminous pajamas hung from his waist like drapery on a French window. "That's nine meters right there, and your *rafiq* is taller than me!" His *kala* was true *kharabati*. The poor man's suit, by the way, contained only four meters of cloth. Each meter cost 90 *rupees*, so now I understand why most *Heratis* wore one suit of clothes for a year, or until they wore them out. We bought materials for two suits each, green and blue synthetic, and grey and brown *Herati* cotton. The time around the Greater Feast was a favorite for buying new clothes; the clothseller's business was brisk.

The tailor proved no less busy. His apprentices scurried underfoot with their oversized scissors and reams of fabrics. "I can't possibly have them tomorrow, *Meestar*. It's before the *Id*, you see, our heads are busy." The tailor measured us, as any custom tailor would, and posed us a bewildering variety of style choices. I had no idea that there was such a thing as style in the shapeless *kala* of the *Heratis*. I had never really looked. We could have plain collars, high collars, V- collars, or cossack collars. I asked for the cossack style; "But that's last year's style," protested the tailor. "This year all the men are wearing the open collar, the way the *badmash* (roughly, "gangster") types wear theirs." I stood my ground.

One of the apprentices, who had measured us, pressed us for a tip. His scissors was as long as he was tall.

Lastly we had to buy belts for our *kala*. The merchants offered us the most expensive, embroidered ones. "What's the point,"

I asked, "of wearing an expensive embroidered belt under the skirt of your *kala?*"

"Men, who are very stylish, they wear these belts under their pajamas, and show them to some close friends." He mimed lifting the skirts of his *kala,* an immodest gesture. We settled on a plain cotton belt.

A Grand Gesture

I was lunching in the main bazaar, in the middle of a day of many purchases, when a timid *bazaari* child came up to my *takht* and took hold of my sleeve. *"Duktur?"* he asked hopefully, indicating my glasses.

"Nope. No." I said, "I'm not a doctor." The child insisted, showing me his complaint; his hand was a mass of old bandages and compresses, almost as big as his head. To the relief of the other diners I led the boy out of the kebab shop, and we sat down together on the curb. "Now I'm not a doctor, but I'm going to take a look at your hand," I told him. I began to unwrap his bandages, finding a fortune in cloth scraps, amulets, camel dung. These, with his permission, I discarded. When I got down to the hand itself, he began to grimace, but kept still. The hand was a mess, battered, broken in several places, and then bandaged by someone into a closed position. I went back into the kebab shop for boiling water, which they gave me in a teapot, and washed some of the cleaner rags to be reused as bandaging. I splintered the broken fingers and wound up the hand straightened out. The child made no complaints, saying nothing until I was all through.

"Don't you give me a pill?"

"No. No pill. Why do you want a pill? Where I come from children hate to take pills."

"Where you come from are there building higher than two stories?"

"Yes, we have eighty-storied and hundred-storied buildings." I shouldn't have said that, because now he took me for a liar, and assumed that children in my country liked to take pills.

He led me to a nearby shop which an older brother owned, to show the man his new bandages. The brother was not at all interested, nor did he approve when the child fetched me tea and sweets by way of showing gratitude. He did not intervene, though, for if the brothers were twenty years apart in age, they treated one another like adults. If the child wanted to entertain a *meestar* as guest, that was his business. My little host had all the mannerisms of the old *bazaaris;* when I asked him how was business, he replied, *"Bi-Khuda,* a man grows grey at the thought of it."

The older brother looked after his business by selling me a chapan, a padded cotton one which I definitely needed against against the cold weather. The child did not seem to approve of my purchase, but said nothing. I thanked them and left.

At the *sarai* Amin inspected my purchase. "How much did you pay for that? Well, it was four thousand *rupees* too much. Look at the sleeve, it's coming off; and the lining isn't cotton, I don't know what it is. Oh, how the merchants cheat some people." By "some people" I knew he meant the gullible. I was furious. Certainly, I didn't expect to be thanked for a small thing like splinting a finger, but still less did I expect to be cheated in the very moment of gratitude. I was always prepared to bargain in the bazaar, but at the one point where I assumed the merchant named an honest price, I had been *faribkhur* (sucker).

I did something I'd never done before. I went back to the bazaar, to the same shop. It was near the old covered warehouses, where dozens of clothsellers' shops formed narrow *cul-de-sacs* off the street. The boy was still there, half-expecting me. *"Sahib,* I told my brother he did evil in his dealing, *bi-Khuda,* he's a dishonest man." The brother sat with his friends in a nearby shop, chatting over lunch.

I stalked up and threw the *chapan* on the ground. "Is this Islam? Is this what the Law enjoins on you? First you deceive me, now you boast about it? May God stint your reward and may you never prosper. *La fazallah jazaka!"* My words had wonderful effect. The brother slunk down sullenly and tried to look innocent.

The other merchants said, "Oh, *Meestar,* forgive us, you are rich and we are poor. What is four thousand *rupees* to you?"

Since it would have been unseeming to admit proverty, I said that I would gladly give the man four thousand *rupees* out of charity, but that the coat he had sold me was worthless rubbish, and he had been a villain to sell it. Opinion turned against the wretch. They murmured, passing the coat from hand to hand, shaking their heads. "You will see, *Meestar,* there is justice in Islam. He will give you back your money." The fellow grew livid and threw a pile of bills into my face.

"That's thirty-five hundred *rupees,* I'll keep five hundred for my troubles." He ran off in a fury.

"May the five hundred go to purchase your winding sheet," I called after him, and took my leave.

I retold the story in the *samovar,* before various of the tenants. Hamid Ullah reflected, "But the fellow still has your five hundred *rupees.*"

I was no longer angry. "Let him keep them, may he be lucky with them."

My neighbors applauded this sentiment. The grand gesture! "He has become a Muslim," said one knowing voice. I had left out the part about "purchasing your winding sheet." In everything, in buying clothes, in dealing with *bazaaris*, the one sure action which garnered the respect of the *Heratis* was recklessness with money. They respected only the rich.

The tenants of the *sarai* learned everything about us in short time. We were open, not secretive like the best *Heratis;* if someone asked us where we were off to, we told him, and on our return there would be no stinting of question. The whole *sarai* seemed to know our comings and goings if we so much as told a single neighbor. They were exceedingly curious about our friends in the city, Abdul Wahid, Daud and Gul Ahmad (who turned up, as will be told). Poor men, strangers, they imagined us to be fabulously wealthy and well-connected in Herat, and they schemed to align themselves with us. In the small world of the *sarai*, all this activity was like a microcosm of an Afghan city: the fawners who stood around and praised our every action, the parasites who invited themselves often into our company, the dreamers who offered wild business schemes for us to finance, even the grand gesture, the offers of arranged marriages, and the cheapest of all gifts: advice. We accepted these overtures as evenly as we knew how, which was mere *naiveté*. After a while, when we did not reciprocate as they had hoped—by making them richer than their wildest dreams—they began to reconsider and ponder why two *meestars* should be willing to live in a poor *sarai* and share their poor meals with them. Unable to fathom the reason, they began to think us odd and to treat us like simpletons. Whoever acted openly in Afghanistan invited the accusation that he was a fool.

The regimentation of life at the *sarai* was extreme, for the people there could not afford the leisure of the prosperous *bazaaris*. First thing in the morning the droshky driver would be up watering his horse from the leaky bucket of the well. We were up as early, watching the man and asking questions about horsemanship, while offering to draw the water. He shrugged us off irritably, and added, "When you two buy your horses, I'll look after them for you." His name was Abdul Hayy (Slave of the Life) and he wore only his single suit of olive *kala* and olive turban, which gave his heavy face a pasty, sick look.

Later on in the morning the teacher would go off to work. With school closed, he had taken a part-time job as a tailor, though he was embarrassed about this and would daily invent some excuse for his early rising during the school vacation. Today it was an appointment in the *wali's* office. The boundaries between modes of living, by trade and by pen, were not to be crossed lightly.

Others set off in the crowd of laborers which now filled the street in front of the *sarai*, waving to us, "Hello *Meestar*," as though we were simpletons, envying us for our leisure.

The litigant never rose before mid-morning, when he would go painfully off to the latrines. I tried to explain to him, and to Hamid, that they mustn't drink the water of the well, which had gathered the contaminated ground water of the latrines and the horses' stables.

"But *Daudjan*," objected Hamid, "once the water is in the ground, it's cleaned."

"A little bit, yes, but after all these years, no. Promise me you won't drink any more of the water. We can't give out any more pills (antibiotics) to the men here if they keep drinking the water."

"Ah, *Daudjan*, if that's what you say, these wretches will drink and drink until their bellies ache, and then they'll say they never tasted a drop of it. Like this complainer here."

"Hamid Ullah, what's that you say? I never touch your filthy well water, which as the man says isn't fit for dogs." The litigant rose with all his wounded dignity and hurried out of the *samovar*, which was difficult because of the tiny door; he banged his head on the low lintel.

Hamid Ullah laughed. "That one is always taking medicines; he's been to every *hakim* in the city. But he'll never get his hands on the best doctor of all . . ." He pulled a roll of bills from his pocket.

When tending the *samovar* grew dull, or business was slow, Hamid Ullah would pursue his hobby: he raised pigeons. He took us up on the roof, where the birds were kept—a dusty mud flat, a low view of the *sarai*, but a spectacular view of the Old City. Here he kept prized sporting pigeons. Released from their cages the birds flew above the *samovar*, turning circles in the air, putting on an aerialist show for their keeper. Hamid smiled and whistled at his flock as they looped and circled above us.

There is a wonderful description of this sport in Ahmed Ali's novel *Twilight in Delhi*. He tells how clouds of swooping pigeons used to fill the skies of that city at sunset, such being the popularity of the sport in the old days. The pigeons swarm with an instinct towards the most powerful flock. The best fed, swiftest fliers will attrack other birds, even from other flocks, and bring them back to roost with their owner. When flying pigeons, one tries to steal away the other sportsmen's birds.

Hamid played a solitaire version of the sport. We saw no other enthusiasts on their rooftops. His only sport was in making sure his pigeons returned. Even that seemed a marvel, when the formation of birds swooped to the roof and marched into their coop. That they should surrender their freedom for this cage was a reminder of how useless a hungry freedom would be in Afghanistan. Occasionally Hamid would lose some, however. I was glad to come down off the roof, since falling off one's pigeon cote was a cliché way to die in the East; Babur the Mughal had perished that way.

Everyone left the *sarai* during the day except for Hamid, the litigant, and the musicians. From near noon we could hear them practicing on the drum and the *dutar* (one less string than a *sitar*). Despite the warning of the other tenants, we began to accept their invitation to watch them play. Amin Ullah, we noted, trusted them as much as he did his other tenants, and he struck us as a prudent judge of character. They were harmless, as long as one kept a sense of humor. They sat around the brazier, warming their hands before they could play. "At night I take off my hands and leave them in the brazier so they don't freeze up," said the *tablazan* (drummer). "Why are you smiling, don't you believe me? It's true." He had a pockmarked face and rag-like hair, with a wild, deep voice. He smoked a lot of hashish, which had aged him beyond his thirty years.

"It's true, it's true," echoed the dancer. He was busy sewing the brass bells onto anklets and wristlets. "It's cold in here. *Daudjan-o-Walijan*, why don't you send for firewood and we'll play for you." This was arranged.

The *tablazan* was the leader of the troupe. "What do you want to hear, *'Bibi Radu Jan'*, *'Shikasta Dil'*?"

"Can you play the song that goes . . ." I hummed something for him. The *tablazan* didn't recognize it. I sang a few lines from memory, but the resolution was all wrong; they still didn't recognize the song, but laughed openly at what sounded to them like my tone deafness.

We had tea reheated off the brazier, in cups that had not been washed in years. "Thank you," I said.

"Thank you," replied the *tablazan*. "Thannnnnnnnkkkkkk yooouuu," he drew out, mocking me. Apparently everything about us struck them as hilarious. *"Daudjan-o-Walijan*, I hear you are looking to buy horses. I have a horse for you." Like a sucker I looked up interested as he drew a knight from a chess set out of his pocket and handed it to me guffawing. More laughter. As musicians, pariah sorts, they had the license to poke fun at everything and anybody they pleased, which explained their low popularity in the *sarai*.

They grew serious when playing, though, and worked hard at their music for the whole day and late into the night, practicing new songs and trying out improvisations and solos. I was impressed with their fervor for music, which was almost a religious feeling, the same sense I had from watching the tradesmen in the bazaar practice their craft. When one's vision of God was very nearly immanent, then whatever one makes—shoes, buckets or music—one feels one is bodying forth something God-like. In this case the musicians gained much of their enthusiasm from hashish, the bad, sick odor of which filled the room.

We thanked them for their performance and they grew mirthful again, mocking our thanks for the playing by repeating, "Thannnnnkkkkkkk yyyyyyyoooouuuu! Tttthhhhaaaannnk you." To their mind, our openness and polite speech were laughable. They thought us likable fools, which was very much our opinion of them. Amin Ullah, as I said, liked them, while the rest of the *sarai* dwellers cursed fortune to have brought them so low as to live by gypsies. Our intercourse with the musicians only lowered the general opinion about us. Abdul Hayy, of all the tenants, gave us the hardest time, which was surprising because he and Amin Ullah were the best of friends.

A Keepsake

Daud and Abdul Wahid we saw regularly, our friendship going on as before. Gul Ahmad, whom we had missed two months ago, I met in the bazaar. For his past absence, he excused himself on account of a sick relative—which meant that I shouldn't ask any further. Oh, the convenient sick relatives of the Afghans. He insisted that I join him for dinner at his home, an unexpected show of hospitality. Two months had acclimatized me, I suspect; Gul Ahmad no longer scrupled to make me his guest. We set off for the house at once, without further making of plans. A real invitation to dinner always saw the host physically escort the guest.

The family was from Kandahar, but Gul Ahmad's father worked for the government here. With the notoriously low pay of the official class, they could only afford quarters scarcely better than those of a petty merchant like Abdul Wahid. Gul Ahmad was visibly embarrassed; he stumbled on the steps leading up to the *mihman khana* and said ruefully, 'This isn't much of a house."

The father was even more apologetic. "You are the candle of this poor house." A thin-faced man with a large "Pox of Aleppo" scar on his cheek, he had the manners of a well-mannered civil servant. For our edification and amusement, he called for reed and inkstand, drawing a number of formal calligraphic compositions, laudable aphorisms from the poets in praise of friendship and learning. I still have a fragile piece of paper with fading blue ink, because he said to me with a shy, sideways glance, "You won't keep this, will you?"

"I certainly will." It was from Saadi in definition of humanity:

> *Each other's limbs are Adam's Sons*
> *Who of one substance were created.*
> *Should Fortune topple one of them*
> *The others cannot keep their balance.*
> *Impassive at your brothers' fate?*
> *You cannot call yourself a human being.*

I took that as a rare acceptance of his son's befriending a foreigner.

Like Gul Ahmad, the father was shy, and little used to confidences. Having a fine mastery of Persian, however, he knew how to disguise his shyness with a facade of volubility. In true Persian style, little was said in a great many words. The two seemed listless, under the surface of conversation, Gul Ahmad with the same reticence as when we had first met him, the father just a fraction more forthcoming.

Dinner was bread soaked in *qurut*, a milk curd dried and then boiled in water. The rich Persicate Afghans, I knew, affected to despise the dish, finding it astringent and greasy. But the combination of milk and wheat made it a basic nutriment, much like our cereals and milk, a carbohydrate and protein diet. The *qurut* was another of the bazaar goods which were provided by the nomads. I praised the meal to my hosts.

"Oh, if we were at home," the father responded, "we wouldn't be serving the honored presence such famine food. The servant petitions, we are not so benighted as not to know how a guest should be treated. In Kandahar we have gardens, fields, trees! We're not poor people, you know. But here, we are almost strangers, like your presence."

"Your presence is very gracious as it is," I objected.

The father and son ate very quickly and licked their fingers in satisfaction, which made me think that they enjoyed *qurut* more than they like to admit. Though *Kandaharis*, they were only the first generation of city folk. They were not Pathans, though, as I had thought. Gul Ahmad explained to me their grandfather was a Baluchi tribesman, one of an Iranian people who inhabited the deserts of Rigistan, at the three-way border of Iran, Pakistan, and Afghanistan. Ravaged by wars, famine, and government persecution, many of the Baluchis in the last century went into mass exile, to Mary, Karachi, Bahrain, as well as into the Pathan homeland. Between the two nomad races, distantly related by language and culture, these existed an uneasy respect. "There must be a balance of terror," remarked one observer to me. In Herat they were considered Pathans, all the same. I wondered if Gul Ahmad's reticence and shyness was inherited, the gloominess of an exiled people living among strangers. I had read some Baluchi folk ballads and remembered how these had a strong tragic strain. I asked them if they knew any.

"No," said the father, eyes lighting up for the first time, "there are singers who do know them, but not in Herat. They are very wonderful songs, sad and heart-rending." Gul Ahmad smiled too, perhaps in a childhood recollection of such songs. Misery can be appreciated as an art.

Holiday Bath

We picked up our completed *kala* from the tailor according to arrangement. In neat, paper-wrapped bundles we carried them to the *hamam*, where we intended to take our pre-holiday bath, before donning our new clothes. We had to be careful not to slip with our precious parcels in the heavy, soapy mud that surrounded the bath building, water that seeped out of the saturated ground. Underneath the baths were great ovens into which ashen-faced men stoked bales of camel dung, heating the water in subterranean tanks. It was hard to believe that one could really come clean here.

Directly inside was a room of flimsy tiling, water inches deep on the floor, steam making everything invisible. This was the public bath, where men stood about in loin cloths and slung water all over themselves in a vain attempt to cleanse themselves without losing their modesty. For more thorough bathing, warm water, and privacy, we had to wait in a long line for a *numra* (individual bathing cubical). This cost an additional five *rupees* over the two-*rupee* entrance fee. The line for the *numras* was long, because of the coming holiday. We waited on a narrow bench in the concrete corridor before the *numras*, steeped in sweat, steam and water dripping off the bare walls.

Waiting in line was a skill; the *Heratis* knew how to look as though they had been waiting in line for hours, when in fact they had just taken a seat. The bath attendant, an oversized boy with a wild look on his face, stripped to the waist, dripping with soapy water and smelling of lye, strutted up and down the line, choosing the next bather for one of the dozen *numras*. While we waited our turn in line, half a dozen newcomers, at least, squeezed in ahead of us by calling to the boy, "For the love of God, I've been here for hours and hours. Justice!" The louder a *Herati* complained, the less one should have believed him.

The bathers entered a metal-doored cubicle and pulled shut an iron bolt behind them. Then, for a glorious moment they would be in a warm room with running water, a rare event in Herat. Here they shaved, bathed, trimmed their toenails, and performed all the other private sanitary functions which faith and custom enjoined on them, for the bath was the only place in Herat where their privacy would not be disturbed. However, after half an hour had passed, the attendant would bang on the door with a length of pipe, making an unbelievable din inside and outside the cubicle. The dawdlers would hurry out, ears ringing with the noise.

We finally got our turns. In the narrow cubicle, to undress, pile dirty clothes in one heap and clean clothes in another, and not get either of them soaking wet was a delicate balancing act. I washed and shaved; immediately the attendant began clanging on the door. It had only been a few minutes. Well, perhaps longer. I felt very strange, alone and undressed for the first time in months. A *Herati* was almost unused to the feeling, and I understood why he did not miss it. Reflecting on my pale, wasted body, I was reminded only of mortality. I took care on the slippery floor as I dressed, since slipping on the bath floor and dying was another cliché way of bowing out in Eastern fables.

I stepped from the *numras* in my *kala* and *chapan*. Since my glasses had fogged, I did without them for the moment. The effect was surprising. The attendant ushered me out of the bath with *"ay bradar"* instead of the usual *"meestar."* He had forgotten me. I saw my friend waiting for me in the main room, wearing his green *kala*, and also without his glasses. We walked out on the street, not far from Amin's *sarai*, where the shopkeepers had long recognized us for *meestars* and were given to calling out a raucous, irritating *"Hellooo Meesttarrr,"* sharing a merry, wicked laughter down the length of the street. We walked past them, the graindealer, basketmaker, blacksmith; and none of them recagnized us. We joined Hamid and Amin in the *samovar* of the *sarai*, and it took them a long, strange moment to recognize who had come in.

Amin complimented us on the *kala*, "May they be *mubarak*." He looked us over, appreciatively. "But come here, let me show you how to tie your *mandil* right." The lesson lasted a while, since the varieties of turban knots were many. "This is the Baluchi," he said, giving my friend a great pouf. "And this is Pathan, like a *Kandahari*"; he had transformed the *poufe* into a long, trailing scarf. "And here is a *mulla*, a tight fold, and an Uzbek, high and round." We tied them on one another; we tied them on Amin. Hamid, worried by the levity, ran up to look after his birds. We tied them around the samovar.

And afterwards, when it was dark, we walked in the New Town by the fruit stands and cafes, lit by their dim electric lights, with the crowds stopping and buying candies and nuts for the holiday. We had to buy *shirini*, the sweets and nuts with which we would reward those who would say, on seeing our new clothes, "May it be *mubarak*." Since many wore new *kala* this evening, the nut vendors were doing a heavy business, weighing out with flat scales the brown nuts in their canvas sacks. We bought pistachios and almonds for our *shirini*. The holiday would be a great occasion of receiving guests and feasting, so men bought fruits and tea sweets, late melons and grapes. There were no women shopping here, since entertaining in the *mihman khana* was a purely masculine affair. The bakeries had even a special cookie for the holiday, which read in green jelly *Id Mubarak*, "May your holiday be blessed."

In the crowded pastry stores, no one took exception to us. On the way home to Amin's, a sentry called and asked us our business. "*Mirim khana akha*, we're just going home." His answer was a relieving silence.

Abraham's Sacrifice

The *Id* was almost upon us, although one could never be sure exactly when it might fall. Like the *Ramazan* fast, and all Muslim religious holidays, the vagaries of the young Arabian moon kept us on tenterhooks. Again, the radios were tuned to Saudi Arabia, the conversation in the teahouses ran only to the moon, in broad daylight, and more and more passersby appeared in new clothing.

Even before the holiday began the city greatly expanded its repertory of entertainments, though most of these could not receive the approval of the puritanical government. We went to see a dog-fight at the Cave of the Bhang-eaters, only to find the police dispersing a crowd of enthusiasts. The word went through the retreating crowd that the fight would be on again, near the Malan Bridge, which was all the way across town. There we found nothing but children playing knucklebone and some indiscreet bathers by the river. Disgusted, we returned to the city and told acquaintances of our misfortunes. "Oh," they said, *"sag-jangi?* The dog-fights are on below Gazurgah, only you'll probably be too late." The road to Gazurgah was jammed with droshkies, streaming with folk in their gay *chapans*. The whole side of the hill, grey and bleak in the autumn sun, became spring-like where we saw the festival-makers walking and sitting about the shrine. From a concerted circle of men, we heard shouts and excitement, mingled human and canine. We forced our way into the group and managed to see the last few fights.

Each fight went quickly. Bets were slapped into the hands of an honest middleman as the two mastiffs were paraded into the center of the circle. To hold their halters took two big men each, who then muscled the animals into confrontation. These were the sort of dogs I had heard howling by Ashab-i-Kahf. I never hoped to see one so close again. Bigger than wolves, spare-fleshed, hideously slavering about their grinding teeth, the two dogs launched into one another.

The men only let the halter ropes out while the animals battled, tearing at ears and folds of flesh (hence the advantage of being lean), throwing each other into the dust. The noise was like the prolonged scrape of a knife over stone. In a moment one of the animals fled to the edge of the circle, tangling his retainers in the ropes, while the victor howled and strained to pursue him.

They played winner fights next, and the top dog crowed at remaining in the circle. They did not play to the death, for the dogs were smarter, in this respect, than the fighting partridges, who battled until dead, and sometimes after. The dogs knew when to run, some breaking instinctively before battle was joined. They aped the Afghan experience in war, amirs like Dust Muhammad and Sher Khan being masters of the strategy to "live to fight another day." The dogs were highly intelligent and the Afghans prized them as such. The contest was not so much the violence, but the betting on the better dog, the choice of the stronger of two monsters.

Not betting, we found the fights desultory affairs, though half the city seemed to have turned out for them. They finished quickly, and the crowd decamped toward the bottom of the hill. We were caught up in the mass, strolling helter-skelter through the gardens and gullies of the *baghat* (the suburbs).

Daud had given us an invitation. "Look, tomorrow will be the *Id*, I want you to come by my house, my father's house, for feast." He had never invited us before, though he was our most frequent companion. We didn't know where he lived. "In the morning I'll send somebody by for you, or I'll come myself."

We had another invitation for the *Id*, Abdul Wahid asked us to be his guests. We could easily manage both visits, as holidays were passed in going from door to door with greetings, distributing cookies and *shirini*. The joke was about the man who rode from door to door on his bicycle, without dismounting, saying to all his friends, "*Id-i-shuma mubarak basha*, May your feast be blessed."

Yet the tenor of the feast was one of gravity. The *Id-i-Qurban*, the Festival of Sacrifice, commemorated *Hazrat* Ibrahim's intended sacrifice of his son, whom Muslim traditions unanimously identified as Ismail (Ishmael), although the Qur'an allowed it was Isaac (Ishaq). In imitation of the first Muslim, those who might afford the cost of a sheep were directed to buy a one-year-old animal, perfect in all its parts, and sacrifice it on this day, distributing the meat to the poor. Families were enjoined to gather in numbers of seven and communally purchase an animal, if they could not bear the cost singly, and celebrate the feast this way. On the day before the feast shepherds drove herds of animals into the city; one could not pass through some of the lanes heading towards the bazaars, and in the dusty squares, family heads milled among the animals and chose their intended victims.

On the morning of the *Id* the city went to prayer. We stole along in the crowd, slightly fearful at the mass of it, and drew near the cathedral mosque. So great was the press outside the ancient building, I grew less afraid of being recognized than of being asphyxiated. Meanwhile the crowd droned the *takbir*, the magnificat of God, and the loudspeaker above on the minaret carried the rasping voice of the preacher, offering the congregation his blessings for the day. The animals we were to slaughter today, he reminded us, would carry us across the bridge over Hell and into Paradise on the Last Day, a sign of our good works. My friend and I did not make it into the courtyard of the mosque itself, not surprising, if all 80,000 of the *Heratis* attended on this day.

At ten o'clock the congregation repairs to the act of sacrifice. I see in one of the small *cul-de-sacs* of the bazaar a communal sacrifice, a most disturbing scene. This is the *Zabh* (Levitical *Zobach*), the ritual cutting of the throat. A man takes the sheep up and trusses it in the air; in height, it is as tall as a child. He pulls the knife across the throat. The onlookers give a start: it is always surprising to see how far the blood gushes out. The air is still so cold, that white steam rises from the warmth of the gore on the ground. I keep my face rigid, expecting the onlookers to be inured to the sight. No one gets used to seeing red blood like their own spilling out. They look at me, to see whether I find it disturbing as they do. Only the children have the cruel look of curiosity, and also hunger. Now a professional butcher steps forward, he hews off the head, and seizing the carcass by the neck, blows into the cavity. The lamb carcass swells up with air, and a few dashes of the knife separates the skin from the body. Another slash empties the entrails on the ground. Now the whole carcass is steaming white clouds, and the lane is enveloped in fog. I go my way, breathing in the sweet smell of stews and griddle cakes which happily wafts from the houses above the lane, trying to forget the awful smell of drying blood.

On the main street of the New Town, in blithe contradiction to the somber mood of sacrifice, the *wali* paraded his military band, looking like a parody of janissary musicians, with an eclectic assembly of East and West in their instruments. The Western instruments and sounds predominated and therefore the marchers outnumbered the spectators, who had a horror of these brass noise-makers.

On such an important feast even the misfits of the *sarai* had their invitations. While we waited for some sign of Daud, one after another they strutted out of the place, dressed afresh in new *kala* and well-groomed. Even the litigant had gotten himself up in forgotten grandeur and gone off for the day, to the house of his attorney, we guessed. Soon, only a spare horse in the stables made any noise; we found ourselves alone in the *sarai*.

Hamid Ullah stuck his head through the trap in the gates. "Are you still here? Come along with me. We're going to my house, with Amin and the rest."

We scrambled out of the trap, to find Hamid and Abdul Hayy, waiting in the latter's droshky. "Don't you look handsome," said Abdul Hayy, sourly. His *kala* was new, though the same olive hue. "May your holiday be blessed," we said to him cheerfully. Snorting, he started the horse off.

Hamid Ullah was telling us what lay in store at the house, "Stew, and sweetmeats, and rice . . ."

"I'm going to demolish the stew" said the lusty Abdul Hayy.

". . . and the musicians are going to play for us. There may even be dancing." Abdul Hayy gave his fat horse a quick whack with the whip.

Amin and Hamid's house was in a village just beyond the

petrol station on the road to the Soviet Union. Closed off by a great white wall, the lanes of the village were quiet, the houses with their whitewashed facades seemed to sleep. Our hosts' generous compound consisted of stables, a cookhouse, harem, stores, and a big, solidly-built *mihman khana* on a second story. We went up the new, clean, pinewood staircase, Hamid beaming with pride as we praised the place. The family's prosperity was recent; they had built the guest chamber only this year.

Upstairs the guests sat about on the carpeted floor, warming themselves in the sunlight that streamed through the real glass windows of the room. We knew some of them, the shopkeeper whose store adjoined the *serai*, the schoolteacher, one or two habitués of Hamid's *samovar*.

As soon as we arrived, lunch was served, lamb stew with squash puddings and plates of rice. We ate quickly, without talking. Amin and Hamid kept a serious overseeing of us, to assure themselves that we commended the meal by our silence and our appetite in eating. As soon as the food was cleared away, those who had been present all morning got up to go, embracing Amin and Hamid, and saying, "We entrust you to God, we entrust you to God" to the general company.

I thought of Abdul Wahid's invitation, but it seemed best to stay awhile, having only just arrived and eaten.

Other guests constantly arrived. Amin Ullah welcomed each with his outspread hands and ready smile. He was everybody's favorite with his easy manners and generosity. More than one old greybeard let it slip out that there was no better host than Amin Ullah. As the guests settled somewhere on the floor, Hamid Ullah served them tea and a dish of sweets. The two brothers spent the entire afternoon running up and down the stairs, bringing on sweets and greeting newly-arrived guests. No one seemed to be leaving at this point.

Talk in the *mihman khana* ranged over many things, though—in obvious deference to the foreigners—world affairs played a larger role than usual. We discussed Afghanistan's chronically bad relations with Pakistan over the Pathan homeland issue. They had heard over the radio how the Pathans of the Northwest Frontier were oppressed by the Pakistanis, and how President Daud was calling for ethnic self-determination for the Pathans. None here were Pathans. They took no more interest in this news than in events in China. Their antipathy to Pakistan was based on a vague contempt for their darker, more prosperous neighbors. But during the Indo-Pakistan war of 1971, many Afghans had volunteered to fight on the Pakistani side (despite the Kabul-Delhi *entente*) in what they termed a *jihad* (holy war). Said one greybeard, "I would have gone down to fight the *Hindis*, just as I did in the days of Aman Ullah *Ghazi*." The Amir Aman Ullah, condemned on account of his "anti-Islamic" measures, was still dignified with the title, "Fighter of the Faith," for his war against the British Raj in 1919.

These were not merchants of the bazaar, but men of the land, with substance, and with a tradition of soldiering. They asked how we had served in the army, and we said there had been "no compulsion."

"The head of your republic (republic was a new word for them, they liked using it), one Jansan, came to Kabul, I remember," one said.

"Johnson? He died. We've had three presidents since."

"Three more? Who is it now?" another man asked. Our reply made no sense to them, and they tired of our conversation. Among themselves, more agreeably, they talked of the price of *ghee* and cooking oil, of *jaribs* of land and of water. The talk of farmers must be the same all over the world.

The light failed and the guest room grew cold. Hamid lit a brazier with firewood, warming only a small corner of the room, though we were near to it. Lamplight soon lit the *mihman khana*.

The last guests to arrive were the musicians. They had been playing for holiday-makers all over the city. Perspired and exhausted, they slumped down beside the brazier, ignoring the company around them, until they had drained the tea which Hamid proffered them. Even by lamplight the alien character of the musicians was clear, with their dark faces, glistening with sweat, and their dilated eyes. There was antimony on their eyelids, which made their eyes seemed wide, rouge on their cheeks, and henna on their hands, to absorb the sweat and cool them. They were bareheaded, like no Afghans, and talked among themselves with rare abandon. Amin came up with their dinners, greeting them with the same graciousness he had observed all day long, "You are our guests now."

After eating, the musicians began to talk to my friend and me, for we were sitting right beside them. For the rest of the *mihman khana*, the proximity was apt: all the freaks in one part of the room. I had begun to feel the "we-ness" of the assembly, now with the musicians I felt the "them-ness" of it. Had we eaten well for lunch? Yes we had. And they? Where they played for lunch the host was miserly and fed them the usual *qurut* instead of stew. "Some people are so tight-fisted," said the *tablazan*.

The *dutarist* left his meal and took the *dutar* out of its wrap.

The sound of his tuning up was like bird calls, echoing in the night.

The *mihman khana* fell silent in expectation.

The *tablazan* looked about the room, sizing up the audience. There were those present with whom he wanted to ingratiate himself. *"Hajji Walid Khan!* May you live long. Are you well? Are you in harmony? May you not grow tired. *Khan Akbar Khan . . ."*

He began a pit-a-pat with his bony fingers on the drums. The dancer, to everyone's extreme interest, was tying the brass bells on his ankles and wrists, while he wore a gauzy, vaguely feminine skirt around his *kala*. A filet disguised the mannish cut of his hair, and heavy rouge was on his cheeks. The audience grew intense. Such dances were forbidden now, and so had become extremely rare. I should add that no women entertain professionally, unless among the aristocrats of Kabul there survive the fabulous *nautch* dancers.

He did not look at all womanly, was without even a suggestion of breasts, and had a big, athletic build. Despite his unhealthy habit of hashish, he had a great deal of energy, which he now unleashed. He began to hop, pounding on the floor with his bare feet, jangling the anklets and, with jerky gestures, shaking the bells on his bracelets in time to the rhythm of the *dutar* and the *tabla*. Then he spun, billowing his skirt into the air. Smiling coquettishly, showing his yellow teeth, he executed leaps in front of the eminences, Amin and Hajji Walid Khan. His hands floated in heavy, wing-like positions, wrists rattling, but inexpressive. There was nothing arousing about the performance. The constant hammering of his feet and the bells fed the intensity of the audience, though. He perspired copiously.

The *tablazan* sang his song, eyes rolling in *shawq*, that fervor which I had observed in his practicing, but now a hundred-fold more acute. He sang and the dancer punctuated his pauses with a great pounding of limbs. Sweat dripped down his face, and the red rags of hair swayed with the tossing head.

The greybeards watched the dancer with riveted attention, inspired at first by prurience, thin-lipped, stroking the ends of their beards. As the pace of the music sped faster, the dancer leapt higher and gyrated violently. The greybeards retreated, instinctively, from the emotional climax, being unwilling to bear with the *shawqis* any longer. They looked uncomfortable, glancing away, beginning to talk among themselves.

Utterly winded, the dancer slumped to the floor. A chorus of *"Wa, wa,"* covered the sighs of relief that the dance had stopped. A plate went around to collect a present for the performers.

Amin had invited them as guests, after all, not hired them. My friend and I had brought no money with us and I shamefacedly handed the plate back to the *tablazan*.

Now I knew how tea could intoxicate. We were very nearly drunk upon it, and sugar, and the madness of our company, the musicians. We rode back to the *sarai* with Abdul Hayy and the troupe, with the *tablazan* crooning through the dark, wailing his sad songs. The dancer coyly asked how we liked the dance. At our reply the *tablazan* carped, "Tttthhhhhankkkkkyyyyyyyooooouu" through the night, mocking us, still wild with his hashish and the music.

We had forgotten to go to Abdul Wahid's, an omission the old man never mentioned.

5.

ON HORSEBACK

Ganj Bazaar

We should have been experts by now, visiting every livestock sale for weeks, always with the intention of buying horses, always returning empty-handed. Not that we did not learn how to operate in the market, the *ganj bazaar;* far from it: we could give lessons. If you want to buy a horse, you go to the *ganj,* held every Thursday in Herat in a ruined corner of the city near the Malik Gate. There are beasts and men in the dusty *maydan,* camels and oxen, goats and sheep. The animals seem to have been assembled for a "visit of the Magi" scene. They are silent and motionless, enduring the heat and flies stoically. A tethered heifer sleeps; some starved goats nibble on the straw which has been strewn around. The animals present a contrast to the men; a sad-eyed camel watches as her dealer throws a wad of money on the ground—an insultingly low bid in his opinion—and stamps on it. The bidder curses him in language mixed from the Qur'an and the gypsies' camp. Their friends pull them apart as they feign coming to blows. The camel averts her head, to the left, to the right, expressionless throughout. Around them, men make further commotion. A wide-turbaned Pathan is praising his skeletal sheep to some skeptical traders; a burly Turkoman is test-riding a donkey—the mount diminutive for so large a rider. No one hesitates to strain the animals; some men eagerly load bales on another camel's back and force the animal to rise up, a test of strength. Two excitable *Heratis* haggle over a dormant bull with sawed-off horns. Everywhere underfoot, gathering up manure from the ground in rubber buckets, ragged, beggar children move with a wildness which surprises even the animals.

You go past this jostling, raucous crowd, past the shepherds and the peasants, the livestock and the pack-animals, to the far end of the *ganj* where they sell horses. This is a different world. Livestock is mere economic necessity, but horses are the nearest thing in Afghanistan to luxury. Customers for horses are few, their trading being a rare event. Mules, donkeys, and camels change hands frequently at the weekly bazaar, but horse brokers must bide their time, balancing a high sale price against long weeks of waiting. They squat in the shade of their horses, holding the nose ropes, under the increasingly hot sun.

A lone Turkoman rides in on his horse and dismounts beside these horse brokers. He squats, like them, waiting through the morning to see if a passerby will make him a good offer for his horse. If not, he will swing into the saddle and ride away. His half-closed eyes betray not the slightest impatience to sell. He may only be curious, you suspect, to learn the going price for horses in Herat. If you offer him 10,000 *rupees* for his horse, he will boast afterward that his horse cost him 10,000 *rupees.*

The trick of the bazaar is to feign the most profound indifference to the animals which are offered for sale. At the mere suggestion of interest in his horse, the broker will drag you into a prolonged process of negotiation, which some sense of bravado prevents you from cutting short. For horses are a luxury; you do not go shopping for diamonds without hearing the sales pitch of the diamond seller.

You must be careful not even to show too much disapproval of a horse, since this is a veiled sign of interest. That horse with burrs on his legs, mange around his mouth and sores on his back: if you as much as say, "Look at that poor nag," the brokers and his cohorts will surround you from all sides and raise a chorus of approval for you and your "choice."

"It's a foal, I raised him myself," says the broker.

"Strong as an ox, for his age," says another.

"What spirit he shows!" General commendation of the horse-cadaver.

You must riposte effectively to show that you know about horses. "What do you say, 'foal'? From whom did you buy this nag? From *Hazrat* Adam? From *Hazrat* Salih (Methuselah)?"

The broker feigns offense. "I grant you, he has been thin lately, but he's a wonder horse."

"The wonder is he stands." This exchange doesn't discourage the broker; it's obligatory, preparing the way for your first offer and his first demand. You know he will ask an unreasonably high price, anyway. If you have no intention of buying the nag, you should walk away at once. But if you had no intention, you should not have begun this banter with the broker in the first place. You can't go away.

"I swear on the Qur'an this is a two-year-old," says the broker, sententiously. Now you must accept the horse's age as moot and consider what sort of mount he makes. The broker's assiduous cohorts ready the horse with a wooden packsaddle, tying it about with a piece of rope, and boost you onto the horse's back. No stirrups, no reins, you make do holding the nose rope or the mane in one hand, while you take a bramble branch for a switch in the other. You ply the switch all over the horse's fore and hind quarters, with no effect. The animal stands in the same position in which he has been hobbled for the last two hours, dimly conscious of the weight on his back. Just as you are about to dismount in well-orchestrated disgust, one of the broker's friends strikes the horse under his tail and he bolts. You are off.

His first leap sails you clear of the crowd which has gathered to watch the transaction. They break into broad smiles, expecting a fall. After bouncing around on the high perch of the packsaddle while the horse keeps up a pneumatic-drill trot, you manage to dig your knees deep into the bones of the horse's shoulder and hang on. You call to him in Turkish, "*Get-get-get,*" and then in English, "Git-git-git." The knees and the voice combine to keep the horse on a semi-controlled career across the bazaar. Every uncertain forward movement tears a tendon in your thigh or your shoulder, but you knot your fingers into the mane and ride him out.

Not having mastered the switch, you cannot control the veer of the horse, blindly dashing through the *ganj*, into the livestock, tripping over sheep, bruising into the sad-eyed camels. You send men and beasts out of your way with the cry "*Ba-khabar, ba-khabar!* (Look out!)." At first this sounds so ridiculous that you swallow it, but later, after running down a few hapless bystanders you call out with gusto, "*Ba-khabar,*" and then "*Get-get*" and also "Git-git." The horse picks up speed as he reaches the walled boundary of the *ganj*, addresses the wall, swerves to the left despite your signals to swerve right, and neatly dashes you against the wall. Hang on, the whole bazaar is watching; the horse turns homeward in a long, open trot. Every old horse remembers the pleasure of a good run, the roll of the rider balancing on his back. The wind breezes by; the rag children put down their buckets of manure to watch the horse-and-rider's synchrony. Even the broker is surprised to see the horse run so well. As you prance up he promptly raises his first asking price by 5,000 *rupees*.

You dismount with as much aplomb as possible in face of the broker's absurd demand, 17,000 *rupees*. Give him the sneer he deserves; the horse is not worth half that. The crowd of buyers and brokers leans in to hear your counteroffer. You must be careful. It is possible, as the broker says, that the horse is merely thin but basically sound. But you cannot tell whether, under feeding, the horse would ever regain his proper weight. A long-mistreated horse never will. If the horse is ailing with parasites or malnutrition, even though you bid a trifling amount, the broker may stick you with him, with the privilege of stabling a half-dead horse. If this mishap should befall an Afghan, he can return to the next *ganj* with the same horse, a fresh coat of oil applied to the hair, several gallons of water bloating the animal's belly, making him look sleek and fat. The once-deceived buyer turns deceptive seller and unloads the animal on another. This expedient is probably beyond you.

The broker waits for your bid, all dignity and probity. The cohorts have assumed an air of improbable innocence. You can be sure the animal has anthrax. He stares at the ground, panting loudly, while the crowd fairly whispers aloud, "Suckersucker-suckersuckersuckersucker." What will you say?

I never knew what I was supposed to say, I broke down, I gave up. My friend, too, wavered here, unsure whether the horse were sound or sick, fat or thin. After weeks of attending the *ganj bazaar*, we still made no single earnest offer, though we were often trapped into bidding on horses we had no intention of buying. Only peasants unparticular about the horses they rode or speculators in suspect horseflesh ever seemed to come away from the bazaar with anything but empty halters.

Eventually, though, we became so well-known in the *ganj* that we no longer had to attend the bazaar; the horses came to us. Not just Thursdays, but every day, brokers sought us out at the *sarai* and offered us animals for sale. Some were droshky drivers whose horses had proved unsuited to the trains, others were horse thieves, and there were the regular shifty speculators from the bazaar. Most of them would go away disappointed, having hoped to hear fabulous bids, in the tens of thousands of *rupees*. One droshky driver grew livid at what he considered our skin-flinting nature. "I swear by the Qur'an I'll sell this horse for twenty thousand *rupees* and not a *puli* less!" Others were less abusive, even shy, in dealing with the *meestars*. Once a horseman rode into the *sarai* without dismounting, asked for us, and inquired politely whether we would pay 40,000 for the horse. We told him, just as politely, no. He smiled and rode off. I was always tempted to express my opinion, that these nags were not worth 3,000 *rupees*, but my friend advised, "If you don't mean to buy the horses, there's no point hurting their feelings."

An Afghan would have enjoyed the process, the wily battle of wits and words over horseflesh. Once a man has bought or sold his mount, he is relatively idle, missing the occasion to visit the bazaar, to chat, to argue, to boast, and most importantly, to sense the mood of the market. The price of horses reflects many things, the availability of fodder, the nearness of winter, the fecundity of the previous springs, the stability of conditions in the countryside. To know the right price of a horse is to appreciate what is going on in the world.

In wake of the famine of 1971-72, the price of a horse had risen from a mean of about 3,000 to 5,000 *rupees*. That bought one a sound, decent horse, with which one could ride anywhere, however far one wished, without worrying that the horse would give out suddenly. For 8,000 to 10,000 *rupees*, one had a horse of elegance, fine-featured, and jittery. "A horse like that," said Amin, "they take five, six men, and they grab him by the nostrils, while he bucks and kicks, and saddle him up, and when the rider gets on, they let go and he rides and rides, like the wind, it were." Above 10,000 *rupees*, there were racers and sport horses, highly intelligent and specially trained. The top of the lot were the *buzkashi* horses, whose worth was proverbially one or two *lakhs*, whose mode of existence was above the animal, even above the lives of most men. The best horses came from the North; I had seen them grazing there on the plains of Balkh. These stood a hand higher than any other horse, growing fat off the lush grass of the plains. They foraged leisurely under the attentive eyes of a groom, whose deference to his charges was considerable. While the horses grazed, he collected choice, juicy bits of foliage to feed the horses from his hand. In the winter he would feed them barley and even animal fat in a compounded mash, to keep them sleek. The horses of Balkh were considered the finest in Middle Asia, having been bred with Arabians over the years by the warlike *khans* of the North and the amirs of Kabul. Such horses used to fetch high prices in India, crores of *rupees*, financing in turn the amirs' purchases of smuggled arms from Anglo-Indian gunrunners. Now the horses served no purpose at all, but were vaunted as highly as ever.

The high value set upon the horse was one of the verities, one of those anchors which the men of Afghanistan used to hold fast to the past. As the army gave up cavalry and the government subsidies for horse-raising gave out, the worth of horses grew greater, not less. A man who could own one was rich, powerful, an upholder of old ways. The language itself reflected this. In

Iran the word *mal* (from the Arabic) meant "possessions." In Afghanistan it had come to mean "chattel," a man's most important possession. This could have been due to Turkish influence, for the steppe-dwellers also said *mal*, the Mongol word for horse. The ancient Turks believed the horse to be a god, who created the first race of men the Turks, in his own image, with fine bones and high, flat cheeks. Most of the language of the stables was Turkish. Horses were named in Turkish, *qara* ("Black"), and *qirmiz* ("Red"). The paraphernalia of horsemanship went by doughty names like *shalaq*, a word which sounded like its meaning, "whip." In Iran people connected the word *khan* with *khana*, "house." But in Afghanistan no one doubted its Turkish origin; whoever owned a horse was a *khan*.

Such was the rarity of horses: in the province there had been 12,000 head, compared to 46,000 camels, 80,000 pack animals, and two and a half million sheep. During the famine of 1971, all the livestock dwindled. The horses, articles of *luxe*, were killed and eaten by the hungry *khans*, though they hotly denied it now. The whole point of being a *khan* was to squander. When we said we wanted to buy horses, it was assumed we meant to spend much money. Surprised when they learned that in our country, too, people rode horses for pride and for pleasure, the Afghans reasoned we were perhaps not so benighted as they had supposed. Again, each civilization considered the other *dahri* (materialist). We had not thought them capable of prideful excess; they imagined us as apostles of *mutars* and machines. Word that the *meestars* would buy horses caused a stir in our neighborhood and among those who knew us.

Kabud, Ablaq

A boy called at the *sarai* for us and begged to bring us to a certain horse dealer, a man named Yusufi. We knew this fellow, an old, very evil-looking character who personified the word "horse thief." We worried about buying stolen animals, about having them restored to their owners without recompense to us; we had avoided such as Yusufi. This time, though, the boy was cunningly insistent, while we had grown long impatient. We let him take us to Yusufi's *sarai*, a desolate, lone lot besides a ruined palace and a Timurid polo field named *Maydan-i-Mila*. The house was surrounded by a wild and weed-swept garden; a couple of old men sat inside listlessly drinking tea. One was Yusufi, with pendulous, carrion-bird's features, the heavy dye in his eyebrows and beard being a fair clue to his honesty. With uncertain

politeness he asked us to come in, sit, and drink some tea. They
had only green, the favorite of hashish addicts. The other man,
yellow and decrepit, poured into two stained cups and offered
them to us. The candies which they sucked with their tea were
black with age and dirt. These we declined. We sat quietly
through this, noting the poverty and disorder of our host's house.
Broken cookingware, miserably poor bedding, moth-eaten rugs,
all were heaped in the *utaq* helter-skelter. The only well tended
object in the room was a bird gun which Yusufi kept beside him.

They were afraid of us, these two men, never having dealt
alone with *meestars*, never face to face over tea with unbelievers.
The gun was for their protection. At a loss for words, Yusufi
motioned the boy to go fetch the horses out of the stable. When
we followed him out, the two men rose so shakily I thought they
would fall.

Outside the boy held the horses. They were not bad. One was
kabud, a grey, a mare, slightly swayback, but plump, and without marks on her. The other was *ablaq*, a piebald mare, looking
rather thin, but strong-tempered and sturdy. That both were
mares pleased us, since we had only one stable for the two, and
males would certainly fight. Playing on our interest, the two
men began to praise the horses. "This *ablaq*, she belonged to
smugglers, a fast horse, strong, used to the *dasht*. The *kabud* is
a young horse, not more than three years, just come from Farah.
She belonged to nomads." We couldn't repress our look of interest.
"See how fat they are, see how sleek," said the withered yellow
man, combing the *ablaq's* tail with his bony fingers. As we
looked, the horses seemed to get rounder and sleeker, fifty pounds
heavier each than at the outset. "This one is *yurgha*," he meant a
trotter, "and that one is *chardast*," a horse that cantered. The
boy saddled both horses.

After weeks of having horses described to us, we thought we
knew what they were about now. I raised my eyebrows at the
word *chardast*, since the canter was not a favorite pace among
the Afghans. The man nervously proposed that we mount the
horses and see how they rode. We needed no encouragement. I
got on the *ablaq*, while my friend rode the *kabud*, which was the
chardast. We walked them out to the old polo ground, a straight
run of about 100 yards. At first the horses ignored our kicks, walking at least half the way down the field. Then my friend gave his
kabud a slap beneath the saddle, and she broke into a canter
which seemed to pitch him into the air. Not to be outdistanced, my
horse leaped forward in an electrically-charged trot, pulling past
him. We breezed to the end of the field, changed leads, and turned
around. We rode back, my friend at a gallop and my *ablaq* still

in a trot but faster, hammering down to where the two men and the boy where standing fitfully waiting. They had been afraid that we would ride off with the horses, having heard that the *meestars* were all dishonest; they were unwilling to trust us further than they could throw us. We dismounted, trying to keep poker faces, though in fact delighted, and rejoined them around tea, which had grown stone-cold.

"They are good horses," said Yusufi, scanning our faces for signs of approval. His yellowish companion said nothing, bared his grey teeth, and popped the candies into his mouth. "Twenty thousand *rupees* Afghani for the two of them," he went on, without changing tone. But the other man's eyes almost popped out of his jaundiced sockets at the mention of that sum of money. I guessed 20,000 was their high price. They were in a panic, since they knew our interest in horses could be their gold mine, yet they were still unsure as to how to clinch the deal. These *meestars*, they knew, were fabulously wealthy, and the thought that they might have asked too low a starting price gnawed at them.

"Ten thousand for two," I said, blandly using a law of halves. It was not only too easy, it was too high. Now we were stuck between ten and twenty. The bidding proceeded, punctuated by our putting aside our teacups, by the two old men spitting out their candies, stomping on the ground, swearing on the Qur'an, and the boy impressively leading the horses away in fine dudgeon. The whole struggle lasted about half an hour. At the last moment the panicky thought flashed through my mind, "Don't buy the horses at all," but Yusufi, clairvoyant, saw me balking and came down to 13,500, "bare, without the saddles."

"Done."

Not quite bare, they sold us. Each of the horses had a wool-chained *tawiz* around its neck, a small charm to assure the animal's good health. The *mulla* who came to witness the deal promised us that the horses were sound—and if not, we might exchange them. I doubted whether we really could, but the white-turbaned witness was reassuring. Yusufi and his friend assumed the dignity of biblical patriarchs now, though when we slapped 13,500 *rupees* into the hands of the witness, who counted the many rumpled bills, tears filled the eyes of the two old men. The *mulla* passed the bills to Yusufi, who counted them again, before handing them over to the third, whose hands were too feeble to count. The money disappeared into his pajama. Then their jitteriness and decrepitude seemed to fade away. Yusufi lost twenty years of age. "By the Holy Qur'an! You have bought fine horses. You will go to the *dasht*, to the mountains! You will be *kalan*, great men, in your times!" he said expansively. We drank more tea, declined the candies again, and hurried back to the *sarai* in the failing light, leading the horses by their nose ropes, which Yusufi in a burst of magnanimity had given us. I felt awed as the breath of the horse warmed my hand; I felt as though I had entered another mode of existence, owning a horse; it was as though I had become a centaur.

We brought the horses back to the *sarai* after dusk. No one was about; no one saw us lead the two animals to the stall Amin had let to us; no one saw how they resisted, shying away from the dark unknown of their new home. They kicked, they rolled, they would not go in. I stood in the freezing night air, holding their ropes, while my friend tried to coax them inside with a sheaf of hay. The commotion roused Hamid Ullah, sleeping in his *samovar*, who appeared with his lantern to appraise the problem.

"So, you've bought horses. *Mubarak basha*, may they be lucky. Look here, they're scared to go into the stables, because they can't see in there. They're scared of the dark just like people." He put his lamp down inside the stable and led the horses effortlessly behind him. "Now, have you got blankets for them? And hay in the morning? And water?" So little had we expected to stable the horses that night, we had nothing prepared for them. Some quick makeshifts provided temporarily, but Hamid gave us a long list of things to buy in the bazaar in the morning. He looked in on our horses and then went back to bed.

My friend and I peered shyly into the stables, darkened again. The two forms lay side by side, looking, in the dark, like small, beached whales.

With the purchase of the horses, our way of life changed as much as it had by our moving into the *sarai*. We could no longer afford idleness. Every morning we had to get up early, draw freezing water from the well in the leaky buckets, and water the horses. We had to feed them, make countless repairs in our gear, worry about the horses' health, examine their stools, their teeth, the gloss of their manes. We had to go to the bazaar and compare qualities of grain, distinguishing old, impure feed from the well-sifted and the fresh. At a late hour, when the air was again freezing, we had to water them for the night. Our lives began to resemble those of our neighbors, the droshky drivers. Our freedom of action, like theirs, narrowed. We seemed always to be looking after our horses.

On the other hand, with the horses, we had a new sort of freedom of action. We could travel anywhere, without relying on the infrequent *mutars*. Our *Herati* friends invited us to this and that village; our easy journeying there being accepted as a matter of course. They thought anyone with a horse ubiquitous. "You can go wherever you please. To the mountains, to Obeh, to Mir Daud, to Iran!" said Hamid Ullah.

"And from there," added a habitué of his *samovar*, "you can go riding to your own kingdom on an Afghan horse."

The greatest freedom the horses provided, though, was indirect. They gave us the excuse to deal with dozens of *Heratis* in their usual pursuits and not as a special imposition. We came to know the blacksmith, the grainsellers, and the bucketmakers in our neighborhood, who left off calling us the odious *meestar*, at least to our faces. In the bazaar the saddlemakers knew us, and we learned something of their trade. We were there often. The apprentice used to try to cadge lessons in writing off me, but his master forbad him to learn letters. "Don't fill his brain with useless stuff. Teach him the numbers." They accepted us as customers merely, which was just as we wished.

Riding Out

At first no one expected that we would look after our animals properly. Hamid must have let out the story of our mishaps that first night. He meant no malice, I'm sure, but the damage was done. If we didn't look after our horses we would be the laughing stock of the *sarai*, we knew. The interest of our neighbors in the affair was very great. I had borrowed a shovel from Hamid to clean out the stables—this was the second day—and some of the tenants gathered around to watch me work. There was nothing an Afghan preferred to watching other people work. I continued to shovel vigorously, enjoying the progress I made in emptying the place, while my audience's mood changed from one of curiosity and amusement to concern and resentment. This was not my *maslak*, my position, they complained. A dozen hands offered to relieve me of the work. In their opinion, I had no right to do the job myself; in so far as I had the money to pay others to do it, I was depriving them of their rights by my activity. They looked on with sad faces, thinking how much money they might have extorted out of me for the work. After an hour, I had pounds of old, sour-smelling manure heaped in front of the stables; the inside was laid bare to dry, sweet-smelling clay. By daily performing tasks like this, we reconciled our neighbors to the fact that we could take care of our horses ourselves.

Sometimes we needed help. When the horses became constipated we asked Abdul Hayy for a remedy, and he quickly suggested adding a certain herb to their feed. Now, thinking us in his debt, he began to insist on all sorts of questions, how much money we had paid for the horses, why wouldn't we hire a friend of his as groom, what we intended to do with the horses when we left Afghanistan. I wished I had never asked him for anything.

He persisted day after day, scheming to learn the price of the horses. He grew sly about it, "What marvelous horse you got your hands on; they're worth at least ten thousand *rupees* apiece."

My friend was prompt. "I'll sell them to you right now for twenty thousand." Abdul Hayy balked.

Amin, overhearing our argument, had a laugh at his friend's expense. "Aye, they'll sell them to you and they'll have an honest profit, too, Abdul Hayy." Only Amin knew how much we had paid for the horses, and he never told anyone. He thought them worth 8,000 together, he told us. For *meestars*, we had not done too badly.

Amin also defended our insistence on not hiring a groom. Would a groom walk off the horses when they had been ridden hard? Would he sift their grain to remove stones and bits of dung? Would he buy good quality barley and hay from the bazaar? The cost of feed was higher than that of a man's daily diet, being about 50 *rupees* a day. The opportunities for a stranger's abuses were too many; the risks to take with a delicate animal were too great. How could we trust a stranger, a poor man, to look after our horses? Abdul Hayy protested the honesty of his protégé, but gave in to Amin's reasoning. "To a relative, to a friend, but never trust your horse to a stranger," he said.

Amin eventually helped us master the complexities of horsemanship in Herat. Weights and measures of barley varied chaotically from dealer to dealer, each of whom had on his scales a *man*-stone—a weight of measure—which varied according to the size of the stone! How much barley should we feed the horses? "Half a *man* of Abdur Rahman's barley, or a bit more of Hajji Ahmad's, less of Abu Bakr's—his stone is very heavy." Other weights, *sirs* and *dastas*, which likewise varied, were an endless source of confusion. Only gradually did we manage to cope with them all.

We hoped to fatten the animals by feeding them carefully while riding them only infrequently. Unused to such a soft life, they became unmanageable. "The barley," explained Amin, "makes them crazy; it has much force."

Abdul Hayy kept a close watch on our mistakes. One day I couldn't get the horses out of the stable, even by going behind and pushing them. Abdul Hayy went in with his long whip and brought them out in a trice. I thanked him, blushing furiously.

"You see, you see, you need a groom!"

He continued to watch as I saddled the *kabud*, mounted and tried to rein her towards the gate. She balked, rolled on me, and proceeded to turn somersaults in the air after I leapt clear. The Afghans looked on askance, while Abdul Hayy snorted, 'You have to beat them more with your whips!"

Afghans were quick to discipline their horses and work them rigorously; these animals were too costly to warrant sentimentality. We would often see old, skeletal creatures struggling under the weight of two riders, or of a big man with a fat lamb slung over his pommel. Once I spoke my mind to an Afghan. "That's a cruel way to use your horse. He's half dead." The rider regarded me as a madman. If a horse was capable of carrying a rider or his load between two points, an Afghan was sure to make him. A horse never gave out and died, though, without the rider's calculation. While the Afghans whipped and cajoled their horses, they kept one eye peeled to the animals' endurance, judging when to go on and when to stop. Horses, unlike donkeys and camels, reflected their state of health in clear signs: the teeth, the eyes, the stools. If a horse could be saved with rest and care, the Afghan would save him. If a horse were dying, no Afghan would scruple to ride him until he dropped.

We had only been used to fat, petted animals, who shied away at the sight of a crop, for whom riding was a brief interruption in a day of feeding and lolling. Our sentimentality about such horses was a luxury few Afghans could afford. Until we had some task to put the horses to, some goal, the horses would neither respond to our half-hearted commands, nor would we understand how the Afghans dealt with their horses. The *kabud* and the *ablaq* needed hard riding and Spartan diets.

My friend knew this. "We'll never get the feel of the horses until we take them on a long ride," he said, "like they're obviously used to."

I was reluctant. Today we had changed horses; I rode the *ablaq* for the first time since we bought her, and I found she would not respond to my reining. I pulled at the bridle until the leather snapped.

"She's draw-reined, like a cowboy horse," called my friend, but it was too late. These horses were still full of surprises to me.

I agreed we should take them for longer rides, but many frustrating delays followed, one after the other. We had to have the bridle fixed. Then Daud asked to borrow the horses for a day and we let him, to the horror of everyone in the *sarai*. "Lending your horses to another? We never do that, unless we are brothers, or blood brothers," went the conversation. Daud returned looking illused; one horse had thrown him, and the stirrup had broke. We didn't complain to him about it, but solicited him. The *sarai*-dwellers gaped and said, "There are not friends in Afghanistan such as there are in the *meestars'* country." But the broken stirrup was vexing and caused another day's delay.

The saddlemaker in the portal of the covered bazaar lamented things were not as they were. "This leather is like paper, it tears like this, and when it gets wet, it's worthless. In the old days, we had good saddles, but no more." One of ours was wooden, painful to sit in but easy to keep seated on, the other was thin leather, under which we felt every bone of the horse's spine.

A friend of ours, a schoolteacher, had asked us to visit him in his village, Ziyaratjah. He would go out by *mutar* and we would follow on horseback. Ziyaratjah (Pilgrimage Place) was a showplace of monuments which he was eager to have us see. The village was about 25 kilometers southwest of Herat, a good ride, which should have taken half a day. "Ziyaratjah?" carped Abdul Hayy. "You'd better go by *mutar*. For you, it's more convenient."

That decided us.

We had wanted to set off early, but time being what it was in Herat, nine o'clock passed before we started down the street from the sarai. Truck and motor traffic crowded the narrow roundabout before the Kandahar Gate, and the *kabud*, nervous and unused to city traffic and loud engines, threatened to bolt. My friend rode her, tightly reining, picking his way between the pushcarts and vendors, overloaded trucks gunning their engines, and darting taxicabs. She frothed at the mouth, but kept her place on the roadside. The physical effort needed to manage her was tremendous.

Once outside the gate, the open plain of the *dasht* offered respite. We could ride at some distance from the pavement where the trucks passed. The countryside before the Kandahar Gate was flat and sunny. The traffic was light, men on donkeys, or afoot, leading their camels laced one to the other, bringing village stuffs to the market just inside the gate. The fallen masonry of the old city walls lay about, clogging a small stream that flowed beside the roadway. Children playing and poor women doing their wash stared at us as we passed.

The stream flowed beside the roadbed in the *dasht* towards the banks of the Hari River. Here the road crossed over the bridge called Malan. We had no choice but to return to the pavement, joining a mass of buses, bicycles, carriages, and trucks which observed no lanes struggling across the bridge. With traffic coming from every direction the *ablaq* went wild, and my friend rode her steadily behind me, relying on my constant pace to reassure his horse. The bridge was long, the heavy traffic taking a good five minutes to cross. Every time a bus or truck drove by, the driver would blare his horn and clumsily change his gears, just to terrify the horses—it was a pastime with them, we had heard. My *kabud* edged nervously and unpredictably close to the embankment, where I saw the water rushing beneath us. A big truck boomed up, shrieking like a banshee down-shifting and shaking the pavement with its weight. I dug my knees into the shoulders of the *kabud* and rode on, faster and faster, hoping to get off the bridge before the big truck passed. In a flash it elbowed by—and when the dust cleared, my friend was no longer behind me. The *ablaq* had bolted ahead, disappearing into the woods on the far side of the bridge.

I caught up with him. Both horses were winded, so we let them walk and drink in the brambles and hedges of the damp riverbank. Looking back towards the bridge, we admired its classical, stone symmetry; the bridge seemed the furthest thing away from a terrifying traffic bottleneck. The *Heratis* imagined the bridge was built by Bibi Nur, a princess who collected cowrie and egg shells for its cement. That was a vivid image suggesting the delicacy and gracefulness of the white bridge of many arches, even if it were only legend. We wandered in the groves of oak and beech trees for a long time, retracing our path back to the paved road only with reluctance.

Towards noon, even in December, the air grew warm in the valley of Herat. We rode at a quick trot, streaming our turban ends and the empty sleeves of the *chapans* behind us. The pace was too fast for the heat. We slowed down, putting off our *chapans* and tying them over our pommels, Uzbek-style. Few *mutars* passed now; we were off the paved road in the immense plain of the Herat Oasis, where irrigation channels from the Hari River crisscrossed around us in a filigree of mud and watery pools. At the interstices of water and dry paths (sometimes the paths were flooded; it was hard to tell which was path and which channel) lay the Oasis's many villages.

A haze on the plain masked the villages from sight until we were upon them. Then we would find ourselves in a maze of mud walls, irrigation ditches, barriers of trees, and the incomprehending faces of the villagers. "*Salaam alaykum*, is this the road to Ziyaratjah?"

Better to answer the stranger, they thought, with silence, so he will ride on. We had to continue uncertain of the way, through the mazing lanes of the villages, and back onto the hazy plain. After passing several villages, we saw the sun begin to set south-westerly, lighting the direction towards Ziyaratjah. We adjusted our path and rode towards the sun.

As the sun fell lower in the sky our way showed more clearly. We did not know how we should recognize Ziyaratjah and wondered how we should see anything in the penumbra of the sunbleached oasis. But in the late afternoon, trotting slowly and scanning the horizon ahead of us, we could make out two slender fingers of dark matter raised to the sky. The outlines of a Timurid mosque grew clear, two minarets rising above the hazy uncertainty of their foundations. We headed towards this landmark, but it took a long time to reach it. The fingers of stone stuck into the air, beckoning but drawing away.

The village, like the others we had passed, was ringed by ditches and walls, reedbeds and orchards. Yet Ziyaratjah had a bazaar, a twenty-yard lane where shops sold kerosene, grain, and sugar. Wooden booths in poor repair suggested that before the *mutar* opened the markets of the city to the villagers they trafficked more readily to this dependent bazaar. We asked one of the *bazaaris* to direct us to the house of Ali Akbar Mu'allim, the teacher. Suspiciously and unwillingly he pointed out a *sarai* at the corner of the bazaar lane. We rode up and dismounted.

Ali Akbar himself came out to stable our horses. His manner was very easy and informal, appropriate to his young age and his "modern" ideas. He had served his army duty in Kabul, studied in the teacher's college, and yet had a cheery affection for provincial life in Herat. He was devoted to his village and therefore delighted that we should have come as agreed.

We drank the customary cup of tea and then, almost breathless, followed Ali Akbar on an inspection of the village. This was a breach of manners (we were tired) for which we readily forgave him. "Ziyaratjah" was an apt name for this village with one cathedral mosque, two elaborate smaller mosques, a dervish cloister and innumerable shrines and tombs. I imagined that the village had been a favorite picnic spot or hunting ground in days passed, for so many courtiers had wished to be buried here, and the sultans themselves used to ride out on Fridays to celebrate the holiday in this cathedral mosque, in preference to the one of the city. Sure enough, a meadow sloped away from the town, where Ali Akbar said game and grass was abundant in the spring. The oldest mosque in Ziyaratjah belonged to the first century of Islam; Ali Akbar attributed it to the Caliph Umar ibn Abdul Aziz (c. 682-720). As the countryside around Herat had scarcely embraced Islam then, the building was necessarily modest. Of brick and mud, beaten by a thousand years of rain and wind, often repaired, Umar's mosque looked, from the outside, like a *tepe* (barrow) while the columned interior seemed a shapeless grotto of primeval stalagtites. Another mosque, Ali Akbar eagerly pointed out, showed hoof-scuffs from the time when Genghis Khan had stabled his horses there as a desecration. This was the famous "Forty-Columned Mosque" with cobbled floors and composite stone columns, just thirty-five of them. The cathedral mosque was more evidence of the Timurid mania for architecture, its distinguishing feature being the lovely reflecting pool, which caught the image of the white *ivan* just at sunset, pooling the golden rays of the sun. This mosque, which from the outside seemed a mere copy of other mosques inside the city, because of the reflecting pool showed itself a forebear of the Taj Mahal. An attendant *mulla* let the three of us up to the rooftop and marvelled, with Ali Akbar, my friend and me, over the beauty of this simple thing, this sunset.

Our host's eagerness that we should see everything worth seeing went further when we returned to his *sarai*, where he took us on a whirlwind tour of the place: his stables, where our horses were chewing on hay, having been fed and watered in our absence; his grain stores, where last year's crop lay low towards the floor; we even stalked through the family quarters to admire his kitchen. The harem looked up at us curiously: a mother nursing a child, two young girls who laughed at the sight of our eye glasses (one pair was not so funny—but two pairs!) and a grandmother too busy darning to notice. "The storehouse, the bakery, the women, the cold storage room," commented Ali Akbar as we followed him at top speed and looked backward, shyly, at the two laughing girls.

We spent the night in the *mihman khana*, where, after dinner, Ali Akbar's father joined us. He was a great greybeard, whose humor seemed very much like his son's. Eager to show off certain treasures of the house overlooked by Ali Akbar, he produced in turn, a Czech Mauser, a German hurricane lamp, and a manuscript book. He described the rifle and the lantern knowledgeably, saying that the Czech model was better than the "Almani," while the German lantern was better than a similar Chinese one. Then we unwrapped the manuscript, each signature of which was kept in a sheaf of velvet, and disclosed the first page, admiring the illuminated design, or *dibacha*. "*Qur'an-i-sharif*," the father beamed. "Where do you think it comes from, and how much do you think it's worth?" He wanted to know the fine points of the sacred manuscript as well as he knew that of the guns and lamps.

"It's from India," I told him, "and it's about a hundred years old."

Added my friend, more diplomatically, "It must be worth many, many *lakhs* of *rupees.*"

The father, torn between wanting an accurate and wanting a flattering appraisal of his treasure, accepted both these statements without protest, smiling, "Hindustan, eh? Many *lakhs?* A man once offered me a hundred *lakhs* for this, but I told him I wouldn't sell it." He paused, waiting for us to offer two hundred.

"We are *dihqan,*" said Ali Akbar, by way of explaining his father's and his high spirits. Nowadays the word meant "peasant," but Ali Akbar meant it in its epic sense of "knight" and "gentry." He said, "We have land, water, house, animals. We have nothing to complain about, *alhamdulillah.*"

"Don't you get dull out here in the village?"

"Bah," said the father. "When I was a young man I used to go to the city all the time. Hated it. Now I never go there anymore. He goes, if we need something. He works there. A man grows decrepit there, I tell you. But here you can live forever. How old do you think I am? Just look at me." He opened his shirt to show a greying barrel chest, an extravagant gesture that caught me by surprise. To further demonstrate the healthy *dihqan* way of life, the father and son began to wrestle Turkish style, where the opponents start from a head-locked standing position. The son threw the father and we gasped, but the old man bounded up, smiling. Then he threw his son and knocked all the wind out of him. He got up, slowly, and smiled, though less convincingly than did his father. We all laughed until tears came to our eyes for the fun of it.

We told stories, fables, about *Hazrat* Ali and the Hindus, about the times of Shah Rukh and Nadir the Persian. We cracked chestnuts in our hands, still later, when our appetites grew on us again.

"*Daudjan, Walijan,* this evening is for us a real memory. I will think of it in years to come," said Ali Akbar, rubbing his bruises and sending the last chips of wood into the half-extinguished brazier.

"Do they have this sort of hospitality in your country?" asked the father. "You know, if a relative comes to visit us we have to entertain him every night like this until it pleases him to go. Is it that way with you? This is the way of the *dihqan.* Even in the city you will not find such hospitality."

In the early morning send-off Ali Akbar's father led out our horses, which looked fresh and spirited, despite their long ride of the day before. Homeward we rode them easily, without haste or delay; we had discovered our pace.

Amin was pleased, Abdul Hayy surprised, to see us return without mishap. The droshky driver debriefed us over our reception. Boasting and complaining about hospitality extended was a common pastime. "What did they give you to eat?" he asked.

"A good meal: rice, salted meat, *rawghan-i-zard (ghee)* . . ."

"*Rawghan-i-zard!*" wailed Abdul Hayy, rolling his eyes with envy. "I can almost taste it, but I haven't had any for so long." *Ghee* was very expensive for those who did not produce their own. The townspeople consumed cheap Pakistani vegetable oil, reluctantly, in its stead.

"Good friends entertain well," said Amin, complimenting us over our acquaintances.

I repeated to him what the father of Ali Akbar had said about hospitality in the countryside, and then I told him how, as we were riding back into the city, a child had thrown a stone at us, making the horses bolt. I saw the child duck into his *sarai*, turned back and banged on the door with my whip. The boy's father came out and told me to go away. I pursued my business, telling him his child deserved a beating. "What for?" asked the father, incredulously. "For throwing stones at a stranger?"

"And they say the people of the *dasht* are wild," I said to Amin, concluding my story.

His half smile had a shade more of irony than usual. "Aye, *Daudjan*, living in a city makes people change. They have no use for each other. That man was a wretch, but that's the sort of people they are."

We rested the horses only a day in our eagerness to explore the new freedom of being outside the city. The Oasis of Herat stretched wide from the city gates. We rode west, this time, along the road to Islam Qala. We had arranged with Sayyid Shafaq to meet him at a town called Zandajan, which lay between the road and the Hari River, some 40 kilometers from Herat. A Saljuq prince had a notable platform-tomb there; the *sayyid* had described it to us enthusiastically and offered to go with us there by *mutar*. Again, we arranged that Sayyid Shafaq should go ahead, to visit friends, expecting our arrival on horseback. We left earlier, along a straighter path to look for a bigger village than before, so we hoped to make 50 kilometers in a day.

The road towards Islam Qala hugged the skirts of the mountains north of Herat, going through a barren space above the river. Tracks led up the side of these mountains, through ravines cut by stream beds which emptied beside the raised road-way. In some places, the force of the flood had covered the road with sand, and we looked up the course of the flood path to the mountain pass, intriguing and alluring beside us. These slowed our going. In the folds of the mountains we saw black hair tents, the *qishlaqs* of nomads, and debated whether to ride into them. This also slowed us down.

When we thought we had been on the road long enough, we turned off into the *dasht*, hoping to come upon Zandajan before we should come to the Hari River. We stopped for lunch in the middle of the *dasht*, feeding the horses some green hay from the bags which we had made for the purpose on one industrious evening at our *sarai*. We both realized we were not making exactly good time. It was unnerving to stand in the middle of the trackless plain, watching one's horses eat and looking at the sun.

In the flat plain of Herat the sunset is famous for both its beauty and its brevity. While you are still pursuing your after-noon, unmindful of the time, suddenly you see the shadows about you yawn and stretch like dogs before they sleep. The horizon goes wildly yellow, canary yellow, gold, pale and silver, but never red or orange. This is a pre-industrial sunset. Over to the east you can see the night; it really looks like a mantle which the sky is pulling over itself, and while you're admiring the eastern sky, the dome above you—and it really looks like a dome arched just five hundred feet above your head—hangs stars out to air. You see them swaying, too, at first dim and sputtering, but soon clear and bright. And you look to the west again; the sunset is over. The whole transition takes about ten minutes.

I admired the effect in the city, in a droshky from the hill near Gazurgah. But now, riding through the *dasht*, I thought on the consequences of losing the light, the road gone, the river nowhere in view, the ferocious mastiffs running free in the villages, to protect the households.

Near at hand rose a *tepe*. My friend decided to climb to the top of this barrow to gain a better view. He scrambled up while I held the horses. For some reason they were not getting along that day. As I held them, they began to fight, to kick; then they both snapped their reins—I cursed the leather how many times!—and darted to graze apart in the *dasht*. My friend descended from his vantage point to see the horses wandering loose and me standing helplessly by. They seemed like mere specks on the horizon, but that was the distance distortion of the *dasht*.

"Don't rush them," he advised, as we crept forward, keeping still and maintaining our distance while the horses grazed around to keep their eyes on us. We got within a few yards of them after several minutes of painful stalking. Then they edged out of the way still further, with the look of "Say, the grass is greener over there" and "By the way, the men are gaining on us." They ambled just out of reach time and again. We were in the middle of a grassy plain, completely lost, still out of reach of our horses.

"I think we should rush them," I said, exasperated.

"Listen to this. I think they're edged east and south, towards the city. You go ahead and drive them in that direction, and I'll get in front of them and head them off." My friend took a while to outflank them, going far and deep into the *dasht* so that the horses should not notice him. I walked towards them slowly, and they, in their usual way, ambled off. I tried to look as wide as possible to deceive them into thinking that their lateral motion was impeded. My friend was right, though, they only wanted to go south and east. They lost ground steadily until they stumbled right into his hands. He grabbed the broken reins.

"Well done!" I cried, except for the fact that the shadows beneath our feet had suddenly lunged forward, and the sky was full of that yellow effulgence, and we were in the middle of the *dasht*.

We rode fast, cantering and trotting them in the direction we knew was south, hoping to find the river and a settlement before sunset. It was not far off. Cultivated fields interrupted the monotony of the *dasht* and then a line of willows, marking an irrigation ditch running perpendicular to the river. A planter, working in the field beside his pair of oxen, looked up at our rapid approach. He was fearful at first, but we salaamed and waved and spoke the words of neighborly cheer: *"Bijuri? Bikhayri? Zanda bashi! Manda nabashi!* Are you well? Are you fit? Live long! Be not tired!"—an endless repetition of politenesses which tugged at my impatience. Finally I said to the ploughman, "Look you, we're travelers on the road to the city, but the night has overtaken us. Can we get to a *samovar* from here, or a *mihman khana,* before nightfall?

"Mihman khanah," said the man, ejaculating much useless talk about his own village and the name of his *arbab* (landlord), Abdur Rashid, telling us how rich the man was and how fine a host.

"Yes, Grandfather, but where's the village then?"

He pointed the way, almost as an afterthought, as though we were rude to ride off from this pleasant converse. We whipped the horses unmercifully to hurry; they seemed also afraid of spending the night in the open. If we could get to the village of this Abdur Rashid before nightfall, the law of hospitality would prevail and we would have, at least, a roof over our heads. After dark, though, prudence would overcome custom.

On the river's edge we saw the village; its walls opened at one narrow path, which led between the high rows of mud walls. Shadows already filled the lanes, only the roofs of houses peaked gold above the darkened walls, and the stars shone overhead yet feebly. There was no one in the streets of the village; all the visible doors were shut and surely bolted. How could we know where the house of the *arbab* was? The horses grew restive in the blind lanes, threatening to bolt out of control. There were perhaps five minutes before nightfall and disaster.

A child carrying a water bucket stepped out from an alley way, looking almost a sprite in the failing light. I would have thought him an angel in our predicament. "Hey! Boy! Don't run away. We're looking for the *sarai* of Abdur Rashid. Show us the way."

Frightened, he pulled his bucket close to his chin and began to slink into the shadows of the alley. We dismounted, which was the best way of showing peaceful intentions, telling him that we were travelers and guests in the village, whom he must protect. *"Mihman"* and *"musafir"* were magical charms, not words. They stopped the boy in his tracks. He took courage and, beckoning us to follow him, set off wordlessly down the street. At the gate of the *arbab's* compound he knocked hard on the door. A voice called out. He answered back, "It's me, I've brought two travelers, horsemen." For a few minutes we stood in front of the gate with our horses nervously shivering in the night air. It was dark.

The gate opened and a servant, silently, took the horses out of our hands and led them into a stable. We stood in the courtyard of the house, very tired, feeling the silence of the darkened *sarai* like a glove about us. The groom reappeared, with our saddle bags and gear in hand, motioning us into one of the houses in the *sarai* compound.

"There's two *mans* of barley in our bags," I told him.

He clicked his tongue; these would not be needed.

The groom seated us in the room, lit a spirit lamp, and propped us up against our bags. Only then did he speak. "Don't go outside again, there's a dog." Then he left us.

The guest room was substantial and well-built. Fresh plaster covered the walls, pleasantly thick Turkoman carpets lay on the floor. Floral frescoes, artless and colorful, decorated the ceiling and the lower panels of the walls and looked newly executed.

There was a *sandali* in the room, which the servant subsequently returned to light while bringing us tea and dinner. When he saw that we were comfortable, he disappeared again.

We had been lucky. To find any hospitality at this late hour was in itself a lucky circumstance, while this particular *mihman khana* was the most comfortable we had seen. I was surprised at its scale: big walls and solid wall-beams, three or four *utaqs* joined together. So close to the city such a guest room had less of a commercial function, since travelers and merchants would not be expected, and more of a status value. Villages without a *samovar* invariably had a *mihman khana* open to all comers, furnished by the richest man in the place, usually, though not always, the *arbab* or owner of the land around. Entertaining uninvited guests was effectively the duty of the landowner, but it was a duty which brought certain advantages: the *arbab* met people from all over the country, sometimes useful contacts in the future; he was the first to get news of the city or the capital; he might buy or beg rarities off the guest which would be unique in the village. These advantages tended to increase his personal power and assure his position as village chief. Anyone who thought he could afford it could build a *mihman khana* and entertain travelers. If the house was not well provisioned, the neighbors ridiculed the host. If he outspent the current *arbab* in his hospitality, he could usurp the prestige first, and then the power of the *arbab* for himself. The *mihman khana* was therefor both a symbol and a means of the *arbab's* power. The *arbab* Abdur Rashid, we could see, was in no danger of being usurped. His house was impressive.

We told him so when he made his entrance. "This is a very splendid guest house."

The *arbab*, a young man in very flowing pajamas, bareheaded, with a fine moustache on a rather coarse face, blushed befittingly. "It is unworthy of such distinguished guests." He meant it, mistaking our glasses for a sign of high rank.

"It is our host who is distinguished," we replied, and let this exchange of flatteries go on for a while. Abdur Rashid was a Pathan, but no nomad; even so, he had the impetuousness and vigor of a tribesman. Quickly tiring of our exchange, he demanded, quite suddenly, "Have you any medicine?"

We asked him the nature of the ailment.

"A friend of mine has a nasty cut. Don't you have any pills for that?"

Pills, we said, are not generally effective against cuts. What sort of cut was it?

"It's a bullet wound. He was shot on the way to Islam Qala. He was driving his jeep along the road when a bullet struck the window, shattering it. He stopped the jeep and threw himself on the ground, while bullets sang around him, but he reached into the jeep for his own rifle and fired back, several times, until the shooting stopped. Then he climbed into his jeep and drove on, peering out the door to see the way. Only after he had arrived at Islam Qala did he realize he had been wounded—in the calf, the fleshy part, the bullet having gone through."

"Your friend is very brave," I said admiringly.

"It's nothing. It happens all the time around here. Raids, kidnappings, ambush." He seemed very pleased with this state of affairs.

"What do they have to fight about?"

"Land and women, also money. There are blood feuds between us, of old. If a man wants to have his honor, it is impossible not to have enemies. They come, and if they hate a man, they try to throw his house down, they take his women and sodomize them, or they steal the man's horses, his sheep. But here it is safe. It is good that you stay the night here."

That explained the thick walls of the *sarai* and the dog inside the courtyard. "Do people often get killed?" I asked.

"No, not often, perhaps two or three a month. But it is a bad thing, because the *wali* comes and pokes his nose into affairs. In this part of the country are many smugglers, you know; they go to Iran with sheep and horses. The price of an animal in Mashhad is almost double what it is here. They go with opium, too, on the fastest horses, or on camels which are called *badi* (wind-like) for their speed. And each one carries a hundred *mans* of opium on its back, though it travels eighty kilometers a day. A camel like that can cost hundreds of *lakhs*, but oh, how the smugglers are rich men! They go to that kingdom and, if they see a gendarme, bang! He is dead. And if the gendarmes see the Afghans, they run away, unless they catch one alone, and then they say, 'Ay, Afghan, your father burned in hell, Dog, Son of a Dog'. And they throw him into jail. And the men of these parts go to the villages there and catch girls, young ones—and sometimes boys, too—and they bring them back here until their parents ransom them. No one in Iran has a weapon, it's forbidden, so they have no defenses against us. The Afghans go and become rich men; it's a wonderful life!"

We were breathless, wide-eyed, as Abdur Rashid paused for breath and settled back on his cushions, smiling and pleased at the effect his story was having on the visitors. I had no doubt everything he said was the truth; it fit into the way the Iranians described the Afghans. Either because Abdur Rashid was young or because he was simple, he didn't feel constrained to withhold anything from his guests. His clumsy story about the "friend's" wound was only the charming equivocation of one who doesn't know how to lie.

Talk ran on late, and we pressed Abdur Rashid for details of his life in the village. He said he had many horses—racing horses, and *buzkashi* horses—but not here, rather at the family estate in Kandahar. "We are men of Kandahar, you know. My father Abdur Rahman lives there. When he retired from government service, they gave him this land in Herat, and he sent me here. But Kandahar is where the real Afghans come from. You should go there: they know how to really entertain a guest."

We asked him how he liked Herat. He related he used to go to the Lycée Jami (that had been Gul Ahmad's school) when he first arrived, but afterward he tired of it, and of going to the city.

"But doesn't it get dull for you out here in the village?"

"Not at all. There's so much to do: hunting, driving, riding." The *arbab's* eyes lit up as he recounted now the licit pastimes of the land. "Do you like to shoot? Tomorrow we can go hunting for partridge and for duck. If my jeep were fixed we could go to the hills and look for antelope." His jeep was in Herat being repaired.

Our host rose to leave, "Oh, about that medicine, for my friend..."

We found an antibiotic paste in our bag and gave it to Abdur Rashid. We could replace this in Herat. "Tell your friend to keep applying it not only after the infection looks better, but for about a week afterward, otherwise it's very dangerous." Half-listening to this warning, the *arbab* snatched up the tube and left us for the night.

The servant brought us a huge breakfast, just when the light filled the windows of the *mihman khana* and the birds of the village raised their song. We sat up and ate with great appetite: cream, bread, raisins, and jellies, the last imported from abroad. Our host reappeared, carrying three guns and a bag of shot.

"I hope you slept well," he said. "I looked in on your horses this morning. They're eating well, but they are awfully thin. How much did you pay for them?"

"Too much," I admitted ruefully.

"It's hard for foreigners to get a fair price on a horse. The people in the *ganj bazaar* are so dishonest. Next time you buy a horse, you come to Kandahar. There we'll outfit you properly.

Now you have to let your horses eat and eat until they get fat again. I'm giving them twice as much hay and barley as usual."

We said we were very grateful, making a sign with hand over chest.

Following the *arbab* we set off for the *shikargah*, hoping to get there when early morning still found the game sleepy and off-guard. The Afghans shot at ducks while they were still on the ground, because shells were expensive and game was required for eating. My friend and I each carried a shotgun and five shells, which Abdur Rashid told us to be sure to save after firing, since he refilled them. I hoped that none of my cases had been refilled, for the chance of their misfiring was high. Abdur Rashid carried a rifle—less effective as a hunting weapon, but more useful for self-defense: it was understood among us that we might run into trouble outside the walled enceinte of Abdur Rashid's village. We fanned ourselves out, stopped our conversation, and crept across the *dasht* towards the river.

At first I could see nothing moving. We passed a series of ravines which the wandering river had cut into the sandy earth. The sides of the ravines were steep, and the brush thick inside them. The earth was faintly copper-colored, the sky cloudy and grey this day, reflecting a nutty, woodlands hue from the earth. Since this was precisely the coloring of our supposed prey—ducks and partridges—I might have been looking right at a bird and not seen it. I looked into the brush as an uninitiate might look at a pointillistic painting and saw nothing but color and texture, no line and no form. The ravines yawned at the cloudy sky, slumbering, without life.

A shot went off. It was my friend, to whom Abdur Rashid had given the honor of the first shot. He missed, and a single partridge flew just over the edge of the grasses of the ravine. "Shoot," they called to me, but I was so surprised at the way the bird kept just at the tips of the grass, moving as on a string, without beating his wings, that I forgot to take the safety off; my trigger clicked uselessly.

More shots. The *arbab* had come upon some ducks. They went flapping into the air, unlike the wiser partridges, presenting a clear shot to the three huntsmen. My friend and Abdur Rashid fired almost simultaneously, bringing two birds out of the sky. I looked up at the ducks, which looked like soot flakes now, and pulled the trigger; another bird dropped down.

We retrieved the birds and stuffed them into our bags, then stalked on across the alluvial sands, by stagnant pools of water, near orchards where peasants, working on the land, stepped out to the edge of the plot and bowed to the *arbab*. They clasped his hand and laid their heads on his chest.

"Sometimes they complain to me about the wolves, and we go hunting for them as well, in the jeep," he remarked, as we left them.

Our few shots echoing in the narrow ravines had driven all the animals into hiding. Abdur Rashid took my friend's shotgun for a moment and fired at some birds in the brush, to no effect.

"How can you eat an animal that hasn't been ritually slaughtered?" asked my friend, suddenly considering that hunted game had not had their throats cut.

Abdur Rashid smiled, "We say they're still alive until we cut their throats, afterward; then we say *'Bismillah'*."

Permitted or forbidden, we ate the birds for our supper, steeped in butter and rice. The pellets which we extracted from our teeth Abdur Rashid collected on a little plate; he would re-load these, apparently. We chatted on with our host in his *mihman khana*. Unlike the *arbab* and people of Ashab-i-Kahf, Abdur Rashid and his villagers were of two races, and the differences between them probably prevented these village people from sitting easily in the landlord's house and visiting with his guests. Part of Abdur Rashid's eagerness to converse with us stemmed, surely, from his sense of isolation within the village. Again and again, he talked of Kandahar, where oranges and bananas grew year-round, and of Jalalabad, the old royal residence, and of the Sulaiman Mountains.

We could not discuss a "subject." Politics wearied him. Anthropology wearied him also. We talked about nomadic migrations in the south, and he said that his family owned so much land and so many sheep that they rented out the sheep to shepherds to bring on migration.

Archaeology he was curious about. We told him we were going to see the grave of the Saljuq prince. "What is this *bastan shinasi* (archaeology)—do you dig for treasure? They say men have dug in the ground and found gold and jewels, and that these things are in Kabul now."

If we had told him that we expected to find gold and treasure in Zandajan, we might have gotten him to come with us, but when he heard that our journey was merely to see a certain platform-grave and meet our friend the *sayyid*, he lost interest altogether. "You really rode out here just to look at graves?" he asked, and mused to himself. Would he have been in a better position to understand the ways of foreigners, he wondered, if he had finished the lycée in the city?

We slept well, breakfasted splendidly again, and received from Abdur Rashid good directions for reaching Zandajan. It was not far, but on the wrong side of the Hari River, Sayyid Shafaq's oversight. Our horses, gorged and rested for a day, were wild and eager for the road, until we led them across the icy, though shallow, fording of the river. Then, wet and sullen, they stumbled into Zandajan.

In the curious *samovar*, we found that Sayyid Shafaq had already returned to the city. I noted a few details of the place to prove to the *sayyid* later on that we had made it there: the *samavarchi's* name was Walid; a mechanical pump worked behind the place. This Walid pointed the way to the platform-grave, and we went to see it, though we much regretted not having the *sayyid* there to tell us about it. The raised slab of marble was surrounded by a railing of stone which had been carved into various letters and scripts of the Arabic alphabet. These were too broken to read. As I had understood from Sayyid Shafaq, this was the grave of a Saljuq prince, but whether the great Tughrul Shah or Muhammad Ghazi (both of them said to be buried thereabouts) I did not know. The platform nature of the grave was usual, being similar to the platform at Gazurgah, the most famous example.

Around the place were scattered ruins and graves. A town, Fushenj, had tumbled mainly into ruins here, and the graves and monuments of its past splendor dotted the plain. Most were of Saljuq provenance, belonging to the eleventh and twelfth centuries. By Timurid times, the towns of Baranabad and Ghuriyan had replaced Fushenj, just a few miles downstream. In both those towns were additional Timurid relics, including a cathedral mosque which was the uncompleted twin of the one in Ziyaratjah. The river's soil was rich here and bodied out a complex of towns, each with a market and samovar. Baranabad even boasted of local poets' graves, one Mirza Arshad and a Mirza Riza. The fact of these towns' past prominence did not mean, necessarily, that they were now contracted in size. I had no doubt that Abdur Rashid and his father, if they wanted, could build a respectable mosque in their smaller village or support a local poet with a gift of land. I had to keep reminding myself that the vast numbers of graves out in the *dasht*, beside these towns, reflected only the centuries of burial and not one-time overpopulation.

We rode back to the city the following day, having spent the night in the *samovar* at Zandajan. The *samavarchi*, knowing us to be the friends of a city *sayyid*, had been as deferential to us as could be. Going straight from the town across the river to the

Islam Qala road, we made the forty-kilometer ride in a comfortable space of time and returned to the city just after dark. We did not fear the dogs here: we pounded on the gates of the *sarai* until Hamid opened up for us. Still, we had to walk the horses off, tie down their blankets around them, and water them; all of this, on top of the long ride, was performed as if in sleep—numbly, automatically.

Sayyid Shafaq required no apologies for our standing him up, since accidents on the road were common. And in the *sarai* confidence in our ability to travel the roads and return grew accordingly; tenants now suggested that we ride to Obeh, in the mountains east of Herat, to Chist, still further east, to Karukh and to Qala-i-Nau. The possibilities swamped us.

But it was already the month of December. One more time we made a shorter ride outside the city, to track down the last of the really impressive monuments of Islamic architecture we could learn about. Ghalwar, just a morning's ride northwest of the city, had a jewel-like Timurid mosque, mostly in ruins, yet still serving as a *madrasa* for a few children and their ragged teachers. They found nothing ruinous about the place; they still slept on bedding in the crumbled *khanagahs* with corrugated roofing to keep the rain off.

Then a vast graveyard stretched across the rocky plain, just west of Ghalwar. For acre on acre heaped the marble slabs of tombs, broken alabaster, emptied coffins, stone dogs which vainly kept watch over their masters. The stone had been quarried from far away, from Obeh, where we would go, up in the mountains to the east. Now the local villagers used the graveyard as a quarry, foraging for lintel stones and thresholds.

A marble slab bearing an ornate scroll of *naskhi* script read:

> *This was the Prince of Heaven's Garden*
> *Who ventured in the World of Be-and-It-Is.*
> *After adorning the World of Shadows*
> *He returned to the Splendor of Eternity.*
> *The Year of his Death was—*

A chronogram based on the words, "Splendor of Eternity," worked out to 876 Anno Hegirae.

Another, less ornate, read:

> *You who read this will join me soon.*

In the fifteenth century Herat was bigger, the main bazaar

coming all the way out of Ziyaratjah. The graveyards were a good distance away from the populated suburbs. Nowadays, the contracted suburbs lie amid ruins of old city walls, while the modern graves press close to the city. There, as we rode back, we saw the tumbled masonry of palaces and garden homes, and the stones which had been gathered to mark the recent graves; no marble for these poorer believers.

A wisp of smoke rising from a shed among the graves caught our eye, and we stopped to detour there. Two young boys gathered brushwood which had been blown across the *dasht* by the west wind.

"*Salaam alaykum.* Do you live here?" I called out to them.

They gathered up their bundles and hid away in the shed. Tethering our horses together we dismounted and knocked at the door. No answer. Looking around us, we saw a small plot of vegetables growing in the shade of the shed, a bucket of night soil, a hoe; to one side, two spindly trees braved the wind blowing off the *dasht*, full of sand. That was all, except for the acres of graves.

I tapped the door with my whip and called in, "We're just travelers who've been visiting the *mazar* (holy burial place). Don't be afraid."

At this the door creaked open, and one of the little boys looked out at us through the slit. Then the door opened all the way. We entered, bending low to accommodate ourselves in the tiny room. One of the boys sat by the fire, whose smoke we had seen, and he fed sticks from his bundle into it. The brazier—a *ghee* tin sawed in half—blazed up whenever he put a stick into it, and then grew cold again. Beside the fire, warming his withered hands, sat an old man, in a simple smock, bareheaded. He looked up dully at us, as though our addition to his environment was of little importance. Besides us, and his two boys, there was only a felt mat, a blackened pot with a lid, some bundles of clothes.

We stared at one another for some time without finding anything to say. The old man looked at us, apparently thought something, reached into the pocket of his smock and produced a small brown bar of hashish. "No, thank you," I said very precisely. "You are very kind." The old man stuck the hashish back into his pocket and motioned to the child by the fire, pointing at the pot. The child took the pot up and left the shed. Silence reigned between us until he returned with water and tried to boil it on the weak flame of the fire. When the water was lukewarm he stuck in some bits of leaves, ginger, some other dried roots, brewing a sort of tea. The youngsters scoured the room for three cups, filled them, and offered the brew to us without ceremony. We nodded to the old man and took the cups to our lips. He drank from the other cup, the children being without.

The tea downed, I expected the silence to break. It did not. So I asked, "Who are you?" of the old man.

"He is *Malang*," said one of the boys, for the old man was unwilling to answer for himself.

My friend addressed himself to the boys, who were obviously eager to talk to strangers, once their shyness was overcome. "What does he do here?"

"He is a *malang*," repeated the other boy now. "That is what he does."

"What do you do then?" my friend asked the boys.

"We are *murids*. His apprentices."

"We serve him, do his bidding," the other volunteered.

The ascetic heard this without comment. He was satisfied to have his *murids* speak for him. Perhaps he had been vowed to silence; perhaps he had nothing to say. He had come out to this place to avoid the commerce of people. His business was meditation, aided by hashish. All he required was a plot of vegetables, a well, and these boys, to run into town for hashish if nothing else. The boys might have been slum children, nobody's children, who discovered the old man in this shed and attached themselves to him. I could not be sure if he had ever spoken to them. They seemed to know or to wonder little about the *malang*. They did not know the man's name. I asked them their names: Abdul Latif and Abdur Rahman.

Our presence hung heavy. The only purpose of our coming would be to give money to the old man, which we did. The boys gathered up our offering and stuck it under the felt mat.

"Tell him to pray for us," I said to the two children. The *malang* made a face, the closest he had come to reacting to anything all the while. His business was not to pray for people. He was simply *malang*, living beyond obligations. We had given freely; now we must go. The boys replied nothing to our inane request.

At the *sarai* I told about the *malang*. "Is he a holy person? Does anybody know?"

"A *malang*?" some said. "No, they're not holy people. That is, some of them are and some of them aren't. Just like anywhere else."

Others said they were simply addicted to hashish.

I told them about the man we had seen in the graveyard. They scratched their beards, "I didn't know about that one, he must be new . . ."

6.

THE JOURNEY

Eastward

Stabled back at the *sarai* of Amin Ullah we spent a few quiet days with our friends of Herat. We discussed the places we had been, the people we had met in the countryside, and I had to repress the urge to draw the unfavorable comparison between life in the *dasht* and in the city. I no longer felt at home in Herat as before; but, restless within the confines of city life, I was eager to return to the *dasht* again for good. Herat lost all its fascination for us; we saw only the same single paved street, the monotonous booths of the *bazaaris*, their sleepy expressions looking out on the street, the slaughtering of animals and the attendant flies. This was all much as we had first found it, only now we had learned we had no business here. Whether traveling through or settling down, we had no way to connect with the still life of the town. We would have to return to the *dasht*.

Our friends, Gul Ahmad, Daud, Sayyid Shafaq and the rest would have had us stay on indefinitely. They warned us against the *dashtis* to delay our going, saying that they were bandits, savages, unclean. We argued; they admitted reluctantly that in some ways the *dasht* bred a better race of men than the city. These friends were sensitive to the ambiguity in the city's attitude to the *dasht*, just as they had been sensitive to the prevailing attitude towards foreigners. They had been our friends; clearly, they were slower to judge strangers than their peers. Did we want to go into the *dasht*? They mused, perhaps we were justified; the ways of the city folk were as devious as the lanes of the bazaars. These *dashtis*, were they not straight and open, as the *dasht*? In the end, our contemporaries, Daud and Gul Ahmad, thought about the *dasht* and envied our going.

A long delay ensued over making repairs in our equipment. We cleaned and oiled all the leather to guard against more snapping of straps; we made extra feed bags of cloth and filled them up with barley and hay. The saddle blankets—felt *namads* stitched in cotton *kilims*—had badly tattered on our previous rides, chafing the horses' saddles, so we spent a long afternoon darning them. We even had to reshoe the horses, with the flimsy chips of tin the Afghans used for shoeing, little better than a glass slipper on the rocky roads of the *dasht*.

The delay gnawed at our patience, just when we should have been quick to go. By early December the cloudy days of winter had set in, portending snows and impassable countryside. Amin Ullah wanted to know whether we would be stabling horses for the winter or would sell them. If we sold them, he pointed out, the price would be greatly depressed, since fodder was becoming scarce and no one would be eager to keep unneeded horses through the winter. "If you want me to, I'll help you sell them. The droshky driver (his friend Abdul Hayy) might give you five thousand for them. They're going to be hard to sell now."

We decided to go to Obeh, 100 kilometers to the east of Herat, in the mountains below the source of the Hari River. There was a famous thermal spring in the town which provided our excuse to go. Beyond that we could retrace my friend's *mutar* trip to the Murghab River, to Abdus Sattar's Bandar and back to Maimana. These destinations passed through our consideration, as we made our thorough preparations to depart, without knowing exactly where or how long we would travel.

Amin noted these preparations carefully. "You will reach Obeh *inshallah* in two days. A day there, and then you will come back. Afterwards, there will be snow and sleet. Hay, barley, straw will go out of sight, and when it snows, the animals can't graze." But he went on, raising the edges of his half-smile, "If you don't come back from Obeh, if you go on farther, let me rent the stables for you."

"Don't tell anyone," we asked him, "just where we might travel." He placed his hand to his eye, meaning, may we pluck it out if he should fail us.

The *sarai* court stood empty; it grew late in the morning before we set out again. The litigant alone sat on the stoop, holding his middle, oblivious to our departure. The absence of formal leave-taking reassured us. We had never belonged here; no one would miss us. Out in front of his teahouse Hamid Ullah stepped out to say good-bye. Had his brother told him of our plans for a long journey?

"You'll be back soon. Go with grace," he said, knowing nothing of it.

"We entrust you to God," we replied.

I looked up at the sky, which was clear, intensely clear; the sun glaring in the northeast really seemed a far-away star to look at. There had been overcast days of late, and reports of rain. I wondered if we would get as far as Obeh before winter set in.

A sense of indecision slowed us down upon the road around the city. We circumvented the trafficked street of the New Town by riding past the *musalla*, over the stream Injil, and through the sleepy villas of the suburbs above the city. When we turned again on the main road, we had to pass a small guardstation which monitored traffic leaving and entering the city. As always, there was a chance we would be stopped. Wrapping our turban cloths around our faces tightly to disinterest the sentry guard in our foreignness, we kicked the horses into a fast trot. For a moment we were by the station, the soldier looking glumly at us and, seeing our saddle bags weighed down with grain and food, probably supposed we were petty merchants. We kept up the trot through a cool, forested park, which inaugurated the highroad, and we broke again into the open space where the *dasht* spread before us. The sense of holding back was gone. The infinity of the road was a challenge. The late morning sun sped us on, and the spirit of the horses, aware they would be in their element, encouraged us to press them.

Winter wheat had already sprouted in the fields around us, showing pale green; the Afghans called this the *safid*, the white crop. There would be no more fresh fodder until this ripened in the spring. We passed the fork where the road led off to Qala-i-Nau via Karukh. No one else was on the road at late morning, neither *mutar*s nor traffic on foot. The quiet of the growing wheat and the white winter sun muffled the sound of our horses' trotting. With no intrusions to fear, we unwrapped our masks and let the sun warm our faces. The air grew warm only late now.

The Oasis of Herat tapers off in the eastern valley of the Hari River on the slopes of the Safid Kuh, the White Mountains. In the last patch of the open *dasht*, one can see in the distance the Hari River cutting its course through the sandy alluvium, surrounded by flat soil. Where the river swells broad, it draws green reedbeds to its banks, and muddy black fields, and clusters of houses. Then, as the mountains close in on the banks, the river turns to shallows, pebbling the earth with white stones from far upstream or choking in stagnant pools. In places where the water runs swift, the slopes of the mountain hem in the land, providing only narrow strips for cultivation. A few cottages stand by the water's edge, overlooking their tiny plots. Still farther up, where the mountains temporarily recede from the riverside, the water moves sluggishly, through a pebbly and sandy waste, without habitations. Leaving the Oasis, one sees that now land and water are rarely to be found in complementary abundance.

We travel over the Center Road, an ancient route which follows the Hari River to its source in the Hindu Kush, crosses the watershed over to the Kabul River, and leads on to the capital. It is an unpaved route, interrupted by streambeds and sandpits, passable only in dry seasons and then only to animals and sturdy trucks. As the principle route to Kabul the Center Road has long been supplanted by the circuitous but metalled road through Kandahar, and even the graded road to the north. Yet it maintains a lingering importance. The Center Road abuts the tribal territories of the nomads; winter and spring they pass along it, their camps and their bazaars feeding off the trade which springs up close to the road. Chahcheran is the main nomad bazaars, high in the Hindu Kush midway between Herat and Kabul. Here the nomads summer their flocks while, from staging places like Obeh and Chist-i-Sharif, city goods are brought to the nomad markets, and the sheep, *rawghan-i-zard*, and other pastoral products are traded to the city. *Mutars* run infrequently now in the late season. Soon, there will be none at all, as the nomads have left the highlands of Chahcheran for lower, warmer pastures. Their *qislaqs* are in the valleys of Badghis and Turkistan.

If we were to find them, we would have to take the road into Badghis, to my friend's Darzak, by the Murghab.

The tooting of a mechanical pump sounded away by the river; a teahouse loomed into view, a single verandaed *utaq* with a corral for travelers' animals. We stopped here, a boy taking our horses into the corral, unsaddling them and turning them loose. I felt uncomfortable to leave the horses in the flimsy corral, but the assured manner of the boy told me this was the way of the *samovars* on the Center Road. We fed the horses from their feed bags of our precious store of barley, and went to our own lunch. Four men sat on the sunny veranda enjoying a meal of eggs and oil. These were locals, waiting for the *mutar* from Obeh to take them into the city. They asked us news of the bazaar, how much was grain, how much sugar; we surprised ourselves by knowing how to answer. News should never be given away for free, but we were too impatient to ask these men any questions of our own.

The *samovarchi* made up for that. A bustling, accommodating fellow, he served us eight eggs in a *sir* of oil, which in our hunger we soaked up with our bread. Then the *samovarchi* told us we were in Zandakhan, a place named for the *arbab* whose diesel could be heard tooting by the river. Because of this pump, the *arbab* had been able to irrigate his flat fields. Prospering, he built this *samovar* to accommodate travelers better than in his own *mihman khana*. Afghans preferred the *samovars* to the private guest houses, for the latter varied in comfort, and left them beholden to strangers. A teahouse on the road signified progress.

The man knew we were *meestars* and was curious about our journey. We were still close enough to the city, though, for him to pretend sophistication and to talk as though *meestars* on horseback were hereabouts an everyday occurrence. By telling him we were on our way to Obeh, the site of a famous thermal spring, we satisfied his curiosity. This Obeh was a local tourist attraction, a reasonable destination, and therefore a good cover. "*Meestar* will reach Zamanabad tonight, a good *samovar*, and on the morrow, *inshallah*," he advised, "you will come to Obeh."

He wanted to know our names, too, which I imprudently told him. My friend had wanted to leave no trail behind us, if possible. "Wali Ahmad and Muhammad Daud," said the *samovarchi* to himself, trying to remember them.

He charged us a heavy tariff for our lunch and for the hay fed to the horses, insisting that, beyond the great bazaar of the city, prices must be higher. I had thought they would go down. He explained, "In the city is abundance—grain, meat, milk. In the *dasht* it is otherwise—hunger, scarcity. *Meestars*, you are unadvised to travel by horseback. God prevent it, there are wolves, brigands, *rahzans*."

We ignored this gloomy prediction and the four wayfarers comforted us: "*Meestars*, with your horses you will fly to Obeh. It's not far from here at all. You'll get there tonight." This was not the last time news of time and distance would vary.

"The hot springs, the water of life, green trees, oh, Obeh is a wonderful place," said another, cheerily.

The post *mutar* from Obeh rumbled up in clouds of dust. The four travelers rose, shook off the dust and the crumbs of lunch, and piled into the van. A stroking of beards, "Go with grace," we said; mechanical delay followed. All the riders got down off the *mutar* and milled about, staring at us, staring at our timid horses in the hay-blown corral. The sound of the engine had terrified them. We tried to hurry, to saddle the horses and get out of these over-curious gazes, but the animals had a case of nerves, refusing the saddles and the reins. The Afghans watched the *meestars* chase the horses about in the corral. Too much time passed.

They fixed the *mutar*, finally, loaded themselves and set off for the city. We steadied the horses, saddled them, asking the *samovarchi* what lay between here and Zamanabad so we might recognize the way.

"There's nothing, *Meestars*, nothing. *Dasht, rigistan*, stone flats." We couldn't count on him for optimism.

The flats were depressing and worked on us a stubborn delaying. To tell what sort of time we were making was impossible, for the unrelieved stoniness of the river valley offered no landmarks to our progress. Two, three clayey paths, much traveled, led off the road to the sunburnt cliffs of the mountains, and the thought of other paths to follow slowed our going, as it always did.

The horses lost their enthusiasm; we could coax them into a faster pace only sporadically. When our attention slipped, they would edge back into a walk. At least we managed to overtake a herd of sheep, trudging along the road. The shepherd boys were bandying insults with one another and singing ribald songs about the sheep. For a while we rode behind, laughing at the scene, the strays slipping out of the boys' reach, bumping into one another and bleating. Our horses preferred to stay behind rather than wade into the flock, and we lost a lot of time before we cleared them, in a broad place in the road.

Towards sunset we approached a hamlet, hardly the big village possessed of a *samovar*. It could not be Zamanabad, so we passed it reluctantly. "Let's keep the horses moving," my friend said.

Coming upon a second village, much larger than the first, we stopped to consider it. The *samovarchi* had said there was nothing before Zamanabad, yet we had already seen one village. In the dusk, how far the *dasht* and stone flats continued was hard to tell. Reined towards the village, the horses resisted; though eager to stop for the night, they were still distrustful of strange stabling places. They felt as we did.

Innumerable lanes closed the village about, walls and channels, which confused us as to the size of the place. Many buildings—where high mud walls gave way to crumbling lots and dust-swept terraces—were in dismal ruins. We cursed the failing light and backtracked helplessly in the maze of lanes, a familiar circumstance. A passerby approached, frightened when he saw us, and we had to shout, heading off his flight, "Where's the *samovar* here?"

He looked back blankly, for there was no teahouse here. "*Arbab, arbab*," he repeated, pointing to an imposing *sarai* among the fallen mud walls, and then he darted off. So we would have to presume on the hospitality of the *mihman khana* again. Why had there been no teahouse here?

Half-darkness, a few whispered explanations, complaints, counterclaims, and the gate of the *sarai* of the *arbab* admitted us. A boy stood by silently as we unlaced the horses' saddles in the dark courtyard. He did not offer to help, but said, "Where are your feed bags?" These we gave him as he led the horses away, leaving us standing in the dark, holding the heavy saddles. Reappearing from the stables with a lamp, he brought us into the *mihman khana*, where we sat down, exhausted. The lamp he left in a wall niche, so we could see the low, wide room, unfurnished but for some straw mats and moldy blankets laid against the wall. We were glad to be by ourselves for a moment, on the verge of falling asleep.

The *arbab*, a young, bony-faced man, clean-shaven in the manner of the town, stepped into the guest room. He asked, abruptly, if we would like to eat. I was not hungry, just tired, but thought to go through the ritual of hospitality. With surprising curtness he told us, "All we have is *qurut*. Will you eat *qurut*?" He left us alone again. My friend said, "I'm not at all hungry." But to refuse now would be offensive to the host, who, we could see, was a man of little patience.

Two returned with dinner, the *arbab* and his brother. The younger man, a lighter, less dour semblance of the *arbab*, sat nearer the door, saying nothing. The *arbab* set the bowl of *qurut* with a pot of tea and half a loaf of bread before us and began to scrutinize our dining with an unpleasant stare. We expected the hosts to join us in dinner; in fact, we waited, but they only looked on. Rolling up the long sleeves of our *chapans* (it was too cold to remove them) we tucked the skirts under our knees and bent over the meal. The *qurut* had been cooked without oil and was thin and acrid, difficult to swallow. It was stone-cold, as was the tea. Nothing warmed us, not the meal, not a brazier—there was none— certainly not the stony stares of our hosts. We said the *qurut* was very tasty, but after a few mouthfuls sat back, wiping our hands with the bread—a sign that the meal had ended. The *arbab* made no attempt to smooth over the awkwardness of our diminished appetites. "We are poor people, you know; *qurut* is all we can afford." I had never heard a host flaunt his poverty like this.

His manner was not hostile or threatening, only sullen. The younger brother sat still by the door, but said nothing.

After dinner we talked. At once we learned that this place was not Zamanabad; it was called Tunyan. The *arbab* quietly jeered at the fact that we had made the mistake, but said, "You were well not to have gone on to Zamanabad by night. *Rahzans*, highway robbers, are about. One has to be careful." He seemed to be warning himself, as much as us. "You are safe here, but in other stopping places, who knows? They are a different sort of people; they do not know the laws of hospitality. We are poor, but at least we know what is a guest." The neighbors, I imagined, must be hard people indeed.

The younger brother produced a revolver from his waitcoat and asked us to admire it. We said it was very fine. The *arbab* asked us why we had no guns. "You should have guns. In the city is it forbidden? What tyranny." He obviously would have liked to sell us the pistol, or an old, mistrusted rifle. "They say it is wrong to shoot these people. They are only *gharibs* (strangers)! How can it be wrong?" By "these people" he meant travelers, such as we were, caught alone on the road, or else neighbors with whom he had a blood feud.

On the Road

Our hosts here, and afterward, lived apart and had little intercourse with travelers. They did not go to the city and had heard little about the *meestars*, so they did not recognize us as such. To them, our glasses, our accents, our features and color were foreign, but no more so than those of a traveler from Nuristan or Swat. Some imagined we were from the east, from Kabul, while others knew we were foreign, living somewhere beyond Iran or Hindustan, it mattering little where. A miss was as good as a mile. Outside the village, outside the *mihman khana*, the world was full of *gharibs*. Cyclops, alone in his cave, vaunts his insularity.

We were joined in the Tunyan *mihman khana* by a third, older man, grand possessor of a lengthy silver beard and a silken turban. He advanced towards us, smiling, "Welcome, welcome." From his pockets he spilled out raisins and pressed these into our hands. "Welcome, *Sahibs*, welcome." He seated himself easily, on his side, well in front of the two brothers; the *arbab* scowled behind him. "I am the father of the *arbab*," he said. "They didn't tell me guests had arrived. May you not be wearied."

"May you live long," we replied, feeling considerably relieved by the old man's company. He lounged in front of us like a friendly lion, showing off his easygoing geniality.

"Have you been given to eat? Are you comfortable? It's cold in here." He sent the younger brother packing for a brazier. Cowed, the *arbab* looked on glumly.

"May you not be wearied," we said, thankfully.

Now custom allowed the old man to ask us our way and our business. He registered each explanation intently, computing an impression; where we were going and what we wanted, whether there were profit in it for him or not. It seemed not.

"Do you think the road is dangerous?" I asked.

"Dangerous? Dangerous? Ay, ay, there was a time when there were raiders in these parts. They used to be bold, coming by night. They would sneak down on their enemies, set fire to their houses, bugger their women. They had good guns in those days, and plenty of ammunition. But now," he exchanged a helpless look with his son, "the government has its telephones and its soldiers everywhere. They come and take such a one and put him in jail until he grows old." He looked sad at these thoughts.

"Before," I asked him timidly, "didn't this village used to be bigger?"

"Before," said the old man evenly, "we were rich, and not poor. We had water for irrigation, all we needed. Our fields stretched from here to the river. But now Zaman Khan has his pump, and all the water. We have to buy water from him . . ."

"But he's downriver from you, isn't he?" my friend interrupted.

"That's Zanda Khan. He has a pump too, for his well. But Zaman Khan's pump is on the river. Zaman Khan is the *arbab* of Zamanabad."

"They were on their way to Zamanabad tonight," said the *arbab* accusingly.

"Oh, well, it is a rich place. There's a big *samovar*." The father tried to gloss over the *arbab's* tactlessness. "Before, there was no village above here, because the river flowed too narrowly and the water was scarce, above hereabouts. But the *khan* set up his pump. I went to the *shahrwali* to complain, but it didn't do any good. They're all Pathans, you know." He said this as though it were a great joke. The *arbabs* were Tajiks, long upon the land, while Zaman Khan was himself a nomad, recently settled.

"They shouldn't be asking so many questions," said the *arbab*, *sotto voce*, to his father. The old man turned aside, pained at the lack of hospitality his son had displayed, and whispered, "Hush, they are our guests."

Now a brazier blazed for us. The old man went on to talk about guests he had entertained in the more prosperous times. We could see the *mihman khana* was wide and at one time grand. He had hosted the *uluswal*, the district governor, and the *kumandan* of Obeh, and they had been his friends. That had been the chief advantage of running a *mihman khana*, making the important contacts which now, in the village's ruinous state the young *arbab* could not do.

"We had *hakims*, too, in days past." He repeated, *"Hakims,"* but we didn't take the hint, so he said straight out, "Have you any medicine?"

We had to see the patient if medicine were required, we told them, causing a commotion, an argument between the father and the son. Finally, the *arbab* produced a young mother with an infant in her arms.

"He's this way," explained the old man. "He won't eat. He screams all the time. It's been five days, maybe more."

The mother, hair streaming over her face, looked darkly at us before handing over the infant. The moment we touched him, he screamed. He screamed at every disturbance, his face going red. The rest of his skin stayed bright orange. Examining the infant just in the manner of the *hakim* in Maimana, to reassure the family, we saw it had no fever, no injuries, no dilation of the pupils. My friend pointed out that his teeth had rotted away; tooth decay from malnutrition, he guessed, which also explained the constant screaming.

The family listened to our strange consultation in English, feeling half-amused, half-revolted by the sound of it. They did not approve our diagnosis. "No, no, it's a fever," insisted the old man. "See, he's turned red."

We told them to bring the baby into town, to a *duktur* we knew there, and to buy him fresh fruit from the bazaar and to feed him milk.

They pleaded poverty. "Give us a *qurs* (pill), *Sahibs*, then all will be well,'" said the old man, mildly. We would not, adamant that a *qurs* would not cure malnutrition. So they left us, the young mother indifferently, who had expected nothing to come of it, the brothers, sneering at our imagined meanness, and finally the father, saddened, as though we had betrayed a trust. He still managed to wish us a good night. We slept in the *luhats* which had been stored in the corner; these were far too thin, so we kept all our clothes on. Tired, we slept heavily.

The old man recovered some of his philosophy in the morning; maybe he had decided we were right about the child. He fed us breakfast, bread and more raisins, saddled our horses for us and saw us to the edge of the village. The horses were jittery, unmanageable. "What's wrong with the horses?" he asked, giving the *ablaq* a great kick to bring her up. We said good-bye, the grandeur of the old man's entrance being repeated in farewell.

But I sensed he was as relieved to be rid of us as we were relieved to go.

On the road my friend could scarcely keep the *ablaq* under control; she insisted on drinking at every standing channel of water. Could it be that they had not been watered last night? Checking, we found the feed bags little consumed: a thirsty horse could not eat very much. Furious at our hosts, we went down to the riverside, where water flowed shallow and rapid, letting the horses drink. Then we fed them, losing thereby a good hour.

To learn that some *mihman khanas* had neither cooking oil nor water to squander on strange guests was both a sobering and useful lesson. We had to learn that, for some of the people we would meet, the laws of hospitality were hard: they would not give but a bowl of *qurut*. It was well to know, too, that there were some, isolated in their small villages, who felt no closer kinship to us than to Adam, who would as soon pillage us as put a roof over our heads. It required a fine sense of decorum and tact to make this journey through a poor land, warding off our hosts' self-interest—the result of their poverty. We would stop in many places, and we always received a cup of tea, something they could not begrudge their blood enemy. *Mihman*, the Persian word for "guest," originally meant "enemy." The ambiguity was an ancient one.

During our brief stopover in Zamanabad I complained to the *samovarchi* of our reception in Tunyan. Not watering the horses, I fretted, might have ruined them. Zamanabad was a big, well-watered village with a new, wooden-pillared *samovar* owned by an expansive, black-bearded Afghan. "Oh, those people downstream are but *gharibs*," the man averred, "but here we are a different sort of human being. We know how to treat a guest." Running down one's neighbors sounded like a familiar litany.

Zaman Khan was not here, but off in the city, where he had gone by *mutar* yesterday. Perhaps he was one of those riders who stared at us in Zandakhan. "If he had been here," said the *samovarchi*, "he would have entertained you himself, important strangers like you (the glasses, again)." Now the question of whether the men of Zamanabad were better than those of Tunyan would remain moot.

In any case we wanted to hurry on to Obeh. The *samovarchi* thought we would make it easily, while another fellow advised the road was longer than that. We went on our way, wondering how it was that all these opinions of one road should coexist—because everyone's horse had a different pace, probably.

On the road my friend said to me impatiently, "You shouldn't have complained to them about Tunyan. What if it gets back to the *arbab*? What if we have to return by the same road?" Keeping one's own counsel was my friend's strongest Afghan strain.

The road led on, the walls of the Safid Kuh rising on our left, the river valley narrowing and gathering into a chasm. The sun began to set, slowly here in the mountains, with the shadows tumbling down the hills like silent avalanches. The level ground reflected the light, with a glow that seemed like phosphorous from afar, only the southerly peaks of the mountains showed direct sunlight, red and orange on red rock. The air grew cold, and steam from our horses' breath showed white in the last rays of sun.

The interval between the gradual sunset and the rising of the moon and stars shrouded us in profound darkness. I had often heard it said, "There was not a light to be seen," but until now had never known what it was like, to be in the world, surrounded by rocks, clouds, mountains, all invisible. I could not even see the road, and my *kabud*, feeling the uncertainty in her reins, kept halting. I gave her a kick, steering to the left of the noise I knew to be the Hari River, whose course still ran beside the road. Sound was the principle sensation, and we began to notice that, however dark the world was, it was still full of noises. I heard brambles rustling, pebbles ricocheting off the horses' hooves, the swish of their tails batting imaginary flies. I could also hear wolves, at some distance. We began to trade wolf stories, in a mordant humor.

"I've never heard of wolves attacking people on the road," said my friend, recalling his days in Northern Alaska.

"I've never heard of such a thing either, but then I've never heard of anyone riding horses in pitch-black."

"When it's pitch-black, though, the wolves' night vision is no better than ours," he comforted.

Then maybe they were overhearing us, for the wolf calls were very loud now, very close at hand. "Look," my friend said, "you ride on my left and hold your whip on the outside, and I'll hold my whip on my outside. If the wolves come we can fight them off from both sides." Our whips were heavy staves, topped with a woven fiber like rattan. We held the ends and brandished the club-like handles. This formation was reassuring, except that on the narrow road we kept stumbling into one another on our horses, bruising our inside legs. After many minutes of this painful riding, the wolf calls fell away. We resumed our ride in line.

I had begun to imagine forms in the darkness when one of the shapes I picked out seemed to get distinctly larger, rather than flee continually toward the horizon, as phantoms do. At point-blank range, with a little light coming up, we stumbled on a large, well-built *rabat*, a fortified caravansary, now in ruins. I listened for the owls which were said to inhabit these deserted places (calling in Persian, *Ku? ku?* Where? where?), but the birds, if they were there, maintained their silence. An arch of brick silhouetted against the dim night sky, and a fallen dome—these were all our senses had to fix upon at that moment. Dreams, I thought, might be the memory of a nocturnal existence, when mankind prowled by night. Everything seemed dreamlike in this unlit world.

The horses, mistaking the ruin for our stopping place, refused for a long time to be led off. My friend, with a memory for poetry, recited the Persian:

The World, Brother, remains to none,
So give your heart to the World-Creator;
Nor rely on the Realm of the Senses,
Which has killed many a semblant of you.

His display of erudition cheered me. For the rest, this ruined place, the dark night, the cold, the wandering on the road, all combined to sap my will: I was on the point of resigning myself to dismounting here in the wind-wall of the *rabat*. "But if there's a ruin here," I mused aloud, "there's probably a village nearby." Inhabited sites tended to swing on axes, a new structure being built near the ruins, and often out of the bricks of the older one. That encouraged me.

The sky grew lighter. Over the Safid Kuh, the dim stars faded. A white glow appeared on the mountain top, a face, a saucer, a bowl of milk. It rose quickly to full height, a great white disk of embodied radiance. All the stars faded from view, the moon rose over them and neared its apex.

"That's the moon, by God," said my friend amazed at the closeness and brightness of it. We had let the horses stop so we could stare at the climbing body. "We can make good time now with that moonlight to ride by." He took his whip into the air again to get the tired horse under him to move. My shoulder was sore from using it.

The horses felt no better for the whips. They did not like night-roving, starting at imaginary objects on the road in front of us that looked like good moonlight to us.

A grove of trees showed ahead, silver pistachios. As we drew near we saw a man, a shepherd, sitting against the trees watching his flock. He held a rifle at the ready, eyeing us silently as we rode by. The moon glowing on the sleeping sheep, the young shepherd wrapped in a wool shawl against the cold might have been a pretty scene, in other circumstances. We said nothing to one another until we were out of the shepherd's sight.

"How far do you think it is to Obeh?" I asked. The road seemed elastic; by some opinions we should already have passed Obeh, riding now for the fourteenth hour on the road.

"About another hour." The moon at least would hold out, even if I were sure I would not. In the dimness ahead of us we made out more buildings, not a ruin but a village, a substantial one. "It couldn't be Obeh," said my friend.

I knew he was right. But afraid of the coming dark, unwilling to discipline my tired horse, I just wouldn't go on. Like those stubborn donkeys that sit down under the blows of their drivers, I stopped in the road.

"You won't be able to stop in that village at midnight," said my friend, angry, trying to keep his *ablaq* on the road though she was following the *kabud* and me.

I thought I preferred the dangers of the strange village to those of a moonlit road. Now, I was not sure. Caught in the maze of the streets, hearing dogs howl at our approach, we poked about in the patches of moonlight, the horses getting increasingly distraught at our indecision. I rode up to the gate of a *sarai* and knocked on it with my whip. No answer. I knocked again, louder, and a voice called back, bidding us depart. I knocked still lounder, calling—like a fool—above the whip, "Is this the vaunted hospitality . . ." After sunset, we were *gharibs*. The howl of the dogs—the fierce mastiffs who did battle with wolves—grew furious. I heard the gate creaking, the gate which now served as much to protect us from the dogs as the *sarai* from our intrusion. The noise of the unleased animals was ear-shattering. I whipped the *kabud*: needing no encouragement, she rode down the narrow lane, plunging right into my friend, whose horse bolted, galloping as I had never seen her do, and disappeared. When I rode under control again, I was alone in the ghostly lanes, surrounded by the howling of the dogs.

I let the *kabud* plod down one lane, then another, hardly guiding her, hoping that she would search out my friend better than I could do by design. I did not know whether he stayed in the village, or whether he had run back to the highway, or even whether he had managed to stay in his saddle. The moon ducked into clouds; everything which could have gone wrong had done so.

Traveling through the countryside was not meant to be easy. Not for nothing did the Afghans prefer the uncomfortable certainty of the *mutars* to the horse ride. Advice on the road had been hard to get, there was no way telling one's time of pace, winter and the early nightfalls contracted the day's ride to the narrow limit, and I had crossed it. When all of this was behind me, later, I asked the Afghans what they would have done, stranded on the road, at night, alone. "Yes, yes, it's very trying," they would admit. "The dark night and the howling wolves. And didn't the dogs cause you a bad moment?"

"Yes, but what would you do?" I pressed.

"Do? There's nothing to do. *Tawakkul billah*, trust in God." They had no sense of the hypothetical.

As I debated whether or not to return to the highroad and go on to Obeh, I made out a light at the end of the lane, then two distinct lights, then three, and three men, each carrying a spirit lamp, materializing out of the penumbra. I accosted them, trying to startle them as little as possible, "*Salaam alaykum*, may you not be tired!"

They started and looked at me, the lone horseman, blocking their progress down the street, and were dumbstruck.

"*Ay Sahiba!* I'm looking for the house of the *arbab*."

The looks they exchanged spoke vividly of fear and mistrust. Stage whispers drifted up to me: *What could this brigand be about, poking in the village in the dead of night? What does he want with the arbab? It could be but a bad business.*

"Will you show me the way?" I sounded impatient, in spite of myself. They were more scared of me than I of them, which which was only a small consolation.

"I don't know about you, Brothers, but I'm not going to trouble Abdul Baqi Khan," a paunchy, shallow-bearded fellow opined.

"We can't let him wander in the village all night, let Abdul Baqi Khan worry about it," put in a second fellow.

"Then you take him," said the paunch, trembling in the cold. "My wife expects me home."

The restless *kabud* began to pivot about, and even to rear. I couldn't dismount for fear of her bolting. The right note, the decorum, the tact, I had better strike now. "*Ey Musalmana*. Is this any way to treat a traveler? If you leave me here, I'll fall victim on the road. Is this *musalmani*?"

The one who had been silent to this point said grandly, "He is a *Musalman*. Are we not bounden to help him?"

"May God speed your reward," I said to encourage him, blushing to have resorted to shaming them, blushing to have misled them into calling me a Muslim, even though *musalmani* meant no more than "humanity." But I had hit the right note with this.

The three of them had just returned from supererogatory prayers at the village mosque; the words of prayer were fresh on their lips, and now a stranger appealed to their *musalmani*.

They agreed to conduct me to the house of the *arbab* Abdul Baqi (Slave of the Eternal), but first we had to detour past the man's house so he could tell his wife he was off to the *khan's*. She heard him from the upstairs window, replying to his explanations with a torrent of high-pitched abuse, the drift of which was, "God knows where you find these wretches! Strangers in the village and you go and leave your women unprotected. May God smite you!" Women did not participate in the ritual of hospitality, so she felt no compunction about leaving me to the dogs. We went on to the *arbab's*.

Abdul Baqi's was a large compound, with a *mihman khana* and a separate stable for his visitors. Anyway, this village had a mosque, suggesting a grand landlord indeed. In the courtyard, where bright lamps twinkled from the doorposts, a trio of young boys stood waiting for us. One of them helped me down from the saddle, another loosened the girth and removed the bit of the *kabud*.

"The saddle's been on a long time, so don't take it right off," I said to one of the boys.

He looked up, smiling, "Of course not."

The smallest boy gathered my gear and led me into the *mihman khana*, followed by my three escorts.

Putting off our shoes and ducking, we stepped into the low-lying room. The guest chamber was long and wide, grand, like the one in Tunyan, but full of lights and people. A huge fire blazed in the middle of the room, smoke billowing from the brazier, and in the glow of fire I saw the many guests gathered in a circle, backs against the wall, lolling beside their teacups, bedding down for the night in *luhats*, or else talking in desultory half-whispers. Baggage lay in heaps along the wall, as though an entire caravan had stopped for the night.

This was the sort of *khan* Abdul Baqi was. The three villagers drew near, whispered something to him under the crackle of the fire. He listened, with a sharp, interested face, understood, and made a series of commands, moving about on the floor with the litheness of a wrestler, flashing a pair of coal-black eyes. The villagers retreated out the door. The *khan* gestured with his eyes that I should take a place on the floor. I sat down in a humble spot and he was satisfied to leave me where I was. Following on his orders, a servant brought tea, and asked me what I would have for supper. The *khan* sat down again with his greybeards, who occupied the place on honor in the room, and engaged himself again in what seemed a pressing business.

The rest of the room was little troubled by my arrival. The anonymity was a blessing now; I sat in the gratifying indifference of the crowd, adjusting my eyes to the light of the fire and absorbing its warmth. I had my tea, sitting cross-legged with my skirts tucked under me, the picture of innocuous repose. I drank slowly, prolonging the period before the *khan* might demand my busines and my destination. I worried about my friend: *Can I ask them to look for him? Is he already in Obeh?* It was difficult to decide, almost hard to remember that I was lost, alone, two days on the road. These thoughts faded dully away. The blazing fire, the hot tea, the grey retinue of Abdul Baqi Khan and their murmured consultation made me forget my woes. Exhaustion had a way of muting cares. The fire blazed hypnotically before my eyes—I was sweating at it now. Fueled with green tumbleweeds of the *dasht*, it crackled far louder than my neighbor's conversations. I drew images from the day's journey around me like a cocoon; they ceased to trouble me personally; they seemed to have been the doings of some other person.

The *khan* had his eye on the stranger arrived after midnight. Seeing that I had had my tea he ordered my supper brought. I dined, trying to show as much gravity and grace as possible, in the best manners of the Afghans. When I finished supper, I reminded myself, I should try to keep my counsel, not giving in to the temptation to voice my predicament. I managed to finish eating without attracting any attention to myself, on account of my manners, which was well.

Now the *khan* began to question me, asking me where I was from, what my destination would be, how I had gotten lost among the roads. I told him I was set on by dogs, which caused some chuckles in the assembly of greybeards, for the Afghans found the idea of being attacked by those animals laughable, no matter how fatal their attack. "So the dogs were very trying, were they," the *khan* smiled. His watchdogs were good; he was pleased.

"Are there Muslims in your country?" he said suddenly, putting me off my guard. He must have guessed, from something, that I was no Afghan. I hadn't wanted to get into the long explanations.

"Yes, there are," I said, saying no more than the truth.

"And mosques? And *mullas?*" The *khan* was in the process

of retaining a *mulla* for his new mosque, one important *arbabal* duty. On this the greybeards and he had been long consulting. "Can you read the prayers?"

"No." There was no point in lying about it, since I might be asked to perform them.

"Neither can we. That is why we need a *mulla*. We sent to Herat for a new one. We sent all these mule men into the city to fetch him and his effects. Fifteen mules! But he changed his mind. He says he doesn't want to come." I had just avoided being drafted as the village *mulla*.

One of the greybeards did not like my looks. "Are there mostly Shi'ites or Sunnites in your kingdom?" I told him the truth, which he doubted.

"There are many Shi'ites in this place," said the *khan*, playing the role of the host, "and we are always fighting with them. They say, too, that in Iran the Shi'ites are innumerable, an accursed place."

When I asked Abdul Baqi Khan who were the Shi'ites in this locale, he answered me this way: "Here there is every nation, *Misihis, Nasara, Yahuda, Kalimis, Aliparastis, Shi'ah*," naming every confessional name he could think of, as if to say, "You see, we are not so backwater, here, as not to know about the nations of the world."

The names of all these exotic tribes was like a sour taste in their mouths. The same doubting greybeard pressed me about my native place. If there were unbelievers there, what sort of excesses did they practice? Bed their close relations, drink blood, eat animals without the *zabh*? I tried to assure him that the customs of people did not differ as wildly as all that, but he remained unconvinced.

Another greybeard asked me the price of bread, of a gun, of a good horse in my country. I told him accurately, and a chorus of whistled sighs breezed through the men.

"Then you have come to trade? To buy things here and return to your home country? You will be a rich man. A good horse here costs only ten thousand *rupees*, and in your country, two *lakhs*!"

"Yes, *Sahib*, except that the way is long. Longer even than Iran, longer than Hindustan."

"If you did not come here to trade, what then?" asked the sour greybeard pointedly.

"Just to travel, to learn the ways of these places."

"Aha," said the *khan*, rising on his haunches vigorously. "Is that what you want? Well, I'll tell you what sort of men we are in this place. We have fields, and water, and irrigation. And we plant, we reap, and we have all we want. We're not poor, thank God, and there's enough for each. That is how we live in this place. Now tell me, how is it in your place?"

"Much the same."

"There, you see. That's all there is to it." The *khan* and I had agreed, we were each human, though the one of his greybeards still suspected me. If I asked no more questions, I hoped, neither would he. The assembly fell silent, and the greybeards rose to go. Most of the mule men had long gone to sleep.

The *khan* had one more question. "That one," he pointed to a sleeping figure on the floor, "is he a countryman of yours?"

I looked at the figure wrapped in a red-brown *barak*, pillowed on the white turban cloth. It was my friend, holding his glases in one hand, his saddle bags beneath him. I nodded.

The *khan* graciously spared me having to make more explanations, but withdrew smiling. In the morning when we set off together he did not wonder at all, though he must have figured we had traveled together on the night before. When we thanked him for his hosting and protection he shrugged his shoulders and smiled, "We have done nothing, forgive me, forgive me. If we had known you were coming we would have prepared a feast."

The third day setting out from Herat, the sky was overcast, making us forget our differences of last night: we had enough to worry about. All morning long it was cold, while clouds, like dragons, curled down the mountainside toward us. The road turned steep, rising and falling over big rocks, or pebbling across dry stream beds. Washouts, where floods had crossed the track, spread out in the sand like veins in the earth. We had the cold comfort of seeing another Obeh post vehicle disabled in one of these washouts, the driver and his apprentice struggling to change a tire. This time the stranded passengers looked enviously at us.

Through the grey fog, a graveyard materializes, also grey, with marble stones, headstones like fossilized turbans, inclining left and right in the wind—waves of the sand. The ground is littered with stone and slate, tessellated scrolls and graven arabesques, all ghostly grey, lying yard on yard. Bigger than any village we have passed is this necropolis. The stone is the famous Obeh marble. It is as though the world grew tired of hauling it from these mountains, instead carting their dead to be buried by the quarry.

The Storm

A dusty *maydan* (square), fronting a meteorological station, guardhouse, and *wali's* office, all looking like Antarctic Quonset huts in the bleak landscape, formed the official town. A scattering of trees, unstrung wicker *takhts*, a single street with booths of vendors on either side, a stucco school house, two small *sarais* with *samovars* and no stables but corrals completed the bazaar. Winding behind this street, a few dusty lanes of houses, mired in mud, looked far older than the bazaar. Beyond these spread a great plain of mud. South, by the Hari River, water ran by bramblers, poplars, and willows, whose branches dipped in the stream. North, layered with mud flats—*dasht*, mountains, and snow peaks. Such was Obeh.

If he were surprised that two foreigners should arrive on horseback and ask for a room, the *saraidar* did not let on. A burly, heavily-bearded man with a suggestion of the sinister, he assumed a forced ease in talking to us, letting us sit quietly and keeping a rein on his curiosity until after our supper. The inevitable questions about our route, our stopping places, and news of our hosts followed.

"Last night, then, you were in Zamanabad?"

"No, last night we were at Abdul Baqi Khan's."

"Abdul Baqi Khan." He registered the information. *Saraidars* along the road thrived on news of the way; it was not merely a question of vicarious excitement. "And what was he like? What did he give you for supper?"

"Oh, he was a *kalan*, a great man. We had eggs."

"Eggs." This also registered, fitting into what he already knew of Abdul Baqi Khan's reputation and riches. Eggs, by the way, short of slaughtering an animal, were as good a dish a traveler, in this season, could hope to have. The *saraidar* extracted the whole tale of our three days and satisfied himself that the information we gave was accurate. Above all, he asked to know the price of barley in each of the *samavars* we stopped at. With winter coming on, and shortages ahead, he had to be sure about the state of the market.

The *saraidar's* boy bandied with us, in the manner of city folk, even addressing us with the hateful *"meestar."* I told him pointedly that was no way to respect his elders. Puzzled, he had no idea that *"meestar"* was derogatory, having seen too few foreigners to have formed a bad opinion of them. If anything he enjoyed being with foreigners, since they were a fixture (he had heard) of his native town Herat and through us he imagined himself home again. He pressed us for the details of the *Id* celebration, the gathering in the cathedral mosque, the eating of sweets in the parties afterward.

The *bazaaris* of Obeh, I learned, had come up from Herat.

Commercial centers spread tentacles into the countryside, from major entrepôts such as Obeh to small samovars in Zandakhan and Zamanabad. In the north, Maimana, Qaisar, and Chikchakto made up such a chain. One could consider the citizens of one city as forming a single tribe. The *bazaaris* were a closed caste, among but not part of the rural landscape. Some towns were only temporary extensions of the *bazaari* colonies. Chahcheran, for instance, was now almost a ghost town, while in the summer merchants from Obeh and even Herat would go up to trade there. In the winter Obeh itself was quiet; the *sarais* empty, the warehouses behind the bazaar shuttered up.

Nightfall. The bazaar unpeopled, without entertainment, the teahouse samovars without fuel, Obeh submitted to night and its coldness. We went out to check the horses—they shivered even under their *namads*—and did our best to adjust the saddle cloths over them. The *namad* stank the sweet, warm smell of horses. To guard against theft from the open corral we hobbled the horses with our heavy *zulanas*. The moon had risen high and full again with a corona bright and sharply defined as a saint's halo. My friend said it was ice crystals. I had never seen such a thing before.

The *saraidar* said, "It means rain tomorrow."

Drizzling waked us, knocking on the flat roof of the *sarai*, seeping cold through the plaster of our *utaq*. Outside, puddles welled in the street; the smell of wet mud wafted through the teahouse. Pouring tea, the boy complained that the hay in the horses' feed troughs had gotten soaked. My friend ran out to look at them. He came back, dripping water, with a dismal report. "They're soaked to the skin, the *namads* were full of water, they aren't eating."

It was cold and we got soaked ourselves, but we went out to adjust the shreds of the *namads*, feeding the horses from our hands, while water poured down their faces. Nothing could match the look of despair on the horses' faces. The *saraidar* came out, too, getting himself wet without accomplishing anything. "Don't worry, don't worry, the rain won't last long," he said lamely.

The rain continued, echoing in the *sarai* as though we were in a seaside place, with a dull roar. I read and I wrote, trying to engage the attention of the *saraidar* with "subjects," but this was not the way he was used to thinking. For him language was an entity unconstrained to depict the world accurately. The connection between two words, puns, rhymes, these might be more important to pursue than a particular thought. Their way of speaking was more musical, more poetic than ours, but made the bare accumulation of information more difficult.

"Chist-i-Sharif, Chist-i-Sharif and Obeh, are like this you see, Chist-i-Sharif is a town, like so, big, but not as big as some. Chahcheran, in the summer, the bazaar is bigger, but in the winter, it's nothing at all. Too cold. This rain is snow on the mountains. If you were to go to Chist-i-Sharif, to the shrine of the holy saint, he was a great man, a Sufi, a *pir*. You have read about him in your books, haven't you?"

Instead of getting a description of Chist-i-Sharif I wound up explaining what I know of Abu Sa'id Abi Khayr. The *saraidar* would interrupt me from time to time saying, "*Sahih, sahih,* you've got it right, you've got it right," as though I were telling him nothing new, as though I were giving nothing away. When one showed surprise, one admitted a debt of information, and the need to respond in kind. For men of the road, the *samovarchis* and *saraidars*, facts were a commodity, traded as any other.

Toward afternoon the rain stopped. The sun showed through and waxed warm. The half misty sky absorbed the dim sunlight, red light on the mud walls of the town, on the rivers of mud in the streets, in the standing pools. Wading in the mud, we freed the horses from their bloated blankets, rubbed their backs with dry cloth, fed them dry hay. Then the sun warmed them. The *namads* we wrung out, then we bore them to the bazaar and found a tailor to darn them. He wielded a comically thick needle and a thread that looked like a rope, making more holes in the *namads* than the riding and rain had done. The drying sun sank low, but we stretched the *namads* out on the domed roof of the *sarai* to dry. From the roof the city looked like the horses' wet feed troughs, pooling, hay-strewn.

In the bazaar of Obeh, with effort, one recaptured the sense of the grand bazaar in the city. Full of surprises, odds and ends which made for a reassuring sense of clutter, the bazaar sold *qalyans*, china teapots, bright fabrics, candies, plastic shoes, tattered magazines faded by the sun, second-hand clothes. Everything cost more than in Herat, since here in the *dasht* one had to pay for the privilege of objects, which distinguished the life of the towns, setting them off from the countryside. Townsfolk had rings, pens, belts, radios, just on their person, which gave them a sense of artificial environment; to envy objects, to acquire them, shaped the subtler character of these people. The *dashtis* had no objects, desired little, plotted to get little; their environment, like their moral landscape, was simple. Not that they didn't enjoy the superfluous: they had the human need for objects. They were fascinated by things we would gift them with—cheap knives, Bic pens, a compass; they would straightway break them: this fascinated them no less. The emptiness of their material lives was their necessity, not, by any opinion, a virtue. That nothing remained, that all would be thrown out in the end, struck them as sad. But they had no interest in anything old. The country houses were absolutely clear of clutter. It sold as junk to the *antik* bazaars of Herat, for tourists to be sentimental over. A small bazaar like the one of Obeh resupplied the few objects of these places, the palm-sized cups, the tinted photographs of the Ka'ba of Mecca, pressure cookers, chintz shawls. I found the bazaar charming; one had to be denied objects to appreciate them.

We bought grain, sugar, loaves of bread, raisins,, and *qurut*. Everything was expensive, and of poorer quality than in the city. The hard sugarsticks were coated with dirt; we rinsed them in tea before eating them. I reserved a few, mindful that Christmas was soon. Milk, fruit, and fuel were close to being exhausted in Obeh, which put us in a thoughtful mood about what we might expect beyond the town. We brought hunting cartridges as gifts, the only costly merchandise which would not spoil, and which was convenient to carry. We knew how pleased any hosts would be to receive something to kill things with.

The young sweetseller from whom we bought the confections turned out to be an Iranian. He identified our accents, ever so slightly, and claimed us as countrymen. He was the grandson of an Iranian, from Shiraz, who had migrated first to Mashhad and then fled to Herat, to avoid the military service instituted by Riza Shah. Of course, he had never been in Iran or he would not have taken us for Iranians. Many people had fled to Afghanistan in this century to escape the powers of the state as they increased in neighboring Iran, the USSR and India. Arabs of Bukhara left Russian taxation for the swamps of Qonduz, Pashtuns from Peshawar moved north to escape British rule. And here was an Iranian whose family had left because of Riza's reforms. Did he want to go back? "Yes, after my service, I'll go there." The grandson had to serve in an army twice as brutal and ill fed as he would have if he had been raised on his ancestral soil.

With his dark olive skin and delicate features, the youth was an exotic physiognomy in this place; behind his musty trays of confection he seemed like a lonely zoo specimen, deprived of space. With nostalgia, cloaked by a sad *Shirazi* smile, he questioned us about his country which he had never seen. Tall buildings, straight gardens, water rippling through the *juibars* all the length of the city, these were harbingers of Iran, the finest kingdom of the world. We left him alone to these images; he said he would come to see us later.

While in Herat I had seen an American black man, a

tourist, in the bazaars near the cathedral mosque. The rarity of these features had seemed incredibly beautiful; the black man looked like some deep jewel found in the sand, surrounded by the pale *bazaaris*. Here in Obeh, a still more monotonous milieu, the boy from Iran bejeweled his surroundings. I had to remind myself that there was nothing particularly extraordinary about him; he was not very charming or very outgoing. But somehow, through the rareness of his face, his distant origins, one felt strangely moved, as though the world had grown larger.

We were soon reminded of the smaller world. The school teacher came to call on us at the *sarai*. We hoped to avoid the official circle of the town, the men who wore astrakhan hats and taxied often into Herat for urban pleasures. We told this teacher we were here to visit the hot springs, and he solicited as though one of us were ill. He was officious, apologetic, insistent, as he took us on a tour of the town we had already seen—the school house, the unfinished hospital. His movements were those of a martinet, softened by age and a drooping moustache. He stayed on in the town during the winter, he explained, in order to trade. He was too old and had been too long in the service to be embarrassed about it; everyone knew teachers made starvation wages. He seemed quite pleased with his trade, back and forth from Herat.

My face was rigid with feigned interest while the teacher made all the invidious comparisons against Afghanistan—"The slave expresses surprise that the presences should chance the rigors of the road, especially in such a savage countryside as lies between here and the city. It's too bad the government allows these people to go on living the way they do, the *khans* robbing the peasants blind and the peasants living like animals."

I wondered if in all his journeys back and forth he had stopped at a single village.

"They are all *kuchis*, you know. They're what keeps our country backwards." The word *kuchi* was contemptuous for "nomad"; on the road we had not seen any. "In Iran there are no more *kuchis*, the villages are neat and clean, they have hospitals—although Obeh, too, should have one soon."

I looked at the frame of the hospital, thinking that here they would struggle to keep alive the nomads whom the teacher would have abolished, or watch over the health of those whose way of life would be destroyed. It all seemed pointless, until I remembered the baby in Tunyan who would not eat.

The teacher searched us for one look of approval, one kind word regarding these pitiful signs of progress, and we didn't give it to him. Looking gnawed by silence, he went on his way.

We were always cruel to such people, I mused, but taking sides was a luxury we could occasionally afford.

We dined at the other *sarai* in the town. Ours was the smaller and unoccupied; we wanted to be in the crowd. Post *mutars* discharged their passengers in front of this other *sarai*, and a good crowd of people bustled in and out of it all day long. We went in, hearing the noise of the loud conversations and breathing the smoke of *qalyans* passed from hand to hand. The late season merchants gathered in groups, sharing their dinner from great, heaping plates. Here one could have *Kabuli pilaw*, with raisins and carrots, an unheard-of luxury in the countryside we had just been through. In the back a boy crouched by the samovar, filling pots of tea, bowls of sweets, and sending them through the crowd on the floor, while the busboy banged the tin trays together, clearing away the meal.

Stares fell on us at our entry, and the *saraidar* steered us into a partitioned *utaq* to take our meal alone. We ate his rice, greasy and thin-grained, but still a luxury food, proportionately dear. I found I had an inordinate appetite for grease, thanks to the cold weather.

The *saraidar* returned to us after our meal and visited in the privacy of the *utaq*. He was a jowly Tajik, with slightly Mongol features, his bulky frame well swathed in heavy cloth. He had grown rich off trading the Center Road. His massively-wound turban proclaimed his prosperity, hard-earned, I imagined, in many trips to Chahcheran, and in hard bargaining with the nomads. His talk and his manners were like the *Kabuli pilaw*—rough, greasy, heartening. His bulk protected him from the cold, and his voice crackled like a warm fire.

"In winter, *Meestars*, these *mutars* go seldom to Chahcheran. What was it you wanted to see? The minaret of Jam? The idols of Bamian?"

For some reason we both trusted the man completely and told him that we wanted to go to Darzak and Bandar-i-Mullaha.

"It can be done. You have to go to the Nayak Pass, spend the night with Hajji Mansur, one of the *kalan*, the great men. Then you'll go to the next district, Qadis, and after that you ride and ride until you come to another *uluswali*, Jawand. It isn't far, maybe a week; there's just one more pass between Jawand and Turkistan. It's nothing, *Meestars*, two weeks at most."

A two-week journey in winter through the Safid Kuh, the *saraidar* was telling us, was "nothing." I liked this man and his advice, the first encouragement we had had so far. I imagined us returning to Maimana, by New Year's, wintering with friend Khalil and watching the matches of *buzkashi*.

"The rain here is snow in the mountains, but in most years the Nayak isn't closed by the first snows. If it's clear tomorrow, you can go across, God willing."

Excited, we returned to our *sarai*, making preparations for departure the next day. I wrote a letter to Amin Ullah telling him not to expect our return, though we told our present *saraidar* we meant to see the hot springs the next morning.

But it rained again. Disconsolate, we sat about in the *utaq*, playing knuckle-bone with the boy, who, even though he never managed to teach us the game, offered the bones to my friend as a gift. The rain oppressed us, the drumming of its drops on the mud roof of the *utaq*, but to the *saraidar* and the boy it was only a nuisance. All winter long life would be lived under such rain, and rarely snow, with knuckle-bone and hashish to pass the time. They did not sense our impatience, and spoke about spring as though it were around the corner.

"In spring, *Meestars*, the height of green, the animals fat and lusty, the *mutars*, innumerable, come up here and go to Chahcheran, and the *Heratis* come to the hot springs, and even the *dasht* is green with fat grass." The *saraidar* smiled weakly, trying to share out his sense of hope, to get us through the winter.

The Iranian youth came to visit, wet and muddy, and we gave him a place by our fire. We ate, and he would not take anything from the same bowl as ours, the religious scruples of the Shi'ites being sharp, I observed. He was going to spend the winter with relatives in the city, where a few more diversions were to be had. Mostly, in the winter, people sat and talked. The women were busier than usual, since they used the long winter nights to plot marriages while the idle men were about and open to suggestion. Was he getting married this winter? The *Shirazi* shrugged his shoulders.

He looked through our books and found a pocket copy of the *Divan* of Hafiz. So avidly did he take up reading the *Shirazi* poet, I thought I had to offer him the book, which had been a gift to me from a bookseller. Our friend was grateful, though for a book one need not be excessively so.

"Your graciousness is great. I have eaten your bread. I would be unjust not to make you my guests, for you, after all, are travelers. When you come back to the city, you must stay in our relative's house. I'll give you the address." He tore a page out of the *Divan*—for paper was scarce—and wrote on it an elaborate address, handing it to me. It read, "Ghulam Husayn Najjari, fourth *sarai* from the Masjid-i-Idgah, Herat, Afghanistan." I think he meant to show off his fine handwriting more than anything else, for he could have made us his guests this night, or stabled our horses from the cold and rain. After traveling as we had done, we became more calculating about the gains and risks offered by others' kindnesses. The image of altruism faded from people's actions.

In the evening, the rain cleared again and we went back to the other *sarai* to get news from that *saraidar*. "It's well that you've come here. I had travelers today from Hajji Mansur. They say there's snow on Nayak Pass, but not much. If you go tomorrow, it will be well."

We thanked him profusely for this news, which he accepted shruggingly. Liberality came easy to him, and thanks were dismissed lightly, as they were almost always in Afghanistan. We gave him the letter which I had drafted for Amin Ullah, and he promised to mail it on the next post. The secret of our destination he alone knew (at least until Amin should get our letter), and we trusted him to keep it. This *saraidar* must have gotten rich off trust, another rare commodity in these parts.

No one else in Obeh thought it possible to travel farther at this point. They all assumed we were going to the hot springs and back to Herat.

"If no one else thinks we can ride out of Obeh, and only that one *saraidar* thinks we can, doesn't that give you pause?" I asked my friend.

"No." We believed what we wanted to hear.

The day dawned overcast but dry. Our *saraidar* asked if we would return from the springs tonight or stay in the small hotel there. We said we would probably stay over.

The horses had cold sores where the *namads* had chafed their skins, open sores for which we could only rub in ointment to ward off infection, without closing the wounds or easing their pain. The saddle chafed them even more, and quickly rubbed off the application. Though we had not ridden them for two days, the bad weather annulled the good effect of the rest period. My friend cursed himself for not having sought adequate stabling for them. "In the whole town there had to be one roofed stable." Some kept the animals in the *utaq* where they themselves slept. That is what we should have done.

Crossing the road, instead of heading back on it, bothered the horses. They had expected to return to Herat, I could tell by their resistance to the reins. We hauled them off the *mutar* road into a flat depression. A last view of Obeh: a crown of spindly orchard trees about the bazaar, the gravelly plain, the necropolis of fog-grey marble, the park of churned mud in front of the birdcage frame of the unfinished hospital, the electric pole of the weather station.

Before us spread a flat alluvium with shallow fingers of streams rivuleting underneath the horses' legs. Great black swirls of mud with traces of silver—rainwater pooling—snared the horses' footsteps, the wet soil clinging to their shoes and being cast out in the air as we rode. Where the water ran clearer we let them drink; they lapped at the water, looked up at the mountains in front of them and ducked their heads down again to drink.

Our path was just the muddy banks of a stream that flowed from the Nayak, a watershed between the Murghab and the valley of the Hari River. We crossed back and forth from one bank of the stream to the other, trying to find the surest footing. At times the stream would go flat and shallow, and we had to dismount and lead the horses over slippery, cold rocks. Or the banks would tower above the stream, with the path giving out in a cliff face, and we had to backtrack to where the stream could be forded. Remarkably, as the stream climbed up the hill, meadows, green with grass, would spread off from the banks, and the horses lunged aside to graze, through their bits, with us pulling hard back on the reins futilely. They might as well eat, we decided, for fresh grass we would not see again often.

The valley narrowed above us, closing in the stream with rock cliff walls. The water cut down through soft rock, leaving us twenty feet above on its banks, hoping against a landslide. There had been landslides here, great heaps of rock blocking the path and choking the stream, where we led the horses afoot. Trees, splinter-like branches, grew straight out of the rock, and we had to dismount to clear them. Each time I dismounted my saddle slipped to the ground, the girth loosened by the strain of climbing. While I tried to shorten the leather my *kabud* kept walking on, leaving me wading up the rocks carrying the heavy wooden saddle and cursing myself. My friend made better time, beating, kicking, and talking to the *ablaq*. I tried to catch up when I tightened the strap and remounted, whipping until my shoulder was sore. The *kabud* trudged, unresponsive.

"You're only hitting the saddlebags," called my friend from up the trail.

Tracks led off in other directions, collateral streams flowing into the one we followed, so that we had a hard time deciding whether we kept to the right trail or not. The signs were few: one path had more donkey droppings than another or its grass was more closely cropped. We chose our path, doubting each time, passing sometimes as much as an hour before the steep, straight slope of the trail assured us we were not lost. We argued bitterly, too, and cursed the animals, and wondered where the sun, which shown out of sight beyond the cliffs of the valley, might be.

The trail led on into a roofless grotto, where the stream swirled into a whirlpool, ringed with icicles, broken trees lying smashed against the rocks. The high walls of the grotto had a crown of pines, bending under a load of fresh snow. Through the trees we could only see straight up into the blue sky. We dismounted and rested against the wall of the grotto, staring up at that sky and forgetting the road for a moment. The thought that this trouble was all self-inflicted nagged me, though with a few more degrees of frost I would be too numb to care. Seeing branches shattered on the sides of the rock face, I felt as indifferent as they to be thrown aside into the cold water. The horses wanted to move on, and we could hardly hold them still to mount them.

Stumbling on the rocky path out of the bottleneck of the grotto, we stopped again. White snowpeaks showed beyond the grey rocks and meadows of the streambed, looking like clouds in the blue sky. My friend, with the instincts of a mountain climber, wanted to head towards them instead of following the trail below them. They towered to 9,000 and 10,000 feet, while we could not have been higher than 7,000 feet.

Here was little natural beauty, I thought to myself, except for sunsets and snow and ice, all things which we would have been better off not seeing. I had often heard Afghans refer to their country as a "big heap of rocks" and "too many rocks," which ought to be sold to Iran. The mountains were only a hardship, an obstacle. The night—the somber, starlit night—meant only cold and a losing of the way, the "separation" of the mystic poets. Ice, which made such a strange ring around the moon, and the snow that turned the bare hills to settling clouds, only portended an end to grazing and a two-month famine of meat. I could not bring myself to love the land. I hated every hard step up, every icy stone, every tangling thornbush. Only these mountains, white with disastrous snow, relieved me with the thought of peace, somewhere else, for someone.

Hajji Mansur's dominion consisted of three *qishlaqs*, lying one above the other up the trail. As the valley broadened a little, we came upon the first of these, a patch of planted wheat, mingled *yurts* and *gach* houses ranged beside the streambed. The *qishlaq* had not drawn itself into an enclosure behind trees and canals like the villages of the *dasht*, but straggled, exposed to curious passersby. From the stone's throw distance of the trail we rode past, looking right in among the houses. Women and children went about their business, mending cloth, gathering firewood, driving a stray donkey. They were unafraid of us, with good right, for they had protection. A huge mastiff leapt out from among the houses, hissing and snapping at the horses' legs, sending them into a panic. A woman sitting in the threshold of one of the houses called him back; he returned instantly to retrieve the scrap of bone which she had drawn from her Nile-blue shawl.

Some children heaped firewood in front of a house, tying it down with rag cord and pressing low to keep it out of the wind. They waited until we were a bit past and one of them threw a stone. Children were hard that way.

A bevy of young girls worked at a loom, squatting on a *takht*, chatting, waving the shuttles, winding the threads. At our passing their talk grew louder, like the warning of birds who have seen a fox, and their curious eyes met ours. Not one raised her *chadri* or turned away, but watched us until we rode out of sight.

Though the hour was late in the afternoon, the men and the herds still grazed somewhere off the trail, for we did not see them in the *qishlaq*. The *yurts*, where the animals stabled, were empty.

The word *qishlaq* is Turkish, meaning simply "wintering," while *yaylaq* is "summering." These Afghan *qishlaqs* were usually permanent settlements, because the winters were so cold. Tents, however picturesque, kept nobody warm. The reason why houses did not replace the *yurts* altogether in such *qishlaqs* was that the wood, for the all-important roof beams, was hard to come by. In the summer, when the men of these *qishlaqs* would go up to 10,000 feet to graze their herds, they would have to leave some families behind to guard the wood in the houses.

An hour more and the second *qishlaq* straggled along the stream bed. We saw no dogs here, since the first *qishlaq* effectively screened travelers along the trail. The sheep had come in, huddling in tiny sheepfolds without roofs, with black cloth bundled over them. A mud-insulated *yurt* lay stocked with hay. Keeping the flocks through the winter required fodder. The herd owner either had to have his own or buy from tillers of the soil. I guessed that Hajji Mansur had his tenants who grew the fodder for his sheep's winter diet.

We reached a broad meadow, grazed to dust, windswept from the north wind, blowing straight down from the pass above. The stream bed gave out and the trail stopped. Looking up at a flattish rock-outcropping, we saw the main *qishlaq* where Hajji Mansur had his *sarai* and his *mihman khana*. The horses stumbled on the steep path which climbed to this ledge. Three sides of the mountain enclosed the *qishlaq* and kept off the winds. Facing the path, well-built houses with sturdy roofbeams emerging from the fresh plaster formed an open courtyard. The main house in the compound had a *gach* staircase on the outside, leading to a second-floor veranda. There sat an attendant, scanning the road for travelers. Seeing us ride up, he descended the stairs and helped us down from our horses.

Hajji Mansur, he said to us, had many guests this night. We settled into a small *utaq* at the top of the stairs, all by ourselves. We could hear commotion in another part of the building; apparently Hajji Mansur's *mihman khana* had more than one room. There had to be a large audience hall from the sound of it.

"*Rishsafid*," the attendant replied to my inquiry, "The council of greybeards." I asked him if we might go attend; he shook his head, indicating a high place in the room and then left us to our quiet.

I thought it was very strange that Hajji Mansur should have two rooms in his *mihman khana*, or that he should entertain his guests and his village council apart.

The establishment we were assigned, however, was opulent by any standards we could remember. The small *utaq* was generously spread with rugs, the brazier well stocked with dry twigs. The sanitary trench, in a narrow corridor towards the exit of the *mihman khana*, gave off a sweet smell of freshly turned clay. A sturdy German hurricane lamp of the best make lit the *utaq*. We ate off plates with a floral design, made in India. Dinner, though, was just *qurut*. All the money in the province could not stock the larder with food in the winter season.

The two sons of Hajji Mansur came to company with us after dinner. Dull-witted-looking Tajiks, they shaved closely in the manner of the town and wore silky, clerical garb. The Hajji had sent them to Qala-i-Nau to learn their letters, which had come about this way: the new government made as minimal requirement that an *arbab* be able to read and write before they confirmed his office, meanwhile the *arbabs* had long been expected to provide their *qishlaqs* with a *mulla*, which hereabouts meant no more than a literate person. By having both his sons schooled, Hajji Mansur trained himself a successor and saved the trouble of having to engage a *mulla* from far away. Abdul Baqi Khan, I thought to myself, had not so much foresight. Yet everything about this *qishlaq*, from its sighting on the rock ledge to the careful furnishing of this *utaq*, spoke of deliberateness and foresight.

The sons acknowledged our compliments to Hajji Mansur with the sort of modesty becoming the heirs of a great man. They called him Hajji Mansur, too, and not "father." The two seemed child-like, bowed down perhaps by the reputation of Hajji Mansur. We had heard how the sons of a great *arbab* did not necessarily replace their father as leaders in the *qishlaq*, since the wealth divided among them might not suffice to keep the *mihman khana* in style. That the sons were literate would help them rule the community when their father passed on, but still they did not have the confidence or airs of the sons of a powerful man. Uncertainty and furtiveness dogged their movements and expressions, as though they had spent all their lives in awe of the man. For a long time after our first exchange they watched us, quietly, shyly.

"Why did you come here, on horse, with the snow?" asked the elder, finally, in halting speech.

"There's not so much snow," my friend said, hedging the question.

The elder son didn't persist, but went on a new tack, "You should have a 'Rover. Horses are not your *maslak*, your trade. With a 'Rover you can go anywhere, *zim, zim*. In Qala-i-Nau, there are many Land Rovers."

"Many?"

"Two or three." The *wali* had one; the chief of police another. The sons seemed to know the town well. I reckoned another reason for the father's sending them to school there had been to strengthen his ties with the provincial government. Of old, the same had been done by means of hostages.

"Whenever our heads are dull," mused the younger brother, "we go to the city (Qala-i-Nau) and sit in the *samovar*, or go to the bazaar."

I imagined I had seen the two there, for it was a common sight in Qala-i-Nau: sleepy youths, put out by the bustle of the big town, sitting shyly in the back of the teahouses or walking hand in hand down the dust-blown avenues, staring at their feet. Even the rich villagers feel daunted by the gaily-dressed merchants, by the self-important officials in astrakhan caps, by the clerics with their mosques and sonorous calls to prayer, which the villages singularly lack. They knew that, compared to the towns, their Islam was a bastard thing, hence much of their respect for the bazaars and the towns.

We could not get a word out of them about the *qishlaqs* of the people of Hajji Mansur. Embarrassed by the thought of the city and its prejudices, they preferred not to talk about their way of life in the mountains. I thought it was ironic that here they lived better than almost all of the people in Qala-i-Nau yet felt diffident before them. The older brother continued his discourse on Land Rovers, a new thing and a great innovation among them.

"Doesn't Hajji Mansur have any horses?" I interrupted him.

"Not that many. He used to have very many, but during the Famine they died. Hajji Mansur, he did not replace them all, since horses are not so useful. A 'Rover is better."

I felt snubbed; they didn't admire the man on the horse.

"And sheep? Does he have many?"

Hajji Mansur had several thousands. He had shepherds to graze them, way up in the mountains during the summer, and also, as I had thought, tenants to feed them in the winter. The sons expanded on his; everyone likes being asked if he's rich.

But then I asked, "Does Hajji Mansur go up to the mountain with the sheep, with women, and everything?"

"We are not *kuchis*. We own the land," said the elder son sharply. The nomads, he assumed, left their settling places because they had no land. That was not precisely right. Among the Pathans, grazing land was communal property, owned by a tribe. I tried to clarify this to them, but they stubbornly replied that as Hajji Mansur owned the land of the *qishlaq* and the land of the *yaylaq*, he had no reason to "migrate." He had been here anciently and the race was an old one. They were very particular on this point, making us note that the countryside was full of upstart Pathans.

"They came to this land penniless," the elder went on, "with nothing more than what they carried on the backs of their camels. We have land, water, livestock. What do we have to wander for?" They scorned the camel, prized possession of the Pathans nomads.

Hajji Mansur put in his appearance unannounced, while his sons humbly retreated. He was a vigorous-looking Tajik with a henna-dyed beard, cut low around the cheeks, giving his face a leonine cast. He wore a pale orange *chapan* and a dark turban, old clothes but dignified. His ceremony was polite and studied, as he asked us whether we had eaten well or if we had any complaints about his hospitality. Beyond that, he only wanted to know about the trail: had we seen others passing either way? Then he excused himself on account of pressing business in his council, and withdrew. Hajji Mansur had no curiosity about our coming, no expansive volubility to converse with us. The sons, too, had found our company uninspiring and followed their father out. An old retainer came in to watch us.

The old man was a talker. An Aymak by looks, he had the young-old, smooth-wrinkly skin of that race and boasted that he was a hundred years old, having served Hajji Mansur for as long as anyone could remember. He had never gone to the city, nor did he show any interest in the outside world, though he said he had seen every nation passing through the Nayak Pass. "Pathan," he said, "Taymuri, Tajik, Sikh."

"And what tribe is Hajji Mansur?" I asked him.

"Aymak. Aymak." This was a medley of tribes which used to

dominate Badghis in the last century, part Tajik and part Turkish.

"And is he chief, *sardar*, among them?"

"No. There are no *sardars* anymore. There is government, and no *sardars*. He is *arbab*." The old retainer answered, not happy to be reminded of changing times.

Tribes were political groups, culturally defined as kin groups. Faced with outside threats of violence, tribesmen claimed ties of blood with whatever group would join with them, and the greatest of the tribesmen, the *sardar*, would assume the position of father of the tribe. This had great emotional appeal to the men, who—after several generations—forgot the kin relationships had ever been fictive. But when the threats of external violence ceased, the disparate elements of the tribe grew apart. A *sardar* could no longer muster the loyalty of distant tribesmen, or those living secure in the protection of the *wali*. With the spread of the provincial government's power into the mountains of Ghur and Badghis, the chieftianships had gone vacant; some tribes had become a dead letter. The chiefly families, though, remained powers in the land, since they were still the richer, and assumed the title of *arbab*, rather than *sardar*. Such had been the fate of Hajji Mansur's Aymaks.

The old retainer talked, and the world he described was far from that which we saw around us. "There were no 'Rovers, no. In those days, hardly anyone went to the city. Hajji Mansur was not the only big sheepherder; there were several, all paladins, with fine horses and good rifles, too. If they said sneeze, the *wali* would sneeze. That was the way it was. Sometimes they fought, among themselves, stealing sheep, and women. Nowadays, if there's a raid, the *wali* comes up here in his *mutar*, that's what he does, can you imagine?"

Hajji Mansur had adapted to the new bureaucracy, with his well-furnished *mihman khana*—for the *wali* I assumed—and with his separate council room, his literate sons. Apparently he was responsible for the traffic on the Nayak Pass; whether he made a direct profit from it or an indirect one I couldn't learn. Clearly, he had an official standing of sorts.

Some of the old ways survived. When the assembly of greybeards broke up, which was late, they insisted on having a look at us. They peered into the *utaq*, demanding of the retainer, "Are they *Musalmans*?"

"They seem so," he said, without consulting us. The assembly departed with heavy footsteps down the stairs, some men walking as far as the first *qishlaq* downstream. The retainer spread three *luhats*; it was a custom for hosts to sleep beside their guests in the *mihman khana* to protect them from harm, though we could not imagine what harm in the well-organized *mihman khana* of Hajji Mansur.

At our departure Hajji Mansur sent the retainer as a guide to show us the entry to the pass. He asked us again to pardon him for his absence the night before, nodding his head with the same dignity and grace, extending the clasped hand of fealty. Some greybeards sat on the veranda, at their breakfast, watching us three saddle up and mount. I could not hear them, but I was embarrassed at the sad state of the horses, who looked very thin now.

The old man mounted more nimbly than we did, on a spirited roan, and led us up the hard-trodden path behind the *qishlaq*. The way was steep, like the ascent to the *qishlaq* itself, opening onto a desolate meadow, a moonscape, framed all around with great slate slabs. The wind whipped across the meadow, chilling and blowing dust before our eyes. Though exposed to the wind, we could see nothing but the grey slabs around us; the wind descended from the peregrine-grey sky, out of the eye of the storm. Snow-bearing clouds swirled above, precipitating and mingling with the snows on the mountaintops in imperceptible degrees. The horizon seemed a depth of white, distantly.

"*Sahibs*! Over that dyke, that *band*, until you come to the girdle of land, the red *kamar*! Then go through the mountain pass, the *kutal*, and you'll see the way down: Qadis, Badghis. Go with grace!" He wheeled his horse around and took it clip-clopping back across the desolate meadow.

After yesterday I thought the pass could not get any steeper. Now each step forward meant a cajoling and kicking of the horses, sweating with the whip and crying, "Git-git-git." At the first obstacle, the *band*, we dismounted and led the horses up the stairway of stone. Without riders on their backs they had a poor sense of their own balance; they wobbled on the stone, staring at it for a safe foothold. The best balance could only be speed and momentum. The steps gave way to a second meadow in a wide bowl, where we let the horses rest and stood on the solid earth for a moment, limbs aching from the relaxed strain. The same rock desolation surrounded us, the same white mirages of snow and mountains flitted distantly away from us. Here were no bearings and no direction. The wind whipped at the horses' shaking limbs, and we hurried on.

The *kutal* was a broken hump of rock, cragged with crevices of vegetation and snow. Our path led indistinctly up its surface like a faint etching, fading towards the summit. Chips of rock kicked off underneath our horses' hooves; we had to place their feet for them, one at a time. When we were nearly at the top, the trail stopped. Around us, the windswept *kutal* flecked with snow, the indistinct horizon, white snowpeaks, and nothing else. The red *kamar*, a belt of cliff-stone, lay out in the fog, invisible. We climbed up farther, pulling the horses with their bridles, eyes fixed to the ground, searching for traces of a path: dim scratches of hooves on rock, trampled grass. Animal dung, almost effaced by the snow and the wind, pointed the way treacherously. Following sheeps' droppings, we strayed far from the path, for the sheep had been grazing all over the *kutal*.

The wind blew in our eyes and in our horses' faces; they blinked, tottering in splayed-legged awkwardness, looking at the ground, clutching at safe footholds on the steep slope of the *kutal*. I worried at any moment they would just give up, relax their balance and fall on the cragged stone. But there was no going forward.

My friend handed me the reins of the *ablaq* and walked off into the fog. He disappeared up a slope, narrow and uncertain-looking.

He was gone a long time. I squatted on the rock, holding the two sets of reins tightly to give the horses a balance, but dreading to be pulled over by them. It stormed around us; the epicenter of the storm drew close, so that far away, to the north, I could see growing distinct white peaks, and hills, lower down, brown-bodied in the repose of the valley of Badghis. And behind them, the sun's yellow disk, pale as the moon, shone on the valleys and cast faint shadows in their relief. Seeing the sun reminded me of Phaethon, holding the reins of the chariot in trembling hands. I looked back for a sign of my friend, and there was none.

The horses' legs began to shake, with cold I hoped rather than from muscle strain. Hours ago, I reminded myself cruelly, I had been safely warmed in the *qishlaq* of Hajji Mansur. Before that, we might have visited the hot springs of Obeh, accompanying a retired and rheumatic civil servant from Farah, listening to his laments about the unsettled state of the country, trading jokes about hashish addicts and pederasts. Or I might have been in Herat, under a *sandali*, playing cards and cursing the overcast sky. I was here entirely by choice; the thought had dogged me month after month. For the Afghans to endure the storms or the nights was different, since they could not blame themselves for the hardships. I had only myself to blame.

The trembling horses slipped a little on the rock, and I steadied them with my weight, pulling on the reins. They stopped shivering and found a balance. I'm glad I'm here, I told myself.

The storm passed over us, and the sun in the northern sky shined more brightly on the valley below me. I could pick out every detail of relief in the sharply-etched landscape. The world below seemed new, untrodden, but it also looked raw and exposed, as though a layer of its skin had been sloughed off. I saw *tepes*, ridges, meandering streambeds, *kutals*, and tracks, chalk-like, where sheep had trampled the earth to dust. All lay close below, as though I could throw a stone across the valley. But how to get down?

My friend walked down from the slope, saying he had seen a *kamar* up there and what looked like the path down. We led the willing horses up the slope, they were more eager to move than to stand, and I saw this *kamar*, which was not at all red, a cliff-face in the mountainside, with a slope leading down below it. The horses' balance in descent was worse than in ascent; they stumbled and fell against us as we led them. Down, down, we dragged ourselves, and in an instant the valley opened before us: Badghis, brown and yellow, the colors of the *dasht*, with flecks of grey where villages lay. Steeply we climbed down, with the valley seeming an arm's length away. The sun shined directly on us now, the storm having far retreated.

But it had left snow on the track of our descent in some places, discouragingly great heaps. Avoiding these, we trod on white patches that looked like a few inches of ice, only to plunge up to our waists, pulling the horses to their knees. Terrified at the slippery surfaces, they balked and would not go on, the *ablaq* especially. So I went forward, packing the snow down with my body and leading the *kabud* behind. In the deep patches, I made only a few feet of progress at a time. The melting snow clung to my *chapan* and soaked into my boots, making each step heavier and heavier.

Someone was making the ascent. Two donkey boys, bare-foot, leading their tiny beast loaded with empty bags of burlap breasted through the snow, which came in places up to their necks. One had a staff in his chapped hand. "What of the path? Is it clear?" he demanded to know. Then, "Where are you come from?"

I forgot myself completely and said, "*Amrika.*"

"And the trail there, is it clear or bound with snow?" His young-old face peered up searchingly, for his life seemed dependent on this knowledge.

"But the road to *Amrika* is farther than Mecca."

The boy shrugged his shoulder and led the way for his beast and his fellow through the path we had cut in the snow. Seeing their footprints bare in the snow, each toe showed distinctly, sobered my sense of hardships endured. It was a healthy slap in the face.

Beyond the snow we mounted—we had not been in the saddle since early morning, hours ago—and rode easily into the sun-warmed valley of the *dasht*. Before us on the trail dust stirred and approached, signaling horsemen. They drew near, and we saw they were armed. They sat bolt upright in the saddle, loaded with bandoliers and cartouches, with tightly-wound turbans; their caparisons were bold Turkoman rugs. At a little distance they halted.

"Peace be upon you," I said, posturing myself high in the saddle.

After a careful eyeing they let out a wary "May you not be tired."

"May you live long," we returned, wheeling our horses about and trying to look less than half-dead. They were magnificent, their horses fat and spirited, each rider steely-gazed and holding an iron hand high on his horse's neck. What must we have seemed to them, with our tottering horses, our threadbare saddle blankets and snow-soaked clothing.

"What of the pass? Were you snowed in?"

"There's snow on the north face, but the sun will melt it. There's no snow yet on the south face, the praise is God's."

"And where did you come from?" asked this same horseman.

"We were guests of Hajji Mansur."

At this name they murmured to themselves, then applied their short whips to their animals and trotted up the path, rifles and bandoliers swinging behind them. 'Go with grace" was exchanged between us.

The further descent foreshortened our view of the valley. *Qishlaqs* and arbors sank from sight, into the penumbra of the *dasht*, and the path led into the trackless, thorny scrub, which stretched on for hours more. Bare *kutals*, nubs of earth these were, all grazed out by the sheep, ravines of spring spill-off, cairns of stones, gravelly stream beds all lay between us and our destination. Only the distinctive folding of the mountains in front of us, on the far side of the valley, guided us toward a straight direction. The *dasht* led right up into the main street.

Prophetic Talk

A town similar in size to Obeh and like it the seat of an

uluswali, Qadis had no Hari River and close-lying mountains to water it. Parched and ramshackle seemed its main street, weathered by wind and unrepaired by a fatalistic citizenry. Official buildings, dingy plaster villas, occupied a barbed-wired *tepe*. The bazaar was a row of booths so rainwashed and dustblown that they appeared to have been carved out of solid mud. The street, wide as though a flood had washed through, clutched a few small, dead trees. The *sarai*, worn to a nub by wind and years, sat amid ruins of older buildings which served as stabling places for animals. These were cavernous and eerie, disquieting even the horses. We tied them up there, beside Pathans' camels and mule trains.

A boisterous crowd filled the *sarai's samovar*, *mutarwans* and donkey drivers on their way to Qala-i-Nau. Travelers, merchants in petty items who arbitraged between the *wilayat* and the *uluswali*, the province and the district, were among their passengers. The serving boy scampered around them, slapping down trays of *shurwa*, dodging complaints of those yet to be served, and threats of sodomization. I could understand their impatience. I had not eaten meat in a long while and had grown weary of stone-cold *qurut*. But the *shurwa* was a disappointment to us all.

"Look at this *shurwa*," bandied a young traveler in the crowd, "it's all bone and water. Do you see any meat in it? Where? And the bones, these were boiled up in yesterday's *shurwa*, son of Satan."

The men laugh at this, with the humor of a people who love to run down their lot, but the fat, slow-witted *saraidar* smiled and shook his head at these complaints. He insisted that these stone-hard loaves of bread were all that could be had in the town.

We had reached a point where the lack of food was on everybody's mind. In the winter, one's appetite increased for fat especially, just when there was no fat to be had. The sheep grew thin on dry, old fodder, and the Afghans rarely slaughtered them, except for celebrating a marriage or for the birth of a son in the home, so men grew lean and chill-racked. *Shurwa*, the specialty of teahouses in the towns, was something these men had dreamt of while they traveled. The *samovar* in Karukh, they said, had good *shurwa*. Talk of food, of once-eaten better meals, filled the room.

The young traveler spoke; he was a handsome, dandishly-dressed fellow whom everyone regarded well and listened to when he told of his travels. "In Iran, I tell you, even the poor people eat rice, three times a day, pure, white as a young girl's hand, with grains so big and this big " he said, indicating with his thumb and small finger. Eyes widened at the thought of such rice, which those who have not been to the city have never eaten.

A Pathan spoke up, in defense of his land. "In Kandahar it's green all year around. They have fruits, *naranj* and *nanana*, even in the winter!" Explanations were required, by some of the men, just what was this banana or this orange, tropical fruits unseen in Badghis.

The Afghans called every meal "bread": breakfast was "bread of morning"; lunch was "bread of noon": dinner was "bread of evening." In the summer I had thought that a very monotonous way of referring to meals, but now in the winter I saw how accurate it was. We were eating bread for breakfast and lunch, hoping for something better by dinnertime. Bread. They harvested and threshed the principal crop in summer, sent it to the towns to be baked into bread, and then stored the loaves in sacks in the bazaar. Fresh bread one had only in the big towns, with their elaborate bakeries, or else the very rich who had ovens in their houses prepared themselves this delicacy; but for the homeless and the travelers of the bazaar, the *saraidar* trucked out brick-hard loaves from his store and warned us that soon this would be exhausted, to justify his high prices.

Feed for the horses was just as dear. He charged us 60 *rupees* a *man* instead of the usual 50 or 55. We were lucky, he said, that we could buy any at all. Another month and he would keep the rest to himself, for his own animals. "What do people do then?" I asked.

"They have their own fields, they lay in early, or they do without."

When the end of the winter comes, the stocks of grain are literally exhausted, except for that fraction of the crop, usually a fifth, which the farmers save for seeding. During the Famine, when the expected stock of grain did not renew itself, the farmers consumed their seeding grain, prolonging their lives only a little while, and then a fourth of the province perished. Famine is a constant subject for discussion in the winter months.

"I myself remembered," says one of the men in the room, "how they asked fifty *rupees* a loaf for bread, during the Famine, at Qala-i-Nau. I could not believe it, I was in a crowd of people, wondering if there would be bread enough for all, and few had fifty *rupees*!"

"That was under the monarchy," said the young man.

"It is all one," said a grizzled greybeard, and none argued with him.

The young dandy talked to us, showing off his Iranianisms and affected, *Tehrani* manners. He called us *agha*, the Persian "sir," and twanged mincingly like the Iranians, saying "Irun" for "Iran" and *"nemidunam"* for *"namedanum."* I wished he would slip out of that absurd accent two thousand miles away from South Tehran, but he seemed to prize it more highly now, like the money he had made across the border. "Do you know Tehrun, *Agha*? I lived in Mawlawi Square. Made a lot of money. Slipped over the line, you know, without a passport. That's the best way. The police, they catch you sometimes, and they say, 'Afghan, your father burned in Hell'. And I used to say, 'Na, Baba, I'm from Gunabad'—that's a town just inside their border and there's no way of telling us apart, you see—only once this *Iruni* policeman said to me, 'So you're from Gunobad, how is Hajji Abtul Hasan?' And like a fool I said, 'He's well'. The damned cop says, 'Son of a depraved mother, there's no Hajji Abdul Hasan in Gunabad' and beat me until I was too sick to die."

"Still it didn't spoil your good looks," said a teasing wag among us.

"No, Father, it didn't. That's what being well paid and well fed does for you, not like these about-to-die Afghans here."

"Too true, too true," they all said, ever enjoying hearing their country run down.

"But those two," said a man of them, "who are they and what are they doing here?"

The young traveler replied without consulting us. "They are archaeologists (no one in the room knew what that meant). They are always coming through here, to go to Langar, to Shaymashhad, to see the relics of ancient times." His manner was so completely assured he convinced everyone, including us. We kept silent.

An old, fanatical person began whining at the outrage done to Islam by the free passage of unbelievers. "They have no prophets, you know, not Nuh, not Zakaria, not Muhammad, nor Daud, nor Isa."

"Grandfather," I said, "what are you saying? My own name is Daud."

"Was he a prophet?" asked another, perplexed.

"They say there were seventy thousand of them before the time of Muhammad." said the same fanatical one, importantly.

"Well, tell me what you know about *Hazrat* Daud!" I persisted.

Embarrassed silence.

The young traveler spoke up, "*Agha,* we are simple folk here, our business is sheep and goats. What do we know of prophets and mullas?"

And the simple one said, "Afghanistan—ignorant. *Jahil.*"

I was abashed.

My friend lit a cigarette and passed it to the young mule boy beside him, who had been silent through all our conversation. He took a few drags on it, before turning quietly green.

The young traveler laughed. "That's strong stuff for you," but declined when my friend offered him a puff. My friend then distributed the rest of his pack through the room, to the amazement of all them all.

"*Sahib,*" said one, "do you mind if we don't smoke these now, but take them home for later?"

Each cigarette cost a *rupee* and would be irreplaceable, but through this gesture my friend had proved our prophets better than I could have done by arguing. I felt doubly abashed.

Later my friend remarked that the two of us were diametrically opposite in the way we traveled. "You go to a place and announce yourself and explain yourself. You ask questions. You get into arguments. It should be possible," he spoke of his own preference, "to slip in, to observe, somehow, without obtruding." They were both useful ways among the Afghans, each in its own place. The Afghans themselves were levitous. Sometimes they wore a brusque *bonhomie;* then we were better off pliant and invisible. Else they whined and cringed, these same rough Tajiks, and we had to be sure of ourselves, to avoid flattery and traps. When they threatened and pried, it was best to react hard and pridefully. To be attuned to their changing moods was a constant psychological strain. Only, between the two of us, we seemed to have each a talent for part of the strain, and so we shared it. Even though we clashed among ourselves, we each needed the other's knack for what we could not handle. The blindman and the cripple, together, stole fruit from the orchard.

The Afghans sat in the *samovar* quietly now, some of them smoking the cigarettes, while others only inhaled the smoke. There was little light in the room, but many smells, that of camel, of horses' sweat and urine, clay, charcoal and green twigs, musty hay, and stale bread, each smell distinct, each smell with its own texture on the air. I breathed them in, savoring each one, thinking them sweeter than the smell of tobacco. Some travelers departed on the stopping-over *mutar*; the door opened and a draught of cold air filled the room; the door shut and the same strong, mixed odors of warm air settled on us like a blanket. Even the tea, flaked with the dust of the air, tasted of camels and old *gach*.

Qadis. The town extended the bazaar of Qala-i-Nau, and most of the *bazaaris* here were from that place, who had in turn moved up from Herat. Even though we had passed through three provinces, Herat, Ghur and Badghis, the lines of supply, the patterns of traffic, kept running back to Herat. That city, with its four bazaars, its satellite Zanjan, its roadside *samovars* and *rabats*, and these far-flung entrepôts like Qala-i-Nau and Qadis, all formed an archipelago of urban life, linked together by the almost sea-like trade through the empty *dasht*. By *mutar* and donkey train they brought the necessities of the urban culture—tea, sugar, and kerosene—even to these remote outposts, so that life could go on with the bare ceremony which they required. The *dashtis* could come to these entrepôts to buy at wildly high prices, if they too wanted to live as civilized folk. It did not seem fair, when one contrasted the cheapness of bread in the city, the abundance of fruit and meat all year round, to the famine in the countryside which had produced it all. The *dasht* was as the colony of the city, with a poor balance of trade. Merchants in Qadis hawked their wares to Aymaks and Tajiks in their mountain fastnesses making only a marginal profit, but introducing the inflated prices of foreign-made objects imported through Herat. Taiwanese china, Ceylonese tea, all drove up the city's surplus of trade with the countryside, which felt poorer and poorer. The big sheepowners with their meat felt still rich, since meat had inflated its price too. The Pathans engaged in trading——and suffered not as much from the arbitrage of the merchants. But for most of Badghis the threat of famine and poverty grew worse every year. Standing still, they found themselves behind, unable to understand what had happened to them. Qadis, full of exploiters and exploited, shared a sense of exile and oppression.

Optimists, like the town's *kalantar*, the commissioner of the bazaar, disagreed. The town was growing richer every year. Look at the new hospital: "almost finished" (it was more incomplete than the bird-cage frame in Obeh), look at the new *mutars*. True, Qala-i-Nau was the *wilayat*, but soon, Qadis would replace it as provincial capital.

"Soon?" we asked.

"In eight or ten years." Qadis was on the up and up; Qala-i-Nau had declined. "Because," the *kalantar* smiled, "their water tastes like piss."

My friend had met this *kalantar* on his way to Darzak, and

they renewed their acquaintance cheerfully. The man had the job of looking into the honesty and right dealings of the bazaar, which involved nothing more than to sit and chat in the *sarai* all day long. He had the right physiognomy for this sort of work, an open, big face, grey eyes, and a dignified beard. He was well informed, as his job required, and we talked with him for a long while. My friend he liked very much, as more deferential to his opinions than I was. We argued over a silly solipsism, which almost led to disaster.

"*Sahibs*, in Afghanistan, it is this way. There are Afghans, and Iranians, and Turks, Aymaks, Mongols, Arabs, Sikhs, Hindus, Jews, I don't know what else. In *Amrika*, what tribes are there?"

"There are no tribes in America," I told him. He didn't believe me, and so we argued.

My friend, in English, said to me, "Don't start another argument, this man is my friend."

"All right," I said. "Have it your way."

"Then there are tribes in America," he pounced on me as though I had been fibbing all along.

"No!" I burst out, and the argument began all over again.

He left, huffing, and my friend said to me ruefully, "He was inviting us to dinner at his house tonight until you got on his wrong side."

What could I say?

What was worse, shortly after the *kalantar* left us so angrily, we received word that the commandant of Qadis, the *kumandan*, wanted to question us. That looked like the end of everything.

All the way to the *kumandan's* office I turned over in my head how it would be; he would take our horses, send us back to Qala-i-Nau on the next *mutar*, and pack us off to Iran, without our having had anything to show for it all. My friend said nothing, but I felt that my tiff with the *kalantar* had done it all. We saw him on the way over; he greeted us and smiled, since one never held grudges here, which gave me a little hope.

The office of the *kumandan* was of *gach*, which years of repainting had turned to shapeless sludge. We sat uncomfortably in steel chairs, on account of our saddle sores, surrounded by the chaos of an Afghan bureau: pajamaed petitioners surging forward with complaints, soldiers slouching their rifles against the wall, a coal stove bellying forth soot, scribes, bristling pens and nibs, wearing a combination of military dress and religious, bearded mullas, long-turbaned Pathans, chained prisoners, a disputed chicken. The chaos of the place heartened me again; it made it easier for me to imagine that the *kumandan*, whose grey, flabby face glanced at us from across his steely desk, was not capable of flogging peasants and throwing prisoners into irons, which of course he was.

"A pity, a thousand pities, that our town should be so unworthy of the honor of your presences," he began. The unsteadiness of his voice surprised me and, I daresay, surprised him. Perhaps he feared some deeper purpose behind our unexpected arrival in Qadis. "Of course the hospital will soon be finished," he droned on.

I thought of Gogol: "A government inspector has arrived, gentlemen, *incognito*, from the capital."

As he went on talking, the sense of the man showed through. The *kumandan* must have been worried, with the *coup d'etat*, with so many shake-ups, how could he know what these scruffy, pajamaed foreigners were up to? He looked at us with deadfish eyes; he was of the old *pasha*-type, trying desperately to avoid trouble with the new regime, those young Turks back in Kabul. For years, perhaps, he cursed his low promotions and backwoods postings. Then came the revolution against the king; flying birds had gotten shot at. But in his humble post, he had slipped by unnoticed, and grown secure, until now . . .

"To what can we attribute the good fortune of this visit?" he concluded his lengthy remarks with a helpless question.

I stated our business as concisely and forcefully as I knew how, hinting that some pressing business awaited us in Maimana, but for our purposes we prefered to travel there on horseback. It was sheer idiocy, so much so that the *kumandan* accepted it gravely.

"Of course, the presences are a cause of considerable concern, due to the uncertainties of the road."

"Why, aren't the roads perfectly safe from bandits?"

If anything were to happen to us on the way he would certainly lose his job, but he didn't dare admit that there were bandits about. The fact that we had already crossed the Nayak Pass lent us credibility. He had thought it closed a month ago. Sensing something in his manner of referring to the pass, I began to brandish the name of Hajji Mansur like a talisman. This tug-of-war went on interminably.

Our manner impressed him, not so much personally, but enough to suggest that we were not to be tangled with. He began mopping his fleshy forehead with a rag and droning even more numbingly, "We can send the presences on to Jawand, if it should seem preferable, but only with armed escort."

Now my friend objected instantly and surely, "How does the lofty state expect to feed a party of soldiers in the *dasht*? In our saddlebags there's no bread for your humble servant, let alone an escort. And in the *dasht*, there's nothing at all."

His excellency backed down, mopping his face and smiling weakly. He would send us with a single guide, a local man, as far as Jawand. We thanked him for his concern and shook his hand, reading on his face a mixture of distrust, fear, exhaustion and envy. We backed out of the door, a usual sign of politeness.

"You did very well," my friend whispered to me. "I don't know what I would have said if he'd wanted to send us back to Herat." That meant I had made up for upsetting the *kalantar*.

The ubiquitous commissioner of the bazaar accompanied us to a village across the streambed from the town, there to arrange with the headman of the *qishlaq* to send a guide along as far as Jawand. The *arbab* complained bitterly against the expense of the horse and the rider, while the *kalantar* doggedly stuck to his demands.

It did us no good to be peacemakers. We said, "We can do without a guide after all."

Both men looked darkly at us, the unwarranted cause of all this trouble.

Finally the *kalantar* said, "These people are guests in this land. If they should go traveling, and something should happen to them, God forbid, men would hold us accountable."

The *arbab* nodded regretfully and shouldered the burden of our safety. His son, a youth named Muhammad Qaus (the Archer), he designated to accompany us. The son had sat at our council silent all the while and accepted his part with a modest nod. I do not think he was excited about the prospect one way or another. His fine horse they led out to be saddled while the *kalantar* watched to see that everything was in order. He did not leave until the three of us were on our way, shouting back, "We entrust you to God."

This Muhammad Qaus knew the land well, and knew horses besides. At his pace we made good time, a fast trot followed by a walk. Leaving the valley of Qadis handily behind, we rose up on the high land which they called the *lalmi*. In good harvest years Muhammad Qaus sowed the unirrigated hills of his *qishlaq*, hoping for rain alone to water the crops. When the crops were bad, they did not risk the precious seed on fickle rains, but planted only by the riverside. But they always planted melons here, for the sweetest melons were from the high land. Muhammad Qaus told us of these things shyly, a few words at a time, more concerned to reach the next *qishlaq* by sunset. When he decided we had made good enough time, we slowed down and relaxed.

"Tell me something about your kingdom, and I'll tell you something about mine, and this way we'll better pass the time," he said easily. "Is it a hot place or a cold place, this *Amrika*?"

"Just like Afghanistan—the South is hot and the North is cold. A lot of it looks like this, *lalmi* and more *lalmi*. We have little irrigation, because the rains are heavy." And we told him how, in the West, the *dasht* stretched on for thousands of miles, and how, before the coming of the plow, the grass on the prairies grew up to a man's shoulders.

"The grass grows so high? Because of the rain. Here, you see, sometimes it doesn't rain at all. One year, during the Famine, it didn't snow. I said to my father, 'We are ruined.' He said, 'Sometimes it happens, God's will.' But then the next year, again, there was no snow, and many people died. Half the world, it seemed."

The desolate grey *lalmi*: tufts of grass knot the landscape, a monotonous patterning. Muhammad Qaus did not find it at all desolate, keeping a lively lookout for game. He spotted partridges, foxes, and hoopoes scampering out of our way as we rode. Even under his tutelage I could not make out these grey creatures. "Look, there's a fox," he would cry, pointing to the ground, while for me the emptiness of the *dasht* was undisturbed. "If you come here in the spring, we can ride out in the *dasht*. And when night falls, we'll hobble the horses, throw ourselves on the ground with a blanket, and sleep, just like that. The horses can forage, too, on the fat green grasses."

And now?

"There's fodder in these quarters, but mostly hay, old hay, without any force. It fills the horses, but they still grow thin on it."

Under the Earth

We spent two nights in poor *qishlags*, directly on the *lalmi*, with no water at all but that which they collected from melted snow. In one tattered assembly of greybeards was a *mulla* who coveted my friend's red-brown woolen *barak*. "There's much blessing in gifting men of religion," whined the *mulla*. "You really ought to give me yours, and I'll let you take mine." With Muhammad Qaus we smiled at this breach of courtesy to guests: the people were very poor. They had no grain to spare for our horses, and when we would offer to buy it from them, they refused, saying that our coins were too large for them to change.

Our horses went hungry then, but for the chaff left over from what we had bought in Qadis, while we broke our teeth on stale bread and sipped cold, weak tea.

The same road-going lay ahead of us, with hungry horses ill-disposed to traveling. Yet Muhammad Qaus insisted on a fast pace, hoping to reach more prosperous *qishlaqs* before men and beasts were exhausted. We met with a dry riverbed, choked with stones up and down its length—red, grey, turquoise, and white—some of them looking precious in the bleak landscape. Sometimes men stopped to pick them up, to carry them a long way into the city, hoping to find them valuable stones, but they were common, all of them.

From the stones shepherds had constructed cairns, guideposts to paths higher up in the mountains, but unfamiliar to men nowadays. "They are *qishlaqs* of old, that are no more," said our guide. The old herders had also left sheepfolds, barely outlined against the hillsides, scarcely distinguishable from random scatterings of rocks. Taking these many settlements from different times as belonging to a single, larger past, Muhammad Qaus wondered that the land should ever have been so rich and peopled. We passed *ziyarats*, the graves of those forty-foot giants, lying surrounded by heaps of carved and broken marble, the like work of which was never seen nowadays. "These are the graves of ancients, of the *kalans*, the great ones," Muhammad Qaus would say.

"Who were they?" I asked.

"The knowledge is lost, if any ever knew."

The graves stretched beside the riverbed, marble mingled with stones, and stone upon marble, until we came to some rude graves which were not old—simply piles of rock heaped in a barrow. That was all, against the grey earth and tufted grass, a sky grey as the falcon's wing, hard and dispiriting. Only our guide did not let himself be affected by his surroundings, but kept a steady pace and urged us to talk less, to ride hard.

The descent into watered valleys was welcome, where narrow, sealed worlds lay between the high faces of cliffs. The *qishlaqs* were fortified with hedges of trees, walnut groves and mulberry clutches, and streambeds with running water where the horses drank deep. High on the face of cliffs stood the houses of the *arbabs* of those places, up steep paths guarded by dogs. Women, washing by the streams as we crossed, looked up and called the dogs away. They did not wear the veil, but velvet capes, and were dark, with hennaed fingers and cheeks. We asked them our way in Persian, which they did not understand at all.

These were Pathans, nomads who had migrated to this

valley from the plateau of Chahcheran. The three-hundred-mile journey had taken them two weeks, as they descended from 10,000 to 5,000 feet of altitude. One did not manage such operation without a firm hand in control. At their *qishlaqs* we met *khans* accustomed to command, whose wealth guaranteed them the compliance of their fellows. A man with 3,000 head of sheep did not risk them lightly. His decisions bore weight in council. When to migrate, how long to tarry in each stopping place, how long to graze a patch of pastureland, dealings with the government and rival grazers, there were the matters in which the *khans* had shown their expertness. One treated them with great respect. Following Muhammad Qaus' lead, in the presences of these *khans* we spoke little, invoked God often, and sat on the skirts of our robes, out of harm's way.

"What do they want, these glasses-wearers?" asked one wall-eyed *khan*. "Do they have glasses that can make people see?" We didn't know whether he wanted binoculars or corrective lenses or what, but we couldn't argue with him. "Give me something for my eyes," he insisted. So we gave him collyrium—more a cosmetic than an eye medicine—which satisfied him.

It was in a *qishlaq* called Garzistan that we met Hajji Aman Ullah Tur. Before the Famine he had been rich enough to buy his airfare to Mecca—first class. "Eighty-thousand *rupees* Afghani," he said matter-of-factly, as though such sums were in the natural realm of things. He was the first of these parts who knew we had flown to Afghanistan by plane. "I was a rich man once and, God willing, I shall be rich again, and fly on a plane, maybe to your country. Would you treat me as a guest there, in your country? Feed me kebab and *shurwa*, and yogurt?" I promised I would, giving him my address, "*Daud Chafiz, 2 Hulyuk Plays, Kamrij, Masachusiz.*" If he still has it, the invitation stands.

Hajji Aman Ullah Tur had once 5,000 sheep, before the Famine. Now there were only 2,000, which still ranked him among the great men of the province. His stables still had horses in them, which were rare, of late; he was not interested in *mutars*. "We have camels, what do we have need of *mutars*? To go to the high passes? You need a camel, I tell you."

"And donkeys?"

"Bah, donkeys are good for nothing." The donkey bore better and walked steadier, but the camel was the animal of prestige. These were the Pathans, the men of Kandahar, descendents of Israel and Hijaz.

Afterward Muhammad Qaus asked me, "Did you really fly from the west of *Makka* or did you make that up?"

"No, we really did."

"*Mashallah*," he exclaimed, considering for the first time how different a people were his traveling companions. "When you get back to that place—it's far away, I suppose— will you write me a letter? I can get someone to read it for me."

"*Inshallah*," we told him, "if we get home."

The nights were cold, bitterly, but the *luhats* of the great *khans*' guest chambers were warm. When one of the *khans* wrapped a guest in the great bear-hug quilt the poor guest cried, "For God's sake, I'm suffocating."

"As long as you're good and warm," said the *khan*. Always, the *khan's* retainers slept in the *mihman khana*, guarding the precious guests.

Travelers we rarely saw on the road, but every night at the *mihman khana* of the nearest *qishlaq* we fell in with other travelers, dining together at the *khan's*. Some were neighbors on social calls, others journeyed far afield, traveling from their *qishlaq* to the *uluswal* Jawand, on a matter of law or for medicine. They were all good-natured about the bad season for traveling, sighing that they had no other choice. We had our choice, but nobody guessed that.

On the last day we traveled with Muhammad Qaus it began to snow lightly. "Don't worry, tonight you'll be in Darzak, that's the *samovar* just before Jawand. I'll go back." What would he do about this snow? Ride fast. He would take nothing from us as a keepsake, saying, "This journey with you has been a memory sufficient. But write me a letter when you get to your homeland." And he made the sign of pen scratching on paper, so we would understand. Then he turned, plied his whip against his horse's flanks, and was gone.

A gathering of telephone wires guiding us to Darzak— "Under the Earth" they also called it—descended out of sight into a sliver of a valley, through which there flowed a collateral stream of the Murghab River. We stumbled into the tail of a camel train, young camels which the herders were recalling from their pastures on the heights above. Now that snow had fallen, even camels could not feed, for all their hardy qualities. (Some said that sheep could forage through snow, though I never saw it.) The herders, boys of ten and twelve years, ran alongside the camels with switches and thorns, whipping them forward. Strays bounded stupidly away, drawing a herdboy after them and blocking the road in front of us.

Night fell, but with the half-moon, we had enough light, walking behind the camel boys, who knew the way down.

Sometimes, in the moonlight, a downy-haired camel foal

would linger behind the herd to watch us, curious at the horses and riders—strange, hybrid beasts to him. Then the herdboys would set on him with switches and drive him back to the herd.

We neared the real cliff where the path corkscrewed downward to Darzak. The boys pulled hard at the animals' muzzles, pad against bare foot struggling for a grip on the hard-beaten earth. Gravity was on the boys' side. The oldest camels began to tumble down, drawing the younger, timid ones behind them. The track was so narrow the animals had to file into a single line and so steep they could not keep their balance at a walk, but had to bound down, two legs at a time. Some camels jumped down and down, making a weird, muffled thump on the dusty path. We followed in the van, entranced by the spectacle. Milky moonlight on the woolly backs of the camels, a steep descent, a gorge too sheer to see the bottom, the *hay hay* of the boys calling across the moonlit mountains, the cliffs above receding into black shadows, the nervous neighs of the horses, and all of us, all of it, the world, plunging down into Sheol with a weird muffled thump on the path.

Under the Earth. The land was made of silver. The moon glowed in the waters of the Murghab River, surging deep and fast, a ribbon of silver, reflecting the mountains that closed us in. Nestling by the ghostly banks, the black hair tents of the Pathans, the nomads of the valley. And the camels, wooly moons of silver light, bounding down.

7.
IN THE VALLEY

A Very Small World

"Under the Earth" had a *samovar*, a single *utaq* with one precarious roofbeam, dimly illuminated by a brazier of green twigs. The *samovarchi* had been expecting us, though he gleefully refused to tell us how he could have known we were coming. His name, Janjal, was a contraction of *jang-u-jidal* (fighting and contending), and it was apt. "Last night you stayed with the *khans* of Garzistan. Isn't that a fact?"

"Yes, but how do you know?"

His reply was a peal of contentious laughter. The hour was late, and we were too tired to drag an answer out of him, but the moment we showed our indifference he explained, "I'm the *tilifunchi*." Every day, at a certain hour, he threw a listening wire over the telephone line which ran through the *qishlaq*, receiving messages from the *kumandan* of Qadis. Mostly, there were no messages, no news. But our arrival had changed that. "The whole valley knows you've come, the *arbab* of Darzak, the *arbab* of Kucha, the *kumandan* of Jawand." It was a very small world.

A ragged countryman had been Janjal's sole client, warming himself at the brazier until our arrival. Now he moved off into a cold corner, imagining that we had driven him there, staring bitterly and hard in our direction. He had a leathery, lifeless face of one who had seen hard times and been broken by them. He did not return our salaams, nor our "May you live long." We glanced over at him, once or twice, meeting his angry stare and holding it, but the man neither blinked nor looked away.

Janjal noticed this and said, "Oh, don't pay any attention to him. He just stares."

All this while we had had nothing to eat, and only hunger kept us from falling asleep. We asked Janjal for bread.

"These people have no right! They have no right. Infidels, unbelievers," the man exclaimed suddenly, not moving a muscle, but distilling an appalling bitterness through his stare. We three looked at him calmly, Janjal because he was used to such outbursts, my friend and I because we were too tired to care. He went on muttering, "They are all rich as kings and they go all over God's world. Unbelievers, infidels."

"Who calls one an infidel is himself an infidel," I managed to say, through my exhaustion.

"Is it true," he demanded, eyes widened like white moons, "is it true that in your country they have conquered death? Do you never grow old and die?"

I felt myself all over, mentally, considering my dysentery, my saddle sores, my hands chapped from weeks of holding the reins, stomach wrecked from the diet of bread and *qurut*. The man didn't deserve any answer. Couldn't he see that we were cold and hungry as he? They all asked us for medicine, envying the foreigners for their pills and their tablets, when what we all needed was food. Nobody had any of that. Janjal fed us all he had, bread and weak tea.

We announced we were ready for sleep, wrapping ourselves in the threadbare *luhats* and turning our backs to the brazier. Janjal retired to his house in the *qishlaq*, leaving a boy to sleep in the *samovar*. The starer would not sleep, but drew close to the brazier and watched us. I woke up in the night, conscious of being watched, and saw the man still awake, hands over the smouldering brazier, his bitter stare still fixed on us. I forced myself to close my eyes and soon slept again.

At breakfast we were joined by the *mulla* of Darzak, a heavy-browed Pathan with a woolly black beard. "How do you like bread and walnuts?" he said with thin humor. "That's what we eat, morning, noon, and night. You picked a fine time to visit us."

Janjal brewed tea, black and bitter, which we wolfed down to warm us. There were mulberries, too. A week before I still enjoyed them, for the sugar if nothing else, but now their dry waxy texture seemed unctuous. We cracked walnuts in our fists until our hands were red and sore. Back in the corner, the starer continued to whine and mutter at us.

"That one is not used to unbelievers," said the *mulla*, matter-of-factly. "As though anyone would become a Muslim, seeing Islam in the state you see it in." That sounded like a challenge rather than an apology; the *mulla* smiled behind his black beard.

He and Janjal discussed the News. The News in Darzak was whether or not the *mutar* from Qala-i-Nau had arrived.

"*Nayamad*, it hasn't come," the *samovarchi* said simply, and the *mulla* nodded. Janjal spoiled for a philosophic discussion, so he could show off his learning to me, my friend, and the *mulla*, the other literate man in Darzak. Janjal asked us about the prophets, the ones we in the West considered most important, Musa, Daud, Isa. The Muslims had their own stories about these figures, culled from the apocrypha of the Oriental churches. One story told how Jesus made birds of clay and breathed life into them; another narrated the tradition that David was the first armorer and ironsmith. "These are the tales we have read," said Janjal, with the *mulla* nodding approval. "Perhaps you have read others." He perched like a crow, waiting to pounce on a kernel of corn.

The principal thing I remembered about my namesake was that he was an adulterer, whom God forgave time and again for his contrition. I told them how David lay with Uriah's wife, then sent Uriah into battle to be slain. The first offspring of this liaison died, but the second, after God's pardon, grew up to be Solomon.

Janjal was delighted by my story, particularly as he had long thought Sulaiman the father of Daud, instead of the son; that was a popular misconception in Afghanistan.

The *mulla* was shocked and disgusted. "That man could not have been a prophet, acting this way. A man inspired by God's word does not stray." The voice of stern orthodoxy spoke, which would not admit evil or paradox to be the basis of human life. Life, ordered in its every detail by the scrupulous exactitude of the Law, should not encounter temptation.

"But don't you see, Daud was a prophet because his contrition was so great and so sincere."

The *mulla* understood me, but disagreed. As a matter of degree, ordinary folk did often stray in their actions, he readily admitted. There were adulteries even here. "A man goes away on a trip and someone visits his wife, and people don't know about it. If the husband discovers, most times he's too ashamed to drag it up in front of the people. But these are not prophets; they are half-infidels, our people."

Still they did not have the luxury of contrition. The husband strangled his wife or shot the lover, risking a blood feud with the relatives for the sake of his honor.

"Aren't we a terrible people?" asked the *mulla*. Again he seemed to challenge us, as he brushed crumbs out of his fine black beard.

By day the sight of Darzak was as striking as that of the night before. The *samovar* lay at the bottom of thousand foot cliffs, above which a patch of sky showed cold and far. A collateral of the Murghab washed by the *samovar* over rapids which stirred and foamed noisily. Down the stream one came to the junction of the Murghab, at a place called Kucha. From there a small track led to Jawand, the *markaz* or center of the *uluswali*. The whole district was sunk beneath these towering cliffs, where the Murghab had cut sharp and deep into the mountains. Between the fast water and the cliffs spread just a little dry land, but room enough for the *qishlaqs* of the nomads. Just upstream from the *samovar* of Janjal the nomads had pitched their black tents; this morning they led their animals down to the riverside to water them, their many camels and sheep spilling over the wet gravel and requiring an army of young boys and men to corral them all.

Their *khan* was Hajji Sarwar, *arbab* of Darzak, possessor of the Qala-i-Nau *mutar*. He was so rich, said Janjal, he had bought the *mutar* with the cash in his pockets. More lately, he paid the bride-price for a fourteen-year-old beauty with his same pocket money. His well-built *qishlaq* stood on protected heights above the *samovar*, walled against the wind with stones and poplar trees. We met the Hajji himself, a tall, scarecrow of a man in his eighties, barefoot and in threadbare winter wraps. The rich men of the town had to signify their wealth with fine clothing to every passerby, in order to command respect. In the small world of Darzak, everyone knew how much Hajji Sarwar paid for his *mutar* and how much for the bride. Display was superfluous to him.

He spoke only of his *mutar*, which he bought to export walnuts and mulberries to the bazaar of Qala-i-Nau and to return with tea and lamp oil. Once a week the *mutar* stopped at the top of Darzak, unable to descend the fissure. "Are there vehicles in your country that could come down here?" That was all he had wanted to know from us. A Land Rover had once penetrated to Jawand, at the other end of the valley, to general amazement.

By the Riverside

Downriver from Darzak, as I said, the collateral stream joined the Murghab at a confluence called Kucha. From there the water flowed the remaining 150 miles to Bala Murghab and the Soviet Union. At the behest of the Soviets, Kabul had set up a hydrological station in Kucha to monitor the levels and composition of the

Murghab, a river important in the industry and agriculture of Soviet Turkistan. The hydrologists, the *abshinasan,* were of course *Kabulis,* strangers to the valley, rotated every five years. At first the nomads of Kucha had a lively suspicion of the station, which was an inexplicable intrusion from the outside world into their hitherto fast retreat. The *abshinasan* learned well how to deal with nomads, after finding themselves cut off from every other form of society. Playing on the curiosity of the nomads with their gadgets, they had taught them to perform the simple measurements of the levels, and even the analysis with litmus paper, though the *abshinasan* still had to record the daily routine in their logs. This done, they had twenty-three hours to pass. For twelve of those they slept; for eleven they ate or talked of food.

The news coming over the wire of our arrival had excited them tremendously, and they remembered my friend and extended him a generous welcome. Sultan, an almond-eyed Hazara, was in charge, sending to the nomads to stable and feed our horses. "We heard of you over the line. May you not be tired. Are you well? The same, the same. The praise is God's. Are you hungry? Would you like to eat soon? Let's eat soon."

A second *abshinas,* Sharif, lolled under a *luhat,* napping. We sat down in their comfortably-furnished, one-room quarters beside a well-stock brazier. The Russians had to foot the bill for the station, so they had built it out of good *gach,* wood, and provided it with snug *luhats* and bolsters, little luxuries, like cigarettes, sugar, and green tea. A chicken coop outside furnished eggs once a day, which we now ate in fried oil, relishing each mouthful. The station was spartan, but for Kucha a considerable structure. Out of regard, we learned, the nomads called Sultan and Sharif both *"khans."* The two *abshinasan* treated my friend as a returning hero. "But you forgot to bring a camera." We had to discuss the News, as usual, but this was far-ranging, heady stuff. They grilled us about world events, the war in Indo-China, the Sino-Soviet border, the *coup d'etats* in Bangladesh. They had both trained in the Soviet Union, which gave their politics a slightly billboard flavor.

"Has United States imperialism eaten defeat in Vietnam?" asked Sultan, without a trace of malice, as though he could not have put the question differently. When I told him yes, he answered, "Oh, I am so sorry, for you."

I had not seen a paper in months, and could not think of anything important to report about the outside world. Around the room were scattered faded magazines, Iranian and Russian, a Marxist glossy in Persian, with colored photographs of the Kremlin and the parks of Leningrad. The world seemed to me to have shrunk down to this: a *kolkhoz* girl in an advertisement for a combine harvester pinned to the wall.

A Pathan entered the room while we spoke and sat down by the door, watching.

"Who's that?" I asked.

"He's from Kucha. They heard about you too. He's just curious." The newcomer said nothing to this, but listened to our conversation, found it incomprehensible, and left wordlessly.

"They're nomads, you know, owners of cattle, innumerable in the valley," said Sultan, enthusiastically. His father had been a Pathan tribesman though his mother was Hazara. He was proud of each heritage. "What do you want to do now? We can go hunting, or swimming in the river (!) or play cards; do you play cards?"

Sharif, old *Kabuli*, lazed back in his place, drawing his fine fingers across the carpet. "Or we can take a nap," he said. "I think it's about time for a nap." He had never emerged from under his *luhat* in the first place.

We felt easy with Sultan and Sharif, as we could not feel with our other hosts, the *arbabs*. They were strangers here too, and we four shared a secret that no one else in the valley of Kucha knew—what the outside world was really like. And further, Sultan and Sharif were both attuned, like us, to feel excited at being in Kucha, to be moved by the sound of the mighty river running by their doorstep, and to admire the haughty pride of their nomadic neighbors. They understood and approved our interest in the nomads of the valley, and they shared their entree into that world with us. Through them we managed to stay and observe life in Kucha as we never else had been able to do.

Much of the time passed with them was dull, of course. We huddled inside against the cold and leafed through the old magazines, looking at pictures of hydroelectric plants in Astrakhan, just for the sake of the picture, the visual image. The eye did grow hungry. We would plan to eat, and then put off the moment of expectation. Sultan told stories of the wars between the Hazaras and the Pathans, tales which he heard from his Hazara grandmother, who had seen Abdur Rahman's invasion in the last century. Himself a miscegenation of hostile bloods, he grew heated and impassioned, describing how the Hazaras had defended their valleys, foot by foot, against Pathan tribesmen to whom the land had been promised as booty. His own father had kidnapped his mother from a village and outridden pursuers, in order to marry her. "They were braves in those days, were they not?" concluded Sultan proudly.

Sharif listened to this with a steady smile, as being miles

away from anything he had ever known. In his turn, he told stories of his rakish days in Kabul before his marriage, of the time he was caught in his lover's house and had to run out in the streets without any clothes on. "I ran all the way home and my mother said, 'What happened to your clothes?' And I told her, 'I was robbed'." Even Sultan laughed, having heard this story before.

The nomads came to visit constantly, by day and by night, unannounced, usually without saying anything. Tea, their due as guests, was served to each, though more often than not they waived the privilege. They had only come to hear the *"gap-gap"* of the strangers, harmless entertainment on these long winter nights when there was no work to be done. Sultan and Sharif treated their guests well, Sultan out of romanticism, Sharif from natural amiability. Often an old greybeard would turn up, wanting to take the measure of the river, being infatuated with the quaint measuring rod and tackle used in the process. Gravely, he would go down to the riverside to measure, get water splashed all over him, take the level, and report his findings, all with an icy formality. But then a smile of excitement would glint from under his grey beard.

Only once could I fault the hydrologists in their dealings with the nomads. A greybeard of Kucha had called on us, silent and unobtrusive as usual. The two *abshinasan*, leering to one another, passed him a magazine to look at. (I noticed that people who didn't read had a hard time "reading" pictures, until they accustomed themselves to the two-dimensional image and seeing patterns in the dots.) The magazine they gave him was *Zan-i-Imruz*, the "Ladies Home Journal" of Iran and the most popular magazine in that country. The greybeard stopped short at a picture of a woman, mostly naked, modeling in an advertisement for shampoo. Sultan and Sharif giggled at the perplexity of the old man, who, they knew, had never seen a naked woman in his life. The greybeard maintained his dignity, but only just. He quickly excused himself, sighing, *"Lailah ilallah . . ."*

As soon as he was gone I said, "You think these cattlemen are so pristine and noble, then why do you show them dirty pictures? Think what they must imagine the rest of the world to be like? What do they think of us, when they see pictures like that?"

"You're right, you're right," said Sultan, his romanticism canceling out the prurience in him.

"Just the same," drawled Sharif, "when you get back to Tehran, Daudjan, will you send us some more magazines like this, with, you know, pictures of women?"

Life of the Tribes

The valley was its own world, a distant island in the archipelago that made up western Afghanistan. Only two tracks led out of the valley that were passable to more than a hardy climber on foot. One of these led to Darzak. Once a week the *mutar* of Hajji Sarwar arrived above Darzak, loading all of those who had made the arduous climb up the fissure. On camels and donkeys they bore up the produce of the valley, walnuts and mulberries, in great burlap bundles; the loading of the *mutar* took all day. Sometimes the *mutar* arrived late, or not at all, having broken down on the high *lalmi*. The travelers from the valley would wait in the *samovar* of Janjal, exhausting his slender store of tea, while as *tilifunchi* he would tap the telephone line and try to get word of the *mutar*. "It's not coming this week, brothers." Uncomplaining, they trudged back to their *qishlaqs* with their loaded animals. After all, before the *mutar* they had been able to go to Qala-i-Nau only in caravan, though few had in fact ever done so.

The valley's other port on the outside world was at the *markaz*, Jawand, where an unmotorable track wound through the mountains of Bandar-i-Mullaha to Sar-i-Hawz and Maimana. This track we intended to take with our horses, after spending a night in Jawand. Sultan advised that the *kumandan* of Jawand was a good friend and would treat us well. The *markaz* was a hard day's ride from Kucha, however. For the time being, we rested the horses.

The Afghan nomads of the valley camped from March to September in high Chahcheran, migrating a little over 100 kilometers to return, each winter, to the valley. The *qishlaqs* of Kucha and Darzak had taken on the appearance of permanent settlements. These were the camps of the lineage group known as the Khayl Umarzai (the Umarzai clan), a numerous kin group of Kandahari origins, recent to the province of Badghis. Their *khans* were rich men, with 2,000 head of sheep each, while the ordinary herder had only 200. Before the Famine, the *khans* had had 5,000 sheep, and horses for riding. Now they coveted ours. Impoverished tribesmen, having lost their herds, served the *khan* as tenants; they tilled the little land in the valley through the summer months, laying up a store of fodder in anticipation of the herds' return from Chahcheran. In recent years the importance of the settlements had grown for the *khans*. The experience of the Famine, in which a quarter of Badghis had perished, persuaded the *khans* to expand and vary the resources on which they depended for survival. Now they farmed; they sold cash crops through Hajji Sarwar's *mutar* to the bazaar of Qala-i-Nau. Some contracted for *mutars* to take their sheep back and forth from Chahcheran, so as not to lose so much meat on the road. They sent their sons to the army and to school; they accepted officials—such as the *abshinasan*—among them, building bridges for the first time to the much-distrusted government. During the Famine, the provincial and district governors, the *walis* and *uluswals*, had turned a deaf ear to the troubles of the starving nomads. Now they were courting the government and placating it. Drawing out of their isolation, the nomads hoped to weather the next disaster.

For that reason alone we had our entree among them, because we were part of an outside world which they had decided belatedly to recognize. They made us their guests, and questioned us pointedly and at length about the world outside the valley. More strikingly, they called us as witnesses to their mode of living and of preserving the ways of their fathers. With them we went shooting and feasting. We inspected their wealth, much reduced since the Famine. They still had some beautiful carpets sewn with cowrie shells. We heard their stories; we shared their pastimes.

They staged camel fights for us, where a female camel would be paraded before amorous males, who set upon one another, biting and cudgeling with their necks, going mad, drooling viscous saliva from their mouths, which trailed on the ground like gauzy silk. And the nomads demanded, "Is this not fine?"

We toured the *qishlaqs* with one of the sons of the *khan*, and he pointed out the well-repaired tents of black cloths, the stores of fodder, and sheep and camels. In the morning they led them down to be watered, amid splashing and shouting in animal-and-man commotion, and he demanded, "Is this not fine?"

The nomads gave me an insight into the whole ragged tapestry of history which we had seen in Afghanistan. In microcosm, the history of the country is played out in every *qishlaq*. The *arbab* is chosen by popular consent from among the richest and most powerful herders. The status is rarely hereditary, since a rich man usually had more than one wife and many heirs, which caused his patrimony to be divided into poor bequests. In nomadism's purer forms, this splitting up of wealth has no harmful economic consequences to the herders, since the wealth, tents, and sheep, are eminently divisible. In fact, a herder's flock can be too large, requiring partition among the sons for better management. But when the nomads own land and houses, the division of the patrimony causes problems, since real estate, broken up, diminishes in value. Already, among the nomads of Kucha, the potential tension between the brothers of the *arbab* was a source of worry. What would the sons of the *arbab* do with the land they would inherit? They would have to cooperate, a thing which came easily to brothers growing up in the same house, less easily to half-brothers of different mothers. In the next generation, among the grandchildren, the truth of the Pashto saying, "Fear your cousin as an enemy," would become clear.

The Afghan monarchy was the same story written large. The chiefs of the tribes acclaimed Ahmad Shah as paramount chief in 1747. Each of Ahmad's sons inherited a province of the kingdom; one son ruled Herat, another, Mazar-i-Sharif, another, Kandahar. Each of these princes in turn bequeathed their domains to their several sons. The cousins began fighting one another for more substantial dominions. Dust Muhammad ruled the united country again until his death in 1863, but then his heirs fought over the patrimony. Aman Ullah came to the throne after the suspicious death of his father Habib Ullah. A cousin, Nadir, succeeded the exiled Aman Ullah. Muhammad Daud staged a *coup d'état* against his cousin Zahir. For these nomads and grandchildren of nomads, too proud to relinquish their birthrights, politics was a quarrel over patrimony. Revolution was Jacob stealing the chrism from Esau.

We witnessed a wedding, favorite pastime of the empty winter months, an occasion for feasting and camel fights. The bride was an Umarzai, from a *qishlaq* down the river. They only marry within their tribe, setting a high bride-price for strangers, and a lower one for coveted kin suitors. Since the giving of daughters in marriages contributed to loosening of family ties, generation by generation, the closer kin—cousins and second cousins—were preferred matches. This bride was no cousin to the groom. Her people brought her to Kucha decked magnificently in silver and lapis lazuli, upon a camel caparisoned in red and purple. We heard the wedding party singing as they marched up the river, and we men (for they had invited us to join them) rushed out and began to reply with priapic songs in Pashto. The women in the wedding party answered with misanthropic gibes, a hostility thinly disguised with humor. The tension between the two parties took symbolic form: the wedding party arrived in military cavalcade, with guns ready; the groom threatened to ravish the bride from her people. Then the in-laws kidded each other in rude humor, masking a suspicion, a reluctance to be involved with strangers.

The camel, groaning under the burden of the maiden's dowry and jewels, was made to kneel; she stepped forward into the sand, barefoot, surrounded by her bridesmaids and attendants. The nomads turned to us and demanded, "Is this not fine?"

After the wedding we feasted. In the *mihman khana* of the *arbab* of Kucha talk turned to the past. A wedding, a break in the straight line of descent, called for a reaffirming of the family, of the common kinship of the Umarzais. I asked after the history of the tribe, whence they came, and how long they had held these winter quarters. The young men of the assembly, the sons of the *arbab*, did not know and had never thought about it. The greybeards admitted that the Umarzais were relative newcomers to Badghis, the first of them coming in the 'thirties of our century, others following after the uprising in Jalalabad in 1947. The events and dates which had set off these tribal wanderings they did not mention by name, but I noted silently as I heard the story from their mouths.

The young men did not like to think that their fathers knew any home except Badghis. The word "exile" had a hard sound to it. I explained to them that my own country was a haven of exiles, but they did not appreciate the comparison. I was a traveler, rootless and wandering. The settled farmers, the Tajiks, accused the nomads of being the same, alluding to their *arriviste* status in the province and their unstable tenure on the soil. I should not have brought it up.

The settled and the nomads displayed small but important differences. We had lived with each and seen no great distinction in manner of living. But the nomads ate more meat and more milk, which kept them in general healthier for their migration to the mountains and more able to avoid diseases that festered in low-lying summer spots. They were also more active, ever searching for better pastures, making better use of water and land. Their *khans* had more power to wield, and their village councils, almost like the board of a company planning its strategy, debated more sophisticated matters. But the constant psychological strain of nomadism was its uncertainty, the homelessness of tribes who had migrated to find better pastures. The Pathans of Badghis, because of their recent resettlement, felt that an ideal—to live and die in the land of their fathers—had been hoplessly compromised.

In response they had developed a strong sense of lineage. The greybeards had a great memory for history, not that any of them could remember the days of Abdur Rahman Khan, but they spoke of it as vividly as if they did. Living long placed the events of one's life in perspective with the events of the past. One forgot one's own age, but remembered the Tajik rebel leader Bacha-i-Saqqao ("Son of the Water Carrier"), whose seizure of Kabul had forced the *padishah* to flee in 1929. They recalled, farther back, the three Anglo-Afghan wars, the *jihads* against the *Ingriz*. For the oldest men, Aman Ullah, Nadir, and Zahir were as yesterday's events, but larger. History was no story, not a chain of causation, but part of the landscape, a sense of place.

An old greybeard recited the genealogy of the tribe, "Umar bacha-i-Abdul Hamid, bacha-i-Habib Ullah, bacha-i-Abdul Karim, bacha-i-..."

"But who was Umar?" I persevered. What did they know about Umar, what did he institute, how did he found the tribe?

"Umar, he was one of the *kalan*, the giants of old. We are his men." They almost said, "We are his children," since their relationship with him was one of adoption. His followers had made him their fictive father, and made one another brothers, to put the patent of kinship on an otherwise political alliance. Kin meant a great deal amongst them, political bonds very little.

Through Umar the lineage group claimed a place in the highly artificial constellation of tribal genealogies which the Afghan *littérateurs* patterned after the equally artificial and literary constellation of the Bedu tribes of Arabia. All the Pathan tribes were grouped into families and lineages, which descended from the sons of one Qays, who migrated from Hijaz to the Sulaimaniya Mountains at the time of the Prophet. The nomads' ultimate unity of blood and kin was an illusion, which again, I improvidently questioned:

"What of the other Umarzais? Are there still some in Kandahar? Do you know them?"

"We are one people," said the *khan* insistently, losing his patience at so impolite a question. It was as though I had suggested the "men of Umar" were a disorganized rabble, like the gypsies, wandering the length of the country, vaunting an empty name.

To retain their good graces I had to ask them a question they could warm to. "What had Umar done that he had to start his own tribe?"

"Blood feuds," said one greybeard enthusiastically.

"Denied patrimony," said another. Feuds, far from being a sign of anarchy, showed the rigid workings of a tribal code of loyalty and revenge.

"They stole a woman," prompted another old man.

"Who?" The story might have been as famous as that of Helen of Troy, needing no retelling. "... and they tried to get her back. And all of them were killed, but Umar. And Umar collected a remnant, and they followed him. And he came down from the mountains of Sulaiman, and went down to Kandahar and lived there." The Children of Israel, recounting to a stranger their genesis: "My father was a wandering Aramaean."

This was one of the traits which set the Pathans apart from their neighbors in the north. The recently arrived were the ruling race of the country. They brought their own language, Pashto, their camel breeding, and the practice of long-distance migration between pasture grounds. In contrast, most of the surrounding folk spoke Turkish or Persian, kept asses for burden beasts, and traveled short distances up and down the mountains to find seasonal pastures. Some of these distinctions were beginning to blur, though. The Umarzais had built permanent homes. All the men spoke Persian. There were Pathan tribes in the north where the use of Pashto had fallen away altogether. The Umarzais' camel herds were greatly depleted by the Famine.

Settling on the land is the first step in the loosening of tribal ties. Ownership of land strengthens immediate family ties at the expense of wider kin relations. At a point, one had to choose between efficient husbandry and obligations to the group. Nomads try to avoid sedentarization, except under the unusual situation where every tribesman can become a landlord. Even then, through the course of time, it is inevitable that some tribesmen become principal landlords and others his clients. In Swat, in Pakistan, the Pathans tried to prevent that evolution by compelling all the tribesmen to rotate their estates every fifty years. The unity of the tribe and the rough equality of the tribesmen is important for them to uphold. It is not atavism; the Pathans do not blindly try to preserve the past. Like Hajji Sarwar they are eager to change things, but they want to hold fast what they know is a good thing.

Across the river lived men of another kin group, the Khayl Alizai, in black tents but with no tilled fields and no houses of mud. Unlike the *khans* of Kucha and Darzak, they retained their old ways absolutely, keeping all their wealth in flocks and tents, removing *en masse* to Chahcheran each year, leaving only the outlines of their tents and charred fires in the sands by the river. They maintained no contacts with the government, except this indirect one: they bribed the schoolmasters to ignore the absence of their children who should have been in school. For this blood money they were as free as the poverty of the land permitted. They paid no taxes (the herd tax had been abolished and they tilled no land), obeyed no laws but their own tribal ones, migrating freely. We saw their tents removed overnight to another place, when whole *qishlaqs* would disappear. The Alizais started their migration toward Chahcheran earlier than the Umarzais, when the road was more dangerous with melting snow, but clearer of other tribes. With the Umarzais their contact was nil, even though they sometimes camped within earshot across the river. Talk of feuds belonged to the past, though every man on both sides of the river carried a gun. Our gift of cartridges had been greatly appreciated. I ask Sultan if we could go across the river or if he had ever done so.

"No, they are a very proud people. They mean to keep their old ways. If you went there, they would kill you for a *kafir*."

Sometimes, ill-advised, I would peer across the stream to look at them; they never looked back. I imagined I saw the look of determination on their faces, as though their continual isolation strained them. Shortly after our arrival in Kucha, the nearest *qishlaq* of Alizais decamped, out of sight.

A Strange Ritual

All at Kucha understood when we said that this day was the feast of the birth of *Hazrat* Isa (Jesus). Naive Muslims of the *dasht* and the mountains, they readily admitted the sketchiness of their religious practice. Did we celebrate the Feast of Isa? Perhaps it was incumbent on Muslims as well. Anyway, we provided the food, so they were bound to eat it.

We rode back to Darzak to buy roosters from Janjal. He pleaded poverty, saying he had slaughtered his last ones. We insisted, and eventually he produced four scrawny ones, at a very high price. I paid him, but voiced a bitter complaint, immediately regretting it. Janjal looked at me with genuine hurt. After all, it was our idea to feast in the near famine of winter. We bound the fowls over our saddlebags and rode off. The birds squawked at each jolt, terrifying the horses who thought themselves pursued by angry fowls; they ran and ran back to Kucha.

There we slaughtered the birds directly, tearing them into a pot with a little pepper and dried vegetable stuffs, all of us sitting around the pot to watch the simmering, savoring the smell of bird fat. In a few minutes we finished off our feast. Nuts and berries, for which I had lost all appetite, were the inevitable dessert. From the bottom of my saddlebags I produced the hay-coated candy canes which I had bought in Obeh and distributed them around. "This is a tradition of ours," I explained. That was all we had to eat that day. We picked our teeth, played wishbone, and forced down the unctuous mulberries.

To amuse our hosts, my friend and I sang carols. They listened, stony-faced, to the brazen monorhythmic choruses of "God

Rest Ye Merry Gentlemen." A *khan* waved his hand. It was a strange ritual. He switched on the radio and, by a bizarre fluke, raised the BBC Christmas Program, which blared out the very same song. They must have thought it our call to prayer, or something else liturgical. From station to station, the *khan* switched the knobs, and we heard signals from all over the world, in different, incomprehensible languages. The *khan* smiled.

In returning our invitation the *arbab* of Kucha gave us a feast, which in that cruel winter was an unheard-of generosity which I will never forget. Sultan, Sharif, my friend, and I were guests of the *arbab* alone. We all ate from a single bowl, squatting in a circle. First there was *shurwa*, with nomad's bread, baked with sweet fat so that it had the consistency of pastry. The grease of the soup and the bread seemed to go right into my frozen extremities, filling me with warmth. I wiped my lips, thinking the meal was over.

A platter of rice was brought out, long-grained and pure, such as I had not seen since our sojourn in Herat; the guests emitted small *oohs* and *wa-wa's*. Rice was the reserved food for the special occasion. The *arbab* dug his hand deep into the heaping pile, pulling out the meat which was cooked inside, and placed it on the side nearest my friend and me; to be fed thus by the *khan's* own hand was a great honor. The meat was salted, yet tender, having been cooked long in *ghee*. Great hunks of sheep's tail fat, pure and white, dissolved in my mouth like butter. What the body lacked and craved tasted rarely good. In the intense cold of the night, to fortify oneself with fat should have been a necessity. Here it was pure luxury. Tea with more sweets followed. I lay back exhausted from the effort of eating, my contracted stomach swelling. The others lolled on their elbows, licking the fat off their moustaches and chins, while the *khan* remained kneeling, watching his guests intently. Though Sharif and Sultan said nothing, I wanted to thank the *arbab*, which was not done. He only continued to look at me intently, without responding. It was not thanks that mattered, but reciprocation.

What we had not eaten, I noted, the famished attendants licked off the bowl, rice and greasy fingerings.

The day of Christmas it had snowed. Where a few stubbles of grass peeked above the fallen snow, shepherds could be seen, foraging their sheep. But the animals moved reluctantly over the cold earth, looking miserable. I had always imagined the shepherds in their fields, on Christmas, knee-deep in snow. But these sheep could not forage in even a few inches of snow. Today was the last day; there would be no more foraging now. For the nomads, an early snow reduced the forage of the present year, but promised more abundant grasses in the next. For us, there was no advantage. I remembered reading in Yate's *Northern Afghanistan* that a big snowstorm had hit his party around Christmastime. If we were to go to Jawand, we would have to go now. There were no elaborate farewells to be said; Kucha went about its business as usual, unmoved by the news of our departure. The greybeards and the *abshinasan* capered at the edge of the river with their measuring sticks.

The pleasant road along the Murghab was lined with trees and scrub, interrupted by rapids and backwater pools, where we could see fish silvering below the surface. It might have been Colorado, the view was so peaceful, with the sun shining through the chasm above. They had warned us, though, of Chihil Dukh-taran, the *kutal* of the Forty Virgins, which lay astride the road. "Its crossing is full of pain," they said. The riverbed narrowed, flowing through a fissure without banks, while the road led up across the *kotal*. This was it. We rollercoastered interminably, dismounting to lead the horses up, then descending to almost the level of the river, only to see more ascents ahead of us. Were there really forty of these hills? After hours of struggling, the truth of the Afghan proverb struck me, "The sky is hard, God is far away." Our groans and curses could be heard by no one in this rocky waste, least of all above the steely empyrean. With blood pounding in our temples we walked down the last of the "forty" rises and back to the streambed, which flowed as calm and lovely as before. A grove of pistachios grew on the banks, looking almost vernal, sprayed with water from the rapid-running stream.

A chasmic gorge held Jawand tight. A clutch of official build-ings, Aymuk *yurts*, a handful of *bazaari* booths, soaked up the deep shadows. "Welcome to Jawand," said one wry townsman, "where the sun sets before noon bread." He was very nearly right; no direct sunlight showed on the town, and the air was crisp. In the bazaars, everything looked ages old: cakes of soap showing grey mange at the edges, rusted tins of *ghee*, cardboard packages of detergent made shapeless from erosion by the wind. Yet the shops were extraordinarily neat. An aging *bazaari* di-rected his boy to sweep the shop at our entry. He had a hurricane lamp a century old and a glass bottle from Tsarist Russia. Once a year, he said, he trafficked to the city to buy supplies.

All are men in these places, whose families stay in big towns. No one is born in Jawand; it is nobody's home, but a gathering of exiles.

The *kumandan*, a *Kabuli* almost too young to feel comfortable with us, entertained us in his office and later in his home. He was earnest, almost dogmatic in his attentiveness towards us. Half of the warmth of his welcome was ruined by his sense of official duty. I felt sadly that, in the new Afghanistan, one would perforce be courteous to strangers, rather than liking them or disliking them as men. I might prefer a rebuff to such treatment.

Our plans to ride on to Maimana disturbed him; he pointed out that two weeks had passed since we crossed the Nayak, which was 3,000 feet lower than Sar-i-Hawz. He had heard that the pass was already closed. We replied that, on the one hand, news of these passes was notoriously fickle, and that over a path nothing short of a blizzard could stop two men on horseback. He acquiesced, agreeing to send a Tajik mountainman from his detachment as our guide.

Over supper we shared the superb nomadic bread, dark and flakey like the richest cake, cooked with *ghee* and fat. When he would go back to Kabul, said the *kumandan,* he would like a supply of such bread. As we ate his salt and visited with him he began to relax, showing off a good humor and a vivacity which the seriousness of revolutionary rhetoric had tried to efface. "And did you really live among the *khans,* the nomads? What do you think of them, are they brave? Did you really sleep in the *mihman khanas?* Didn't the dogs give you a lot of trouble?"

"The dogs were terrible."

He laughed at this, as all Afghans did.

In the morning he gave us a great sack of the bread to carry up the pass with us, in case we found no other food. The Tajik soldier turned up with a strong-boned horse weighed down with burlap sacks.

"What are you carrying?"

"Merchandise. Trade," he said, tight-lipped. The man was a local, probably well-to-do, whose army service would not inconvenience his business of trading. As the *kumandan* ordered him to Sar-i-Hawz, he intended to bring the produce of Jawand with him to trade: mulberries and walnuts. Over there, he could buy raisins and tea.

"What's Sar-i-Hawz like?"

"It's a town, then. Not so big as this. Bigger than some." His wiry, weathered face contracted a bit at the effort to do all this talking.

The Tajik led the way out of the chasm of Jawand. One more mountain pass, I thought, and I never want to see the mountains again. I wouldn't have to, for we would be in the warm plains of Turkistan. Our trail wound toward Bandar-i-Mullaha (Port of the Mullahs), which Abdus Sattar had once described to me, then over the high peak to Sar-i-Hawz and then down, after two days, to Maimana. We never made it, not even to the first stage.

Snowflakes began to fall thick and heavy around us. The Tajik knew what this meant, but rode on with the easy fatalism of the Afghans. The *sahibs* were in charge; if they wanted to ride through the snow, he would ride. I brushed the flakes off my *chapan*, off the horse's mane, sticky, wet clumps of them, but they redoubled each time. The white clouds of snow sat low on the brow of the mountain, showering their whiteness heavily. The pistachio scrub beside the road began to sag under the weight of snow. The trail ahead of us vanished into the white mist.

I dismounted and led the horse, putting my one foot in front of the other to test the ground in front of me. The path hugged the edge of a cliff, the fall-off enveloped and invisible in a cloud of snow. Not being able to see the bottom was somewhat reassuring. My friend and the Tajik plodded on ahead of me, so I only had to keep their vague grey forms in sight, hoping they stayed on the sure path. I drew closer to them and saw they had stopped.

We stood together on the narrow path and peered into the opaque whiteness around us. Wet snow had cased us like many layers of outer clothing, and had tangled icily in the horses' manes. It did no good to brush them off now.

"This won't do," my friend said sourly, as though mildly inconvenienced by the snowstorm.

"*Sahib*," said the Tajik in his plain way, "I told you, you can't travel in winter. And you said, 'Oh, we're young, it doesn't matter.' Do you see how it is now? We'll never make it to Bandar tonight."

"Then let's go back to Jawand."

"If we can!" said the Tajik, smiling through his many wrinkles. The snow in his beard looked like glass. We bundled ourselves around on the trail, the Tajik leading, followed by me, then my friend. Sliding on the snow, the horses walked slowly. We strung out along the path to give ourselves more room to slip and fall. The way down was harder to follow than the way up, the paths bifurcating to one side and another, into banks of snow which concealed deep ditches, into abysses filled with wispy snow clouds. I stumbled into the snow time and again, climbing up weighed down with wet snow, struggling to keep up with the sure-footed Tajik, whose swift descent was as steady and as confident as his ascent had been. His horse kept under the weight of the burlap bags without stumbling, while mine fretted at the burden of just my saddle and a sack of bread. I was glad to know that between the three of us, we had a good deal of food. The

Tajik, I noticed, took little, light steps on the snow, like a walking toy, and kept his horse on a long rein. I tried the same.

We reached the bottom of the trail, he and I, then turned around to wait for my friend. The snow poured thick and fast, reducing our visibility to a few feet. We expected him to materialize out of the whiteness at any moment. A minute passed, then another, and there was no sign of him. I began to worry.

"Where is your friend?" asked the Tajik.

"How should I know?" I fretted.

He spoke not accusingly, but simply stating facts, "You should not have lost track of him. After all, he is your *qaradash*. Two people could make it down when one person would get lost. You should have watched him, while I was watching the road ahead."

The Tajik was right. I had been so busy trying to get down and out of the snow I had forgotten about my friend. He was usually the first one finished with anything, while I lagged behind. Now he was late.

"Real friends stay with each other on the road. This is the way we are. Perhaps in your country," mused the Tajik, "it is not so." They had this ability, the Afghans, to speak brutally, but impersonally, meaning no malice.

"Here," I gave him the *kabud's* reins and climbed back up the path to look for my friend. I called out, but the snow muffled me, as though the mountains themselves were rumbling. Without a horse I made my way more easily, and pushed far back along the path. The snowscape began to look familiar. I looked for our tracks, but they were snowed over. Then I saw him, struggling along in a snowbank, with the *ablaq* up to her hocks in the stuff.

"Hey!"

"Yes?" He answered me like someone just awakened from sleep, who's not quite sure yet if the waking world exists or not. Snow caked him from head to foot, while his hair and his turban had frozen with ice, blinding him. I took the *ablaq* and had him walk beside me.

Now when I looked for the trail down I could see nothing. The wind blew from downhill, snow blinding us in our descent. The snow blew at us, the pistachio groves peaked black over the edges of the drifts, while my fresh tracks had already been filled with blizzarding snow. My friend only dimly realized we were lost, and stumbled beside me mechanically. At last resort I let go the horse's reins and forced her to go down in front of us. She started off after I kicked her cruelly, and we trudged behind.

"Where are we going? Where's your horse?" my friend asked.

"Down, down, I hope." I wondered if the Tajik would still be standing where I left him, with my horse and my bags, or would he ride back to Jawand. Would we be able to find him at all?

The *ablaq* looked around at us, asking for directions I couldn't give her. Reluctantly she descended, picking her way in tiny steps along the white walkway of the mountainside, and at the end of the path I saw the Tajik squatting between the two horses, who were whipping their tails and shaking the snow from their heads.

In Jawand the snow was rain, and no one was out in the puddling streets when we returned.

I hated returning over the paths already taken. My spirit drained out of me as we recrossed the Chihil Dukhtaran, going back to Kucha. Would we have to do everything again, even crossing the Nayak? That was the penalty for turning back. Where we had struggled sweating before, we ambled down, and where we had descended easily, we trudged up, temples vibrating with blood, hands chapped from pulling the horses' frothing bits. We crossed half of the "forty virgins."

A horseman rode down from the next rise, while we rested in a low place. A traveler, like us, laden down with baggage, he salaamed as he rode by, then stopped and looked back at us. We blinked.

"Are you Muhammad Daud Khan and Wali Ahmad Khan?" said the stranger, eyeing us from head to foot.

"Yes, yes. That's who we are. Do you know us?"

"No. The *samovarchi* of Zandakhan sends his salaams." We wondered, dumbstruck, where was Zandakhan and who was its *samovarchi*. The horseman noted our confusion and went on, "I passed through Zandakhan a few days after you did, and they were all talking about two horsemen, from far away, who went riding to the town of Obeh. And through everywhere I passed, I heard of these two. So now I am on my way to Jawand, and I heard you had gone there too. Was your trip successful?"

Until now I had thought not. "Yes, it was as we wished. The praise is God's. We wanted to go through Sar-i-Hawz, but a blizzard stopped us," I continued, not making any sense.

"What God wills," he replied. We wished him luck, and shouted felicitations after him, until he climbed up the *kutal* and became a pinpoint out of sight; then we still waved. The Chihil Dukhtaran seemed reduced in number, afterward, and we reached the straight road by the river and wended home. Our return, like our departure, was unremarked.

The Shah of Mashhad

A drizzling morning gave way to a sunny afternoon. We walked out of the *abshinasi* station to see the rainbow bridging the Murghab. Clear weather came only in spells now, and there was no passing up these opportunities to move about, before the next storm. Since returning from Jawand, our welcome had worn thin. Food supplies in Kucha were short, in spite of our gift of bread. We saddled our horses and rode past the Kucha *qishlaq* to the ruins of Shah-i-Mashhad, a long-postponed pilgrimage to a monument on the river, famous among the local people.

"There are ruins, ancient places of kings," a greybeard of Kucha had told us, "and the story is known." Once, in this valley, lived a princess, beautiful and heart-snaring. And there was a monarch in the city of Mashhad, which is in Khurasan, a great ruler in his day. And this king saw in a dream how the princess lived in this valley, and fell in love with her, with the phantom he saw in his dream. Far and wide he inquired of her, learning of her dwelling place, and he found her here in Kucha, and they lived together in the valley. He built a great palace for his queen, filling it with precious objects and treasures. Then he went back to Mashhad, to his own kingdom. Before he left, he showed her a ring, saying, "By this ring you will know me always." The story went on; one lost the thread of it, for such stories were old, retold and often respun. The king perished in battle, his hand was cut off, and they sent it back to the queen, who recognized it and fell dead. The palace was in ruins, intact the hidden treasure. Yet the old knowledge of the place was lost.

"I have tried to read the writing of the place," said the *mulla* of Darzak, "but it's very difficult. Maybe, if you can read it, you'll discover the treasure."

"But many strangers have come to find treasure. One had a camera. Two more were Chinese. The other had a horse, finer than yours. There were six, seven in all," said the *arbab*.

The valley is full of legends, caves where treasure is stored, megaliths which the men of old, who were giants, erected as cairns. A great boulder, sitting in the middle of the river, they tell, was a pebble in the shoe of a giant, which fell out one day when he crossed the river to go amorously courting. Where did they, who had been here no longer than a man's lifetime, learn all these stories? Who lived in the valley before the Umarzais? Hajji Sarwar, eighty years old, claimed not to remember the autochthons, or whether they had any stories. For a man of his age, the legends of one valley are mixed inextricably with those of the next. The world is a mystery; it takes eighty years to understand that the mind is fallible. These strangers ask too much.

The track runs alongside the river with just a few yards of rubble between the riverbanks and the cliffside. A higher path leads up the edge, for trafficking when the spring torrent overruns its banks. Up there we see cairns, sheepfolds, and ruins of more substantial dwellings, *qishlaqs* with stone parapets. A fort, pillaged and burnt, but unmistakably walled, crumbles on the cliff overhead. The river goes into a bend, flowing deep and fast. The water is pure blue, the color of the cloudless skies, while the cliff-faces are brown and grey, the color of mulberries, the color of walnuts, of animals' dung, of camels' wool. The rain has washed away the last snow.

Beyond the bend lies Shah-i-Mashhad. A portal rises twice a man's height in the air, framing the blue sky and the brown hills about it. The ruin is fragmentary, with only two contiguous walls standing. Around it, the rubble has been cleared away, so the place does not have the look of a ruin, but of a complete structure: two walls and a portal, four arches and an incomplete dome. Under the dome an *utaq* has been built of stones to serve as a sheepfold.

The arches are all exquisite, midway between the sinuosity of Indian marble and the orthodox symmetry of Iranian brick. They lead impressively nowhere.

The structure is of fired brick, unornamented but for the rich patterning of the brick itself and the gentle grafting of stucco into the brickwork. Matter is become a calligram, first in the geometric relief of brick and stucco, where there are pentangles, seals of Solomon, hexagons, endlessly snaking ladders and cautiously organic arabesques. The restraint is inherent in the modest substance of the material itself, poor brick, but the imagination which conceived it had no restraint. Mazes and floral symmetries give way to script, monumental lettering of Kufic style, wavering between the abstract and the word:

IN THE NAME OF GOD THE MERCIFUL THE CLEMENT . . . BUILDING THIS MADRASA SHE THE BLESSED THE EXALTED ORDERED . . .

The name of the queen was effaced; was this the bride of the King of Mashhad?

A sensuous line of stucco covers one entire wall, rounded, fat-bodied letters in Sulus style. There is nothing inhuman about the workmanship, or the abstract design, for the love of the workman himself is as fresh as though the stucco were unset still. These lines recite the Victory from the Qur'an:

YEA WE GRANTED THEE A CLEAR VICTORY, THAT GOD FORGIVE THEE THY SINNING, OF WHAT THOU HAST DONE AND DID NOT DO, THAT THOU MAY COMPLETE HIS FAVOR TO THEE, AND GUIDE THEE ALONG THE STRAIGHT PATH.

The dates read some eight centuries ago, when the Ghurids, cattlemen and nomads of an unknown race, ruled Herat and Kabul from this mountain fastness. Their capital, Firuzkuh, had never been identified, though it was known to be somewhere in these valleys of the Murghab and the Hari Rivers. Those who had gone by plane above or by Land Rover through Ghur and Badghis looking for the city's ruins had been stymied. Firuzkuh, I think, would have been a *qishlaq* like Kucha, a camp like that of Hajji Aman Ullah Tur, where a man carried enough money in his pockets to buy a plane fare to *Makka*, a *mutar*, to build a splendid *madrasa*, or fill a poet's mouth with pieces of gold in reward for a sweet ode, or commission an epic poem about the conquest of Hindustan. The nomads of Kucha knew it was nothing for kings, if they wished, to ride into a valley and wed a princess, distributing treasure and building palaces. They did not find Shah-i-Mashhad remarkable, though the few outsiders who had seen it told them it was the finest work of its kind in Afghanistan.

Hajji Sarwar and the *arbab* of Kucha might have built these monuments, if they had any victories to commemorate. Shah-i-Mashhad commemorated the victory of the Ghurid sultans over a tribe of Turkish raiders. Hajji Sarwar was only thankful for handing off a bribe to the *wali* of Qala-i-Nau, or lambing an ewe. Whoever built Shah-i-Mashhad had confidence, which Hajji Sarwar singularly lacked. His exiled tribe's hold on this valley was fresh, with hostile tribes, government inspectors, and quarreling heirs to undermine its control. The memory of the Famine was strong, as were the misgivings about the new ways of doing things, the planting of wheat and the selling of crops by *mutar*. Uncertainties abounded in the world of the nomads of the valley, a Ptolemaic earth with no planets circling it. One heard many things, but could trust nothing. Strangers came, took photographs, and were gone. No one understood why. A revolution took place; a *shah* lost his throne. Perhaps the Alizais were right not to build themselves houses of stone, for nothing could be relied on. The booths of hair, the burdened camels, and the road to Hazarajat were the only verities one could rely on. In the spring, if it snowed, the earth would be green.

Shah-i-Mashhad belonged to that past when there were certainties, in rulers, in bloodwhit, in tribal loyalties and family. If they knew the word, they might have called it civilization.

They regarded the works of the rulers of old with a kind of envy, like lost angels looking back at Paradise.

We spent the afternoon here, tethering the horses until sunset, surrounded by the mountains, by straying sheep, and by the numbing noise of the river. So high up in its valley, the Murghab flowed broad and deep and swift towards the Turkistan steppe. We might have thought of Bala Murghab, only two days distant, on the road to Maimana. But that was not what we considered, looking at the river. We saw how it reflected the hills, patterning its own blue against the sunlit gold of the cliff-faces, still uttering its low hum, with the sound of the mountain. The sight of so much water rushing to some quieter land, far away from the bitter cold and the snowpeaks, beckoned us to come home.

We had never broached the subject of returning before, knowing that as soon as we spoke of it, everything would be over. Now, spontaneously, we could speak of little else. The cold sores on the horses' backs, the lack of fodder, the poverty of our hosts, the certainty of more snow, our own poor physical condition, urged us to return. I was almost too sick to ride any longer, having hourly attacks of dysentery. My friend was not much better off.

The words of the Victory burned in my ears with a bitter irony, "WHAT THOU HAST DONE AND NOT DONE."

So many things had gone wrong; a sense of failure, of irreparable mistakes, of time lost, of chances passed up, welled forth in us strong like the current of the river. These were more compelling reasons to give up than any practical ones. Standing there in the growing shadows of the Victory, we felt as envious and uncertain as the nomads. The bricks said: "You did not build us. You have come as others have come, and you will leave as they have left." It was time to stop being strangers.

We talked of places which never existed but in imagination, places that had seemed as phantoms to me a week before: Mashhad (would we see the King there?); Tehran; our bank, a glass building on Boulevard Elizabeth II, Paris (where they would be having a New Year's party now). America was too far away to think about. The last words of the Victory—GUIDE THEE ALONG THE STRAIGHT PATH—offered comfort.

The greybeards at Kucha understood. The season was late, all agreed, and the weather cruel on the horses. How would we dispose of them? Let a man be appointed to keep them for us until we should return, they said. Only we would ride them back to Qadis and leave them there with the *kalantar* of the bazaar. From Qadis, Qala-i-Nau, Herat, Mashhad, Tehran. It seemed like a dream.

Riding back over the same grey *lalmi* had one effect on the

horses and an opposite effect on us. We had seen this road before and loathed it, finding the unending monotony of grey sky
and grey earth a torture. But the horses recognized the trails
and hoped to be home. They went faster, without encouragement,
and we made good time. We stopped at different *qishlaqs* on the
way back, so as not to make hardships for those who had hosted
us before. But we met one of the *khans* we knew in another
gishlaq and he said, "It's your right to return among us, if you
have to."

At the stream beside Qadis we decided to race. I felt so sad
when I saw the town through the poplar trees, knowing that here
we would give up the horses, the life of the *dasht*, and the nomad
camps for long, for good. I drove my *kabud* on, half with tears
and half with laughter, for we were neck and neck along the
stream, clattering into the town looking like scarecrow cowboys,
whipping the horses, kicking up clouds of dust and screaming at
the top of our lungs. When we stopped in front of the *sarai*, a
crowd gathered to put a bid on our horses, such a brave show we
had made of our entry, but we stuck to our arrangement with the
khans of Kucha and gave the horses to the *kalantar* of the bazaar.
He led them off into a stabling place and we never saw them
again.

The next day the *mutar* from Qala-i-Nau arrived, not Hajji
Sarwar's, but another. It did not go to Darzak, but loaded passengers directly for the provincial capital.

8.

LEAVING AFGHANISTAN

A Handful of Dust

The decision to leave Afghanistan, once it had been made, assumed a life of its own, an urgency, and a whip. We had to wait for three days in Herat while we collected our belongings from friends who had been keeping them for us while we traveled on horseback. Gul Ahmad had books; Daud was keeping our clothes; Amin Ullah, for some reason, had my friend's belt. As we managed to say our goodbyes and to gather all our luggage into a hotel room—we did not return to the *sarai*—I grew uneasy as the stack of bags piled higher and higher. In the end we managed to collect everything but the belt, which Amin had sent up to his village for safekeeping. Many things we left as keepsakes—a pen, a compass, a waterproof hat. I was ready to leave it all; I wanted to fly away like a bird. What was weighing us down now was neither our bags nor our friends, but a sense of failure, of lost tempers, spoiled chances, untraveled roads. My health, which had been wretched, suddenly improved, and it seemed for a moment that we might head east, buy new horses, outfit properly, and take to the *dasht* again. But the decision to leave was greater than these dreams. It demanded we go.

I shall never wash off the sweat of my departure from Afghanistan. I slept very soundly on the eve, a rare experience for a restless traveler. As we had used shavings from a rubber tire to light a fire in our heater-stove before going to bed, the fumes from the smoke had stretched over the room like a glove. Dreaming something about the sea (here, two thousand miles from the ocean), I was awakened by the sound of a pounding surf, which turned out to be a boy from the hotel, banging on the door to warn us that the bus to the border was leaving imminently, and that we would surely miss it. My friend shifted gears from "sleep" to "last minute panic" and rushed off to retrieve his belt from Amin, who promised to bring it down from the village. I rose and dressed calmly, my slowness being perhaps an after-effect of the rubber fumes. I shouldered all the bags, saddlebags, bales of Afghan clothing, horse hobbles and bagatelles, then trudged down the stairs, dispensing with my free hand *bakhshish* to the help of the hotel.

A line of Hafiz went through my mind, "The caravan bells are singing, 'Bind on your burdens'." I walked over to the square in New Town, not to meet a camel train, but a Mercedes-Benz minibus.

The bus for the border is ready to leave. My fellow travelers, both native and foreign, all smile with anticipation of putting Afghanistan behind them. They are disappointed when the driver honors my petition to wait a few minutes for my friend, not yet returned from the matter of the belt. I keep my eyes beaded on the streetcorner from which he must come. Meanwhile, I am surrounded by and ignoring a dense crowd of street beggars and moneychangers. The beggars insist that I must give them good coin for the security of my journey, while the bankers warn me that if I don't buy my *rials* here, when I get to the border the rate of exchange will be very unfavorable. Neither God's grace nor Iranian *rials* are on my mind now. I stare out and get a last look at Herat's timeless, urban *paysage*. The clatter of droshky-horses' hooves rings on the pavement, and the drivers' whips crack as they bring the astrakhan-hatted bureaucrats to their offices. Across the street are tiny files of identical shops vending sweets and haberdashery, each one dominated by a single turbaned shopkeeper, gazing listlessly out of his financial empire, thoughts immemorially turned to the profit and the loss. In their eyes I read only a faint resentment, faint because their awareness is vague, against those of us who enjoy the privilege of youth, money or foreign citizenship, and are leaving Afghanistan today. *Biman-i-Khuda*—We entrust you to God.

The driver insists on leaving. "For God's sake," I plead, "he's coming." In fact, he is nowhere in sight. It dawns on me that I would just as soon leave my friend as be stranded here. An unreasonable fear of being left behind begins to choke me; the decision to leave drags me, slowly, onto the already lurching bus. Just then, I see my friend; he sees the moving bus and breaks into—an amble. Settled aboard, he says he hasn't managed to retrieve the belt: Amin gave it to Abdul Hayy, the droshky driver, who was entrusted to return it. Instead of the belt, my friend has a small bag with him, something he picked up in the bazaar on the way back from Amin's. White dust flaked out of the bag onto my hands.

"What is it?"

"*Qurut.*"

Would I have left him behind because of a handful of dust?

The beggars bless us, the men piously stroking their beards with the words *Bismillah*—In the name of God.

We drove away. We passed down the wide traffic-less avenue of the city, with its shoddy white villas and tall, sleepy pines. Then we were resolutely in the *dasht*.

The *Heratis* call it *dasht* and mean "the desert." They never penetrate the *dasht*, convinced that the villagers and nomads are wild, undignified by the name *Musalman*. In the *dasht* there is no running stream, no public bath, no sweet bread of the bazaar. At night the wolves howl, the shepherds eye you suspiciously, rifles cocked. The sun beats down by day, drying the landscape until it looks like the surface of the moon. But we remember the city as a place of squalor, of sewage backed into the wells, of waifs and maimed ones hurtling themselves after foreigners, screaming "*Meestar, Meestar,*" of hash addicts steaming, oblivious, in the sun.

We loathed the city and missed the *dasht*. Here, where the minibus ticked off miles in a few minutes, we had come painfully across on horseback, lost for hours in what seemed like an uninhabited waste. Then the signs of life appeared—animal droppings, a graveyard, a parched streambed. The road led us on, with frustrating aimlessness, hour after hour. But when we would arrive, the welcome would always be commensurate with the hardships of the journey: "*Salaam alaykum,* is your soul in harmony? You've come from where? May you live long, *Sahib!*" Our hosts were rich and poor, mean and liberal, but now that we would see them no more, we began to fiercely idealize them. When we returned to Herat, our city-slicker friends were genuinely surprised to see us alive. "They are such people there," we told them of the *dashtis*, "as nowhere else in the world." And a few of our friends, disquieted, stroked their beards. Now, in the company of sleepy-eyed merchants and greasy clerks, we peered at the *dasht* through the smudgy windows of the bus while the nomad tents and villages fluttered by.

The bus. We were marvelously self-contained, our suitcases and our fates taken completely out of our hands. This was modern travel, a thing to which four months here had entirely unaccustomed us. The bus sped on willy-nilly. The *dashtis*, who had his possessions and destiny firmly in hand, scarcely noticed the passing minibus and scorned the tourist who seemed to be blown in and out of his country like leaves on a wind, wandering and homeless as he was not. I stared, unseen, into the passing landscape; the skirting mountains seemed close, although one never could estimate true distance in the *dasht*. Intriguing paths led off among the foothills, perhaps over some snow-blown pass into an oasis in a secluded valley. Those paths once might have delayed us, but now we were in the bus, so we simply followed the road. Our voyage picked up speed, like a horse heading back to the stable. It was a week ago that we had decided to go home.

Madmen

The trip from Qala-i-Nau had been a nightmare. We sat in the van of an old lorry, without seats, squatting amid people and sheep, while a soldier terrified us all with his sullen expression and clumsily held gun. He had a prisoner, a ghastly mess of rags and chains. Those sitting alongside the two were disgusted at the smell of the rags and at the festering sores caused by the chains on the prisoner's limbs, and complained bitterly against him. We set off in a foul temper, some men cursing the sheep, who were defecating, others cursing the hard ride, while one bitter man sat and cuffed the prisoner who gaped helplessly. The soldier ignored this brutal treatment of his prisoner, but fingered the rifle and glared at the passengers.

The prisoner wore hobbles, such as we used for our horses, which bound his arms and legs together. The chains had been on him so long that where the skin wasn't absolutely raw it showed black and shiny, like patent leather. The man had a mild face, his hair streamed long over his shoulders, and his eyes were intelligent and sad. Only his gaping mouth and his weirdly-cocked head made it clear he was a madman. His neighbor kept cuffing him with a satisfied look on his face, as though getting his own back for something. The prisoner seemed not to feel the blows, but his eyes grew sadder, as though a small flicker of consciousness asked for our pity.

My friend said to the soldier, "Why are you letting him beat your prisoner like that? Isn't he a human being?"

"A human being? Eh, well, he's mad. He doesn't know anything," said the dull soldier.

The prisoner must have guessed someone had taken interest in him. He let out a wail, a strange unearthly cry for help. The man beside him slapped him cruelly across the face, and many others in the van now cursed and complained.

My friend leaned closer to the tormenter. "If you hit him

again, I'll . . ." then he waited for his foreign looks and authoritative voice to make an impression.

"You'll what?" replied the man. "You'll do what to me, *Meestar*? Will you jail me or flog me? Nothing could be worse than what this man has done to me. He's my own brother and he has made my life a living death. For a year he's been like this. Mad. Now thank God I'm taking him to the hospital in Qala-i-Nau. I should have shot him!"

The madman cowered fearfully at these words, and slobbered some, at which the other men about him looked distastefully away.

"What do you want, *Meestar*?" said one man to my friend.

"Look at these foreigners, trying to make trouble," said another.

The madman, dimly aware that the argument was worsening against his defender, smiled even more sadly than before, as though to say, "This is the way we are. Why struggle against it?"

They kept off cuffing him the rest of the journey, but they gnashed their teeth at my friend's interference, and we stared at them, stony-faced. In Qala-i-Nau, a *mutar* driver recognized us from our trip north months ago. We rode in his truck back to Herat; he cheated us on the fare, but I did not care: I had my mantra, the stages of our return—Herat, Mashhad, two days; Tehran, two days; Paris.

I was reciting the mantra now, when I realized with some disappointment that our minibus had only reached the Afghan border. We had to carry all our baggage off the bus for contraband inspection, and then carry it right back on. The baggage grew heavier and heavier in my hands.

I bought a hard-boiled egg from a vendor, putting it in my pocket. The egg was raw, and broke apart. Fearful Afghans swarmed around me, desperate to be off. Each one clutched his passport in hand, a slip of paper which had cost him many years and a fortune in bribes and fees to obtain. Some had been anticipating this trip for years, and it seemed too good to be true. *Mashallah!* They gazed at the horizon intently. A young Afghan student, turned back for lack of one of his many visas, was utterly downcast. I licked the remaining egg off my fingers and reflected on what a little thing my passport seemed to me.

The minibus reloaded its passengers and baggage. Infinite times we had to stop and show our passports to rude and curious soldiery along the highway. Being unable to read, they collected all the passports and compared the total with the number of passengers on the bus. I was always grateful and surprised to get my passport back from them, and kept a sharp eye on my friend's, his third in two years.

A shadow in the desert deepens; a graveyard and a flock of sheep are harbingers of habitation. Then the differences: the metal highway sign (in Afghanistan they were of concrete, metal being too rare), a mesh fence, highway lamps, trees exploding into view, followed by a trickling stream and a customs house, surely, *bi-Khuda!* a mirage. The two-storied neo-Achaemenid glass and concrete pavilion looms under a huge neon sign announcing the Empire of Iran. Eyes are glued to the windows: "*Wa, wa*, this is Iran! Well done," we purred. The smartly-uniformed police officer signals the bus to pull alongside tanker trucks, huge carriers, tour buses and diesel trailers. A sign reads, WELCOME TO THE IMPERIAL KINGDOM OF IRAN.

"*Wa, wa*, this is Iran! THIS IS IRAN!"

As our innoculations against cholera had run out, we were compelled to receive a "shotgun" injection by the health authorities. The imaginary symptoms of cholera already gripped me, along with the real fear of hepatitis. I rolled up my sleeve and, God works wonders, the doctor used a disposable needle peeled from a neat yellow plastic like a banana.

Elated by the free innoculation and famished, we went to have tea. As unused to the Iranian teashops as the Afghans around us, we, like they, ate the large chunks of gratis rock sugar from the table before the tea arrived. In Afghanistan one had had to pay extra for it. Unheard of luxury, this! Then came the tea, not a pot but a single glass. Unheard-of parsimony! The Afghans' wildest fears were realized when the sneering busboy told them how much each glass cost. The merchants, who were rich men in their own land, counted out their *rials* tearfully. From a vendor my friend bought two sandwiches, complete with pickles. We devoured them quickly. "What kind of meat is this?" he asked the vendor.

"Spam, *Meestar-agha*."

"But Spam is *gusht-i-khuk*!" That was pork.

"Not so loud, *Meestar-agha*, please." And he watched the pious but ravenous Muslims defile themselves in the name of progress.

The customs people were unspeakably polite, if not obsequious, asking each young European in an intimate, offhand way if he or she were carrying any hashish, making each traveler feel as though they had taken him into their confidence. 'So that's how they trap people,' I said to myself.

We inquired at the tourist office how to spend a few days in Nishapur and Mashhad. But the moment we arrived in Mashhad, numbed by its size, the factories, the streetlights, traffic, and prosperous shoe-wearing people, we stumbled right onto a bus bound for Tehran that very night. Not for the last time we hauled that baggage, symbol of our homelessness, running and puffing to catch the gunning bus. Dusk deepened, and city and mountains vanished into the night and the glare of highway headlights. In the void, my mind had nothing to fasten upon, neither to convince me that I had really left Afghanistan, nor that I was on my way home. Reality remained in abeyance, no longer the felt tents of the nomads, nor yet the steel and glass offices of Tehran.

Echoes and Apologies

Our host raised his full glass of wine and spoke in his habitual voice, which was half intimate, half formal. His eyes twinkled, like the crystal of his glass; he was clearly enjoying his role as he proposed the toast. "I want to drink to our two guests, welcome back from Afghanistan. We're very happy to have you home."

I was one of those being toasted. I knew how heartfelt his expressions were, and knew, too, that the moment called for a response over and above the etiquette of replying to a toast. I cleared my throat and tried to say, "I can't tell you how happy I am to be back." But first I looked out across the table, into the bland, smiling faces around me awaiting my reply. Too much smoke rose from cigarettes held by jeweled wrists, too much glass—as though a neo-realist painter had set the table—glittered amid the silverware, white napkins, and decanters of red and yellow wine. I lost my focus in the penumbra of the dinner's setting and said nothing, but fiddled with my knife and fork. This was the only sound to be heard. I withdrew my gaze downward and looked at my soup, a plain broth. We had had plain broth in Afghanistan, too. I tried again to say it, "I can't tell you..." The rest was mumbled. That was all they heard. Then I began to eat my soup hungrily. Conversation at table that night was trying. Someone encouraged me to visit Guatemala, claiming it was just like Afghanistan. Someone else told me about a relative who had been to one of those countries. A third knew the woman from New York who had become queen in that country. An older man asked me to explain why it was that the Mohammadans and the Islamics were always fighting one another. I listened to all these things dumbly, like a schoolboy taking a quiz. Then and afterward, if someone so much as said, "He has been to Afghanistan," that plain four-syllabled word marked me for a *farfelu*, and people searched for queer facts to share with me.

A woman told me, "My great-grandfather was consul-general in Persia. That's why we have all those wonderful Persian carpets. You mean you didn't bring back any carpets? Then what did you bring back?"

I thought about this. No photographs; I am too embarrased to take people's picture. No souvenirs; it was tiring enough to haggle for necessities, let alone keepsakes. We set out with a few things, left some along the way, and returned home with objects which, out of context, had no meaning at all: horsehobbles, riding crops, turban cloths, knucklebones.

I had not brought back anything, not even stories. That was perhaps a more important omission than I had first thought. It was the stories which assured the traveler, in telling them, that he had really been to those now distant places. The stories equally reassured the listeners that the traveler had really been absent, had exchanged this familiar life for another, different one, that there is some escape. Not to bring back stories was to make the listener anxious, to awake him to the fact that life is inescapable, to say, "I saw stars, waves, sands, and despite unforeseen hardships, it was often very dull, like here."

I remembered emotional sensations, but these were more difficult to express than items in the itinerary. We crossed certain geographic boundaries, which could be easily explained. But in life we crossed boundaries unmarked on any map; dejection such as we had never known, also fear, triumph, and joy. Those were regions besides which Darzak was unexotic indeed. This intensity of feeling could not be spread out on the map. We could not say, "Here I sat down and wept. Here I was happy." My friend could not have explained it to me before he brought me back to Afghanistan. Now I understood why he had wanted to go there, but could not explain it to any other.

There were other reasons for my reticence. Daud had wondered if we were taking our Afghan clothing back with us. "When you get to your own country, will you wear your Afghan clothes as a joke?" Or in what other way would we make fun of Afghanistan? He assured us this was only natural. "I know that for your countrymen everything we do here is crazy." I thought of all the *mihman khanas* where we had found such safe haven: a crazy custom no doubt, this extending of hospitality to those who would never reciprocate. It seemed the best way to reciprocate was not to tarnish the memory of those hosts with frivolous recollections.

And I always intended to go back to Afghanistan. My friend

had understood, from the last day at Shah-i-Mashhad, that one does not get another chance. I was hoping to go back, and didn't want the Afghan government reminded of our illegal journey in Ghur and Badghis on horseback. There was a slim chance that neither Qadis nor Jawand had reported my trespass, and that I might still be free to enter the country. For even the Daudi regime was organizing its police and issuing its identity cards and travel passes, insuring that travelers would see only sights and not people.

Finally, I was reticent because I heard people say, "He has been to Afghanistan" with a certain tone of voice, which meant there was nothing to report about that distant country. Its impact on the history in which the rest of us lived was so marginal, and the events which occurred there had no wider echo. A member of the royal clan said to me, "So when were you in Afghanistan? Oh, but those were normal times." Normal times, prince? A famine had decimated the hillfolk, a king had been overthrown, an eastern province was in open revolt, communists were rioting in the streets of the Capital. But those were normal times for Afghanistan, as unremarkable for the people who lived there as for the rest of the world.

When events took such a decided change of course in Afghanistan, many of these inhibitions of mine became void. Afghanistan was no longer the subject of levity. Its people and their customs had become an issue of global concern. The fanaticism, or patriotism, or atavism of the Afghans, which had been an object of popular derision or condescencion, was suddenly, widely, praised and admired. In the shrillness of our jingo-enthusiasm for the freedom-loving Afghans, I heard a familiarly dehumanizing, alienating message. They were not fanatics; they were not untouched by history; they were not beyond the pale of our experiences. "Are we not like yourselves, all sons of Adam?", they had asked. Surely they were, and surely there was a tale to be told about that.

I knew that my journey had become irreplicable. Whatever government emerged in Afghanistan, unrestricted travel would never resume. No one would penetrate the old city of Herat now, or find his way into the Cave of the Sleepers, or ride through the *dasht* on horseback. I was free to be a witness to the things I saw. The Afghanistan which had existed once, like the Cloth Hall of Ypres in another war, had to be reconstructed in the imagination.

As my journey through Afghanistan became more remote in time, the tangible reminders fell away. Daud, predictably, did not write ever, but Gul Ahmad, who had always been so reticent in person, proved to be a prolific writer. He never gave any news, but sent some photographs of himself next to the *musalla,* of his father, of a new baby brother. Gul Ahmad would also write to ask when I was coming back to Afghanistan. Once I went back as close as Tehran, from which I sent him a card. Another time I went back as far as Kurdistan, which is farther away than Tehran in one sense but closer in another. But after the troubles in Afghanistan started, there were no more letters.

Then, not long ago, I had a phone call from an Afghan. The voice was of an older, tired man, who first spoke to me in Persian, and then, with some disappointment, in English. He told me he knew me from Afghanistan. In between snatches of speech I heard him wheezing, as though the effort to talk was very great, or as though he could not stop sighing. I did not recognize his name, and he could not recollect for me the place or occasion of our first meeting. I had met so many people, and had obligations to so many of these, I had to accept this man's claim on me, no matter how obscure. I urged him to come and see me, and to tell me where he was now. He refused my invitation, and was unwilling to tell me where he lived, or where he could be found. We went on talking for some time, he parrying my requests to meet him, and I trying to understand who he might be. Then he announced, "I don't want anything. Just to talk. I will call you again, so we can talk and remind one another how Afghanistan used to be when you traveled there."

GLOSSARY

alman	Germany
aqrab	Afghan month
arbab	title of respect
bagh	gardens or orchards (pl., baghat)
bakhshish	charity, bribes, tips
barak	heavy overcoat
barakat	charismatic religious power
barikollah (Ar.)	'God bless' (approving ejac.)
bast	inviolate sanctuary
bazaar	the market
bazaari	shopkeeper, market folk
bi-khuda	'by God' (pious ejac.)
bi-nam-i khuda (Pers.)	'In the name of God'
buzkashi	Afghan national game
chadri	veil; Iranian chador
chapan	silk cape worn by Uzbegs
dagh	fever
dahri	materialist
dargah	threshold (esp. of a saint's shrine)
dasht	uncultivated countryside
dasta	measure of weight
div	demon, jinn
dutar	two-stringed instrument
faransavi	French; France is Faransa
gach	plaster
ganj	livestock
gharib	stranger
hafiz	reciter of Quran
hajj	pilgrimage to Muslim holy cities

hakim	traditional medicine man
hamam	bath house
haram	religiously prohibited
hazrat	title of respect for prophets
hindis	Hindus and Hindu Indians
id	religious feast day
ishan, muqadir	said to encourage performers
inshallah (Ar.)	'God willing' (pious ejac.)
ivan	architectural portico or facade
jan	familiar term of endearment, e.g. Ahmadjan
juibar	gutter
kala	clothes
kalan	great (said of saints)
kalantar	bazaar official
kariz	underground aqueduct; Iranian qanat
khan	title of respect
khanagah	cloister
kharabat	decadence, extravagance
khatna	circumcision
kitman	dissimulation
kuchi	nomad (derogatory)
kutal	mountain pass
la ilah illa lah	'There is no God but God' (pious ejac.)
lakh	unit of 10,000; any large sum
lalmi	rain-fed crops
luhat	blanket
madrasa	religious upper school
malang	acetic, dervish
maldar	cattle breeders
man	measure of weight
mandil	turban
markaz	center (said of district or provincial offices)
marmar	bride price
mashallah (Ar.)	'What God wills' (approving ejac.)
maydan	square, playing field
mazar	shrine
mihman	guest
mihmankhana	guesthouse
mir	title of respect
misihi, isawi	Christians

mubarak	blessed, lucky; cf. barakat
mulla	man of religion (casual)
murid	follower of a pir
musafir	traveler
musalla	open air place of prayer
mushaira	poetry contest
mutar	motor vehicle
mutarwan	a driver
namad	felt
naskhi	ornamental script
nautchee	dancing girl
nawbahar	spring season
payghambar (Pers.)	prophet
pir	mystic religious leader
qalyan	water pipe
qaradash (Turk.)	comrade
qaymaq	heavy cream
quishlaq (Turk.)	winter quarters
qurut	dried curds
quti	tin, flagon
rafiq	friend, buddy
rahzan	brigand
ramazan	Muslim fasting month
rial	Iranian currency
rishsafid	greybeard, village counselors
sahib	title of respect
samovar	a teahouse
samovarchi	teahouse keeper
sarai	house, usually large, whence seraglio
saraidar	here, an innkeeper
sayyid	title of respect
shahid	witness, martyr; cf. Grk. 'martyros'
shahrwali	mayor
shalwar	pajama trousers
sham	evening hour
shawal	Month of religious calendar
shikar	hunting
shinas	-ologist; abshinas = hydrologist
shirini	sweets
shurwa	soup
sir	measure of weight
tabla	drum
tablazan	drummer
takht	platform, usually wooden

tepe	mound
turbadar	keeper of a shrine
ulama (pl.)	religious scholars
uluswal	district official
urupa	Europe
utaq	cell, room
wali	governor
wilayat	province
yahud, kalimi	Jews
yaylaq (Turk.)	summer quarters
yurt	Central Asian circular tent
zabh	ritual preparation of meat
zulana	horse hobbles